The Colonization of Psychic Space

The Colonization of Psychic Space

A Psychoanalytic Social Theory of Oppression

Kelly Oliver

University of Minnesota Press
Minneapolis • London

An earlier version of chapter 10 appeared in *Philosophy Today*.

Published by the University of Minnesota Press
111 Third Avenue South, Suite 290
Minneapolis, MN 55401-2520
http://www.upress.umn.edu

Library of Congress Cataloging-in-Publication Data

Oliver, Kelly, 1958-
The colonization of psychic space : a psychoanalytic social theory of oppression / Kelly Oliver.
p. cm.
Includes bibliographical references and index.
ISBN 0-8166-4473-X (hardcover : alk. paper) — ISBN 0-8166-4474-8 (pbk. : alk. paper)
1. Oppression (Psychology) 2. Dominance (Psychology) 3. Alienation (Philosophy) 4. Social psychology. I. Title.
HM1256.O44 2004
302.5′4—dc22

2004010513

Printed in the United States of America on acid-free paper

The University of Minnesota is an equal-opportunity educator and employer.

16 15 14 13 12 11 10 09 08 10 9 8 7 6 5 4 3 2

For my parents, Virginia and Glen Oliver

The real revolution could only be won by the imagination.
—Julia Alvarez, *In the Name of Salomé*

Contents

Acknowledgments

I would like to thank Lewis Gordon and Cynthia Willett for their continuing support of my work and for their extraordinarily thoughtful comments on an earlier draft of the manuscript. Thanks also to Robert Bernasconi, Penelope Deutscher, Betty Josephs, Chad Kautzer, Shannon Lundeen, John McCumber, Eduardo Mendieta, Ellen Mortensen, Mary Rawlinson, Kalpana Seshadri-Crooks, Lorenzo Simpson, Benigno Trigo, and Lisa Walsh for comments and conversations that helped me improve and finish the book. Thanks to Steve Edwin, Jennifer Matey, and Julie Sushytska for research assistance and to Matthew Meyer for indexing. Most important, immeasurable gratitude to Beni and Kaos, who sustain and inspire me.

INTRODUCTION

Why Turn to Psychoanalysis for a Social Theory of Oppression?

Many theorists who approach social theory using a psychoanalytic framework do so by applying psychoanalytic concepts to social phenomena.[1] They take concepts like melancholy, desire, or abjection and extrapolate from the individual to diagnose particular social situations, cultural productions, or the psychic formations of certain groups of people.[2] Although such concepts have been developed critically, they rarely have been transformed into social concepts; rather, theorists either apply psychoanalytic concepts to the social, show the limits of applying psychoanalytic concepts to the social, or combine psychoanalytic theory with some particular social theory, such as Marx's or Foucault's. In this way, either psychoanalysis is abandoned for its inability to move from the individual level to the social, or its fundamental concepts remain intact (and therefore limited) even after their social applications.

My project here is not to apply psychoanalysis to oppression but rather to transform psychoanalytic concepts—alienation, melancholy, shame, sublimation, idealization, forgiveness, and affect, as the representative of drive—into social concepts by developing a psychoanalytic theory based on a notion of the individual or psyche that is thoroughly social. If the psyche does not exist apart from social relationships and cultural influences, a social psychoanalytic theory is necessary not only to diagnose social phenomena but also to explain individual subject formation. We cannot explain the development of individuality or subjectivity apart from its social context. But neither can we formulate a social theory to explain the dynamics of oppression without considering its psychic dimension. We need a theory that operates between the psyche and the social, through which the very terms of psychoanalysis are transformed into social concepts. To this end, I develop social notions of alienation, melancholy, shame, affect, sublimation, idealization, and forgiveness—concepts underdeveloped in psychoanalytic theory that are key to transforming psychoanalysis into a useful social theory.

Even though Freud discusses civilization and the infant's move into the social, traditional Freudian psychoanalysis rarely addresses social problems, particularly oppression and its psychic consequences. As many theorists have shown, however, psychoanalysis can be deployed in interesting ways by applying it to nontraditional objects of study such as immigration, assimilation and depression, homosexual melancholy, racism and desire, lesbian disavowal, and lesbian fetishism.[3] Many of these applications of traditional psychoanalytic concepts, however—whether taking on concepts wholesale or rejecting the concepts as inapplicable—risk presupposing or implicitly accepting the psychoanalytic notion of the individual psyche as fundamentally at odds with the social realm. And when they do consider the social conditions that produce the psyche, most still employ Freud's family romance or some negative version of it.[4] Although Freud acknowledges the effect of social conditions on the psyche, he and his followers rarely consider how those social conditions become the conditions of possibility for psychic life and subject formation (outside the family drama). Like Freud, contemporary psychoanalytic theorists, including object relations theorists, consider the social as founded on the relationship between the infant and its caregiver; the social, then, is defined as a relation between two people. But there is another social dimension to consider: the larger sociohistorical context and political economy within which that relationship between these two develops. Although object relations theorists, especially feminists, do consider how patriarchal culture affects the development of a gendered subject, too often they reduce the psychic dimension of the equation to sociological facts about the gender of caregivers and imitation of gender roles.[5] So, while they consider the subject's social position, they give a simplified account of subjectivity.

Elsewhere I have introduced the distinction between subjectivity and subject position as the difference between one's sense of oneself as a self with agency and one's historical and social position in one's culture (see

Oliver 2001). Subject positions, although mobile, are constituted in our social interactions and our positions within our culture and context; history and circumstance govern them. Subject positions are our relations to the finite world of human history and relations—the realm of politics. Subjectivity, on the other hand, is experienced as the sense of agency and response-ability constituted in the infinite encounter with otherness—the realm of ethics. And although subjectivity is logically prior to any possible subject position, in our experience, the two are always interconnected. This is why our experience of our own subjectivity is the result of the productive tension between finite subject position and the infinite response-ability of the structure of subjectivity itself.

The subject is a dynamic yet stable structure that results from the interaction between the subject position's finitude, being, and history and subjectivity's infinity, meaning, and historicity. Architects and engineers have worked with the principle of tension-loaded structures that use tension as support. A classic example is the Brooklyn Bridge. In a sense, the subject is a tension-loaded structure, but its flexibility makes it more like what architects call a *tensile structure.* A description of the difference between the two structures by the architect Frei Otto (1967, 15) is suggestive: "The capacity to transmit forces and moments by tension-loaded materials is found in animate and inanimate nature," while tensile structures "are found more frequently in animate nature. . . . Flexible tension-resisting skins and sinews are necessary whenever the supporting system is movable." The stability of tensile structures is the result of opposing forces pulling in two directions, through which a membrane's double curvature receives its structure and resistance. Subjectivity is analogous to the structure and resistance that result from a membrane or skin being stretched in two directions and held together by tension. Like Otto's famous architectural design using the tension of two opposing axes of force to support a fabric (which architects call a membrane, or "flexible stretched skin" [12]), the subject is a tensile structure. The two axes whose tension supports the subject are subject position and subjectivity.

One's sense of oneself as a subject with agency is profoundly affected by one's social position. Indeed, as I have argued elsewhere and continue to argue throughout this book, we cannot separate subjectivity from subject position; any theory of subjectivity—psychoanalytic, phenomenological, poststructural—must consider subject position. While Freudian psychoanalytic theory has addressed itself to questions of subjectivity and subject formation, traditionally it has done so without considering subject position or, more significant, the impact of subject position on subject formation. Even most recent applications of psychoanalysis to the social context of subject formation have not reformulated the very concepts of psychoanalysis to account for or explain how subjects form within particular kinds of social contexts. Instead, such applications use psychoanalytic concepts to diagnose certain kinds of psychic or social formations. But to explain the effects of oppression on the psyche—why so many people suffer at the core of their subjectivity and its concomitant sense of agency when they are abjected, excluded, or oppressed—we need a psychoanalytic social theory that reformulates psychoanalytic concepts as social and considers how subjectivity is formed and deformed within particular types of social contexts.

Theories that do not consider subject position and the role of social conditions in subjectivity and subject formation cover over not only the differential power relations addressed by some contemporary theorists using psychoanalysis but also the differential subjectivities produced within those relations. Theories that do not start from the subjectivities of those othered but rather start from the dominant subjectivity presuppose a defensive need to abject or exclude some other to fortify itself. Without considering subject position, we assume that all subjects are alike, we level differences, or, like traditional psychoanalysis, we develop a normative notion of subject formation based on one particular group, gender, or class of people. Instead, we need to start from the position of those who have been abjected and excluded by the traditional Freudian model that normalizes a male subject. Without a psychoanalytic theory for and revolving around those othered by the Freudian model subject, we continue to base our theories of subjectivity on the very norm that we are trying to overcome; in this way, our theories collaborate with the oppressive values that we are working against. A psychoanalytic theory of oppression must consider the role of subject position in subject formation, that is, the relationships between subject position and subjectivity.

Some philosophers and cultural critics maintain that the subjugation and violence that result from oppression are just different forms of originary subjugation and violence inherent in all subject formation. Theories that level suffering by proposing that all subjectivity is born from subjection and exclusion, however, cover over the suffering specific to oppression.[6] In so doing, they risk complicity with values and institutions that abject those othered to fortify the privilege of the beneficiaries of oppressive values. For, if various forms of social or political oppression are just reiterations of subjection or alienation at the core of subjectivity, then there is no reason to think either that some forms of violence are unique to particular situations and that therefore some forms of violence are unjust or that we can overcome social and political subjugation or alienation.

Some members of the Frankfurt school, along with some object relations theorists and other critical theorists following them, focus more on the relationship between the psyche and the social than traditional Freudian theorists do.[7] They insist on accounting for subject position in their analyses of subjectivity. In general, however, their theories too often either merely extrapolate from the individual level to the social level, oversimplify the psychic dimension of life in favor of the social dimension that determines it, or insist on or presuppose the dichotomy between the social and the psyche, or ultimately reject the possibility of formulating a psychoanalytic social theory altogether.[8] While Freudians overemphasize the psyche apart from its social context, some traditional critical theorists do the same with the social to the point that it completely determines psychic dynamics. If Freudian psychoanalytic theory leads us to assume that psychic transformation can take place only on the individual level (usually in therapy), some critical theorists and object relations theorists lead us to assume that psychic transformation can take place only on a grand social scale. Rather than privileging the individual ego and psyche, or social institutions and political economy, however, we need a psychoanalytic social theory that develops concepts between the psyche and the social by socializing psychoanalysis.

Most psychoanalytic models of subjectivity and subject formation, including both ego psychology and object relations theories, suppose a primary struggle between the individual and the social order that is constitutive of subjectivity.[9] Such models propose that subjectivity develops through alienation from, and/or subjection to, the social realm. Here, I argue that it is not alienation or struggle but forgiveness that is constitutive of subjectivity understood in a new way. I develop a psychoanalytic social theory of forgiveness as an alternative to both philosophical and psychoanalytic notions of subjectivity as based on struggle with, and alienation from, others and the world. Much nineteenth- and twentieth-century psychoanalytic theory and continental philosophy (including existentialism, poststructuralism, deconstruction, and critical theory) are based on, or presuppose, an antagonistic relationship between self and other, between subject and object, between individual and society. My project is to develop a theory of subjectivity that is relational but not fundamentally antagonistic, or at least not constitutionally antagonistic.

Many post-Hegelian theorists who recognize the intersubjectivity of subjectivity—Freudians and post-Freudian psychoanalytic theorists (including object relations theorists), phenomenologists, and critical theorists—have not taken the relationality of subjectivity to its limit.[10] To do so would mean going beyond intersubjectivity and admitting that there is no subject or individual to engage in a relationship with another subject—to engage in an intersubjective relationship—prior to *relationality* itself.[11] It is relationality that is primary, not one subject or the other, or two self-consciousnesses encountering each other and looking for mutual recognition—this can only come later after the foundation of subjectivity has been established (if only provisionally). Representation, language, or other nonlinguistic visceral and more bodily forms of communication and meaning always mediate this relationality—it is always mediated by our attempts to respond. Responsivity is both the prerequisite for subjectivity and one of its definitive features. Subjectivity is constituted through response, responsiveness, or response-ability and not the other way around.[12] We do not respond because we are subjects; rather, it is responsiveness and relationality that make subjectivity and psychic life possible. In this sense, response-ability precedes and constitutes subjectivity, which is why, following Levinas, I argue that the structure of subjectivity is fundamentally ethical. We are, by virtue of our ability to respond to others, and therefore we have a primary obligation to our founding possibility, response-ability itself. We have a responsibility to open up rather than close off the possibility of response, both from ourselves and from others.[13]

If Freud normalizes a white male European subject, and we risk perpetuating this normalization by using his concepts without transforming them, then why turn to psychoanalytic theory at all? Even if we could do away with the prejudice of Freud's nineteenth-century theories and their twentieth-century versions, psychoanalysis still deals with individuals at odds with society, so what can we gain from turning psychoanalytic concepts based on individuals into social concepts? How can we balance the social and the psyche to develop concepts that articulate the relationality and link between the two? My hope is that this book implicitly answers these questions by developing social psychoanalytic concepts of alienation, melancholy, shame, affect, sublimation, idealization, and forgiveness starting from the subjectivity of those othered and by analyzing the colonization of psychic space. Although the text that follows provides the flesh and fluidity of the answers to these questions, something can be gained from addressing them head-on at the outset.

There are two primary facets of psychoanalysis that make it crucial for social theory: the centrality of the notion of the unconscious and the importance of sublimation as an alternative to repression. Both facets come to bear in important ways on the fact that all of our relationships are mediated by meaning, that we are beings who mean. As beings who mean, our experiences are both bodily and mental, and unconscious drive force operates between soma and psyche, and unites them. Our being is brought into the realm of meaning through drive force and its affective representations.

The psychoanalytic concept most appropriate to this discussion is sublimation. Although the notion remains underdeveloped in Freud's writings (Freud supposedly burned his only paper on sublimation, thus subjecting it to literal sublimation by fire),[14] and it has been used without much further development since, it is central to social theory, especially to a social theory of oppression.[15] We need a theory that explains how we articulate or otherwise express our bodies, experiences, and affects, all of which are fluid and energetic, in some form of meaningful signification so that we can communicate. Oppression and domination undermine the ability to sublimate by withholding or foreclosing the possibility of articulating and thereby discharging bodily drives and affects. The bodies and affects of those othered have already been excluded as abject from the realm of proper society.

This project is an exploration of sublimation and how oppression undermines it. Not only do I develop a sustained analysis of sublimation, something much needed in psychoanalytic literature, but, more important, I develop a social theory of sublimation. I reject Freud's notion that sublimation is the result of redirecting sexual drives in particular and his notion that the drives originate within one body. Rather, I propose that all forms of signification presuppose the sublimation of drives and their affective representations into the realm of meaning. Unlike Freud, I focus on the affective representations of drives as the link between drives and signification. My conception of drive is much more fluid than that of traditional psychoanalytic theory, in that rather than employ specific drives—anal, oral, sexual, death, life, etc.—I prefer to talk about drives as bodily impulses that cannot be so easily categorized. If it is true, as Freud suggests, that affects are representations of drives, then it is also true that our greatest access to drives should be through the affective realm. In fact, if drives remain unconscious until brought to analysis and subjected to interpretation, it makes sense to focus on affects in order to begin to understand our bodily impulses and experiences. This is why here I focus on the affects of oppression rather than on drives in particular.

In addition, I maintain that drives and affects do not originate in one body or one psyche but rather are relational and transitory—they can move from one body to another. Indeed, following Frantz Fanon, I suggest that the negative affects of the oppressors are "deposited into the bones" of the oppressed. Affects move between bodies; colonization and oppression operate through depositing the unwanted affects of the dominant group onto those othered by that group in order to sustain its privileged position.

Diagnosing the colonization of psychic space demands a close analysis of the affects of oppression and how those affects are produced within particular social situations.

Sublimation is the linchpin of what I propose as psychoanalytic social theory, for it is sublimation that makes idealization possible. And without idealization we can neither conceptualize our experience nor set goals for ourselves; without the ability to idealize, we cannot imagine our situation otherwise, that is, without idealization we cannot resist domination. Sublimation and idealization are necessary not only for psychic life but also for transformative and restorative resistance to oppression. Sublimation and idealization are the cornerstones of our mental life, yet they have their sources in bodies, bodies interacting with each other. It is through the social relationality of bodies that sublimation is possible. But in an oppressive culture that abjects, excludes, or marginalizes certain groups or types of bodies, sublimation and idealization can become the privilege of dominant groups, and idealization can become a cruel, judging superego. Here, I redefine the psychoanalytic notions of sublimation and idealization as fundamentally social concepts necessary to subjectivity and its concomitant sense of agency. Sublimation is necessary for beings to enter the realm of meaning. The first acts of meaning are available through the sublimation of bodily impulses into forms of communication. Moreover, sublimation allows us to connect and communicate with others by making our bodies and experiences meaningful; we become beings who mean by sublimating our bodily drives and affects. Sublimation, then, is necessary for both subjectivity or individuality and community or sociality.

Subjectivity develops through sublimation, through elevating bodily drives and their affective representations to a new level of meaning and signification. In addition, sublimation always and only takes place in relation to others and the Other that is the meaning into which each individual is born. Sublimation in the constitution of subjectivity is analogous to sublimation in chemistry, which is defined as the conversion of a solid substance by means of heat into a vapor, which resolidifies upon cooling. Sublimation transforms bodily drives and affects that seem solid and intractable into a dynamic vapor that liberates the drives and affects from repression (specifically, the repression inherent in oppression) and discharges them into signifying systems that then resolidify them. This process continues from birth to death. Because we can never fully "speak our bodies" or our experiences, we continue to try. We continue to attempt communication precisely because we never succeed, which is not to say that we completely fail. On the contrary, we not only fill our own lives with meaning through sublimation but also make communication with others possible, if always tenuous. The process must continue because the bodily drives and affects are fluid and like vapors, dynamic and volatile; therefore, they cannot be fixed or resolidified in signification without a remainder or excess. But this excess is not an alienating lack; rather, it is precisely what motivates us to continue to communicate and commune. This excess is the unconscious itself, that which can never be fully brought to consciousness, that is, the singularity of each individual. And, as I show, the continual attempt to express this singular excess presupposes forgiveness.

Without accounting for the unconscious processes inherent in sublimation and thereby necessary to becoming beings who mean, we risk falling into the all too popular discourse of autonomous self-governed individuals that covers over how that sense of autonomy, self-governance, and individuality was formed. This discourse erases the unconscious processes by virtue of which we become subjects with a sense of agency. We are not born with feelings of autonomy and self-governance. Rather, they are the effects of sublimation and idealization. Autonomy, sovereignty, and individuality are effects—or by-products—and not causes of becoming a being who means, of becoming subjectivity.

No one, including neuroscientists and anthropologists, can say how we originally became beings who mean—when and how did we acquire language? No one can fully understand how our meaning systems work, or how or where meaning might be located in the body. Is the mind the brain? Can desires and affects be reduced to chemical processes in bodies? If they can, we aren't even close to understanding how. As advanced as they might seem, modern science and medicine barely understand the workings of the body, particularly the brain. Yet most scientists and physicians recognize the existence of psychosomatic symptoms. Today in popular culture and in medicine, many physical problems are attributed to "stress," which is conceived of as a mental state. Indeed, Freud's theory of the unconscious has made its way into popular culture so that we often talk of Freudian slips and ulterior motives. Certainly, the advertising industry believes in the unconscious or at least in the subliminal effect of images and sounds that go unnoticed even as they affect the recipient's behavior and desires. Influenced by Freud, popular (Western) culture believes in the unconscious, not fully realizing the implications of this belief.

If we analyze the social merely in terms of bodies and behaviors without accounting for the unconscious, we cannot fully explain the contradictory effects of oppression. To explain the bodies and the behaviors of those oppressed, not to mention their oppressors, we need to account for the unconscious effects of oppression. We need to understand how oppression causes alienation, depression, shame, and anger. But only a theory that incorporates an account of the unconscious can explain the dynamic operations of the affects of oppression. To understand the relationship between oppression or social context and affect, we need to postulate the existence of the unconscious. Without this postulation, we become complicit with those who would blame the victims, so to speak, for their own negative affects. Even if sociological or psychological studies demonstrate a higher incidence of depression, shame, or anger in particular groups, this information cannot be interpreted outside a social context and without considering subject position and subject formation. Certainly, affective life is caught up in one's sense of oneself as a subject and an agent. And oppression and the affects of oppression undermine subjectivity and agency such that even those very affects become interpreted as signs of inferiority or weakness rather than symptoms of oppression. In other words, only by postulating the unconscious can we explain why many people who are in some way excluded, oppressed, or marginalized at some level blame themselves for their condition. In general, our culture blames individuals rather than social institutions for negative "personality traits" and "flaws." The psychoanalytic notion of the superego is useful in diagnosing how and why those othered internalize the very values that abject and oppress them. Without the psychoanalytic notion of the unconscious, we could not adequately explain the conflicting, especially self-destructive, desires of those othered. Even the Marxist notion of false consciousness implies not only that we are not transparent to ourselves but also that there are parts of our mental lives that we repress or cannot access without intervention. There is a complicated relationship between cultural values and our sense of ourselves as agents; this relationship goes beyond the internalization of abject images.

In the end, I argue that ethics—or, making politics ethical—requires accounting for the unconscious. Only when we believe that we are not transparent to ourselves will we also believe that our bodies and behaviors demand incessant interpretation. If there is part of ourselves that always remains inaccessible and to a greater or lesser extent resists any one interpretation, then we will be compelled to continually question our own motives and desires. And only when we engage in this continual self-interrogation is there hope that we can become an ethical society; only then is there hope for anything approximating justice.

Here, I argue that it is a social process of forgiveness without sovereignty, forgiveness beyond recognition, that creates the effects of autonomy and individuality important to acting as an agent. The unconscious processes that create the sovereignty effect cannot be governed by the self but rather produce the self and its sense of self-governance. Popular Western notions of the individual and individualism cover over this process and fix the subject as self-contained and opposed to others and society. This fixed notion of the individual denies the unconscious processes that sustain it and by virtue of which it exists. And by so denying the unconscious, this individual denies what motivates its actions and relationships behind the scenes of conscious life. This individual lives with the illusion that it is (or can become) transparent to itself and self-governing, in control of itself and therefore in control of others and its world. This illusion, however, can be dangerous insofar as it can lead to a sense of entitlement and privilege that comes from the confidence of one's own boundaries, a confidence that covers over the fears and ambiguities that haunt those boundaries, fears and ambiguities that are disavowed to maintain the illusion of self-control. This unforgiving illusion of entitlement and privilege leads to self-righteous killing in the name of justice, democracy, and freedom, which requires disavowal of not only conscious ulterior motives related to political economy and maintaining domination but also unconscious motives related to repressed fears and desires. We need to critically examine not only our conscious motives and reasons for our actions and values but also our unconscious drives and affects that affect, even govern if not determine, those very actions and values. Without such self-examination and questioning, without continually interpreting and reinterpreting the meaning of our own actions and values, we risk the solidity that prevents fluid, living sublimation and idealization and leaves us with empty and meaningless principles in whose name we kill off otherness and those others who embody it for us. This is the burden placed on those othered by privileged subjects who believe their illusions of independence and entitlement.

To imagine what Derrida calls a justice "worthy of its name," we need to take responsibility not only for our actions and values but also for our unconscious desires and fears. We need to go beyond traditional moral theory that holds individuals responsible for their actions within the limits of their reason, beyond even an existential ethics that holds individuals responsible not only for their actions but also for their beliefs, desires, and values, beyond a Levinasian ethics that holds the subject responsible for the other's response, to a truly hyperbolic ethics (borrowing from Derrida) that holds us all responsible not only for our actions, beliefs, desires, values, and the other's response but also for our unconscious bodily drives and affects. We are responsible for the effects of our affects on others. We are responsible for what we do not and cannot ever completely know about ourselves. This is radical ethics, an ethics that demands an endless responsibility so that we might imagine response-ability itself as constitutive of subjectivity, so that we might imagine our indebtedness to otherness and others whose provocation and responsiveness give birth to subjectivity and the singularity of each individual. Only by acknowledging this singularity beyond recognition, beyond conscious reasons, beyond and yet constitutive of bodies and actions can we hope to overcome oppression. This acknowledgment is an endless task, which is why we continue to live, to speak, to act. This task, the task of acknowledging the unrecognizable singularity of each individual, a singularity beyond individual rights or the law, is what gives meaning to our lives and to our relationships with others. We do not know or understand ourselves. We do not know or understand others, perhaps most especially those closest to us. Once we fall under the illusion that we do, that we understand ourselves and others, then we lose the possibility of communication, of communion, of love, of the forgiveness that makes it possible to continue to be beings who mean. Acknowledging that we don't understand or know, and moreover that we can never fully understand or know, provides the impulse for interpretation. Because we cannot know, we interpret. Because we cannot know, we mean. Because we cannot know, we are beings who mean. And through endless interpretation, our lives become meaning full.[16]

Part I

Alienation and Its Double

Some contemporary cultural theorists maintain that forms of psychic domination are not unique to oppression but affect all human beings; or, oppression is the fate of all of us. Some have even suggested that alienation is inherent in the human condition and that oppression and violence are just repetitions of the founding violence at the core of subjectivity, nationality, and humanity.[1] If this is the case, then resistance to domination is futile. As I have argued elsewhere, to delineate the psychic and physical affects of oppression, it is crucial to distinguish constitutive violence inherent in subjectivity and human society from the violence of oppression, domination, and colonization, which may be necessary to the lifestyles of their beneficiaries but are not necessary to life itself.[2] Indeed, I have tried to show that domination and subjection are not necessary to subjectivity but, to the contrary, undermine it.

Here, I would like to take these arguments further by demonstrating that the European notion of an alienation inherent in subjectivity actually covers over a more treacherous form of alienation, the alienation unique to oppression. Existentialist and psychoanalytic notions of alienation as inherent in all subjectivity are constructed against a dark and invisible underside, the alienation of domination, slavery, and colonization. The late-nineteenth-century and early- to mid-twentieth century fixations on alienation, anxiety, and dread are much more than the result of modernization, urbanization, atomization, and mechanization. These theories of alienation (beginning with Hegel) were also born at a time when the practices of imperialism and the slave trade had been called into question as inhumane. The free-floating guilt and anxiety inherent in the human condition described by philosophers of alienation can in itself be diagnosed as a symptom of a concrete guilt over the oppression and domination that guaranteed white privilege. The thesis that alienation, guilt, and anxiety are inherent in the human condition works to cover over this guilt in the face of specific others against whom the white subject has constituted itself as privileged.

Perhaps it is no accident that the heyday of Sartrean existentialist theories of alienation and freedom tied to the look of the other coincide with women's movements and civil rights movements in which women and blacks demanded freedom from sexist and racist alienation. Maintaining that alienation and subjection are inherent in the human condition and in the constitution of subjectivity not only covers over how, historically, subjectivity and humanity have been the privilege of a few but also levels different forms of alienation, subjection, and violence and thereby continues to render invisible forms of alienation, subjection and violence unique to oppression. Such theories, which maintain that alienation is inherent in the human condition and that all forms of alienation are merely versions of this primary sort, are symptomatic of an anxiety and guilt in the face of racial difference and racism and sexual difference and sexism. In the chapters that follow, I argue that European notions of alienation describe only a privileged subject and cannot account for the underside of that privilege, the alienation of those oppressed precisely in order to shore up such privilege. Of the so-called existentialist philosophers, only Frantz Fanon diagnoses the underside of privileged alienation by articulating another more dangerous and real form of alienation that cripples not only the body but also the psyche of those colonized and oppressed by the agency and arrogance of a privileged white subject.

CHAPTER 1

Alienation as Perverse Privilege of the Modern Subject

Although Frantz Fanon's work remains at the margins of mainstream philosophy, critics have variously claimed it for Hegelianism, Marxism, Sartrean existentialism, and Lacanian psychoanalysis. While Fanon engages with these traditions, his writings suggest a notion of alienation unique to colonialism and oppression. Going beyond the alienation identified by Hegel, Sartre, and Lacan in particular, Fanon points toward a debilitating alienation inherent in colonialism that not only adds another layer to the idea that alienation is inherent in the human condition but also works against that primary alienation. What Fanon identifies as the difference between *the black man* and *man* turns around this difference between originary alienation and its double, or underside, the alienation of colonization and oppression. Fanon suggests that the black man is denied the form of alienation so precious to subjectivity according to various European philosophers. Rather, the black man is the dark, invisible underside of the privilege of subjectivity constituting alienation. For him, the alienation of oppression does not constitute his own subjectivity but undermines it even while it is constituting the subjectivity of his oppressor.

If "the black man is not a man," as Fanon claims at the beginning of *Black Skin, White Masks*, who is he? Fanon (1967, 8) answers, "the black is a black man," and he suggests that the rest of the book is his attempt to delineate the difference between a *man* and a *black man*. Echoing Sartre, Fanon describes man's confrontation with "a zone of nonbeing, an extraordinarily sterile and arid region, an utterly naked declivity where an authentic upheaval can be born" (8). But this echo rings false and becomes more and more ironic as the book progresses. In response to the idea that man is a confrontation with nothingness, that man is a return to himself from the alienation in front of the other who provoked this confrontation, Fanon says that "the black man lacks the advantage of being able to accomplish this descent into a real hell" (8); that is, the black man lacks the advantage of a confrontation with his own freedom by asserting his subjectivity against his alienating otherness reflected in the white man. If a man goes through alienation to become a being who, as Sartre says, makes himself a lack of being so that there might be being, for Fanon, a black man's alienation within a racist culture prevents him from making himself a lack of being. Fanon says that the black man is "the result of a series of aberrations of affect, he is rooted at the core of a universe from which he must be extricated" (8). And to extricate him from this core in which he is rooted, Fanon proposes "nothing short of the liberation of the man of color from himself," that is, the liberation of the man of color from the world of being in itself into the world of meaning (8). In other words, Fanon proposes nothing short of giving the black man back his lack, which has been the perverse privilege of the white subject. Going beyond Fanon's engagement with his contemporaries in philosophy and psychoanalysis, I attempt to show in the sections that follow how the notions of alienation proposed by Hegel, Marx, Sartre, Heidegger, and Lacan presuppose a privileged subject and cannot account for the subject of oppression; moreover, some of their theoretical moves not only cover over the alienation inherent in oppression by postulating a universal alienation that renders invisible concrete forms of alienation but also appear as symptomatic of the privileged subject's anxiety and guilt in the face of those others on whose backs that privilege is built.

Colonial Perversions of the Ideal of Mutual Recognition: Hegel

The separation between the world of being in itself and the world of meaning is variously described by Hegel as the difference between in itself and for itself, by Heidegger as beings in the world and *Dasein* whose being is meaning, by Lacan as the fundamental division of the subject or alienation itself, and by Sartre, echoing Hegel, as the difference between being in itself and being for itself. In *Phenomenology of Spirit* Hegel (1977, 111) says, "Self-consciousness exists in and for itself when, and by the fact that, it so exists for another; that is, it exists only in being acknowledged." The acknowledgment or mutual recognition is motivated by what he calls desire, which is always the double movement of a return to the self of, or from, an alienating otherness inherent in self-consciousness. As we know, for Hegel the movement from in itself to being for itself, or self-consciousness, finally comes through activity or work. Work allows the negativity or alien objectivity inherent in consciousness to become explicit. This in turn allows one to make negativity or alien objectivity one's own and in so doing to make one's existence one's own: "In fashioning the thing, he [the bondsman] becomes aware that being-for-itself belongs to him, that he himself exists essentially and actually in his own right" (118). Consciousness overcomes its negativity or alienation by making its own negativity an object for itself, that is, by turning back on itself through the movement of negativity or lack that is desire.

In *Black Skin, White Masks*, in a section titled "The Negro and Hegel," Fanon (1967, 216) summarizes Hegel's notion of man: "Man is human only to the extent to which he tries to impose his existence on another man in order to be recognized by him." But since Fanon insists that within racist culture the black man is rendered not a man, what Hegel says about man does not apply to the black man within colonial ideology. More specifically, Hegel's analysis of the master-slave dialectic that gives birth to self-consciousness does not apply to the white master and the black slave. After describing the conflict essential to the Hegelian dialectic of lord and bondsman, Fanon says that "there is not an open conflict between white and black. One day the White Master, *without conflict*, recognized the Negro slave" (217). Fanon points out that for Hegel this type of recognition without conflict cannot yield independent self-consciousness (219). Even when black slaves are freed and recognized as persons or *men*—or, as Fanon says, "the machine-animal-men" are promoted "to the supreme rank of men"—they still do not have independent self-conscious existence in Hegel's sense because they do not act (220). They do not gain their freedom through their own activity or work, and by implication they do not make their own negativity an object and transform their alienation into independent self-consciousness. Rather, Fanon says, "The upheaval reached the Negroes from without. The black man was acted upon. Values that had not been created by his actions, values that had not been born of the systolic tide of his blood, danced in a hued whirl round him" (220). Insofar as the black man was "freed" by his white masters, then these values are still the "values secreted by his masters" (221). To become independent, the slave needs to create his own values. Without doing so, he has not moved from the world of being into the world of meaning.

In a footnote, Fanon says, "I hope I have shown here the master differs basically from the master described by Hegel. For Hegel there is reciprocity; here the master laughs at the consciousness of the slave. What he wants from the slave is not recognition but work. In the same way, the slave here is in no way identifiable with the slave who loses himself in the object and finds in his work the source of his liberation. The Negro wants to be like the master. Therefore he is less independent than the Hegelian slave. In Hegel the slave turns away from the master and turns toward the object. Here the slave turns toward the master and abandons the object" (220–21).[1] I have argued elsewhere that Fanon is not merely opposing the Hegelian ideal of mutual recognition to the reality of black slavery and oppression but also suggesting that the ideal itself becomes corrupt and pathological in the colonial situation.[2] Insofar as the demand for recognition is created by the colonial situation in which the recognition of humanity is denied to the colonized, the demand for recognition itself becomes a symptom of the pathology of colonization. Fanon insists that "the former slave wants to *make himself recognized*" (217; my emphasis) and that his sense of his own self-worth must come through his own action and meaning or values, which can come through violent resistance to dominance.[3] For Hegel, overcoming the alienation inherent in confronting another self-consciousness initiates in one's own consciousness of self. For Fanon, overcoming this privileged form of alienation is not possible for the black man within the colonial logic because as the white man's Other he is not permitted to overcome otherness and regain himself—he is the Other against whom the privileged subject feels alienated and then recuperated. The black man, on the other hand, can only overcome his debilitating alienation by breaking out of the colonial logic; Hegelian alienation becomes possible only outside colonialism. Within the colonial logic, the struggle for mutual recognition becomes part and parcel of the pathology of colonialism.

It might be tempting to read the debilitating alienation that results from colonial oppression as a form of Hegel's unhappy consciousness. After all, Hegel describes the unhappy consciousness as a split, or double consciousness, that continues the struggle between master and slave within one and the same consciousness that has yet to experience its unity. The unhappy consciousness experiences itself as made up of dual forces in opposition: the unchanging, essential, universal, or objective, on the one hand, and the changing, contingent, particular, or subjective, on the other. The unhappy consciousness identifies itself with the changeable and contingent because it finds itself in this contradiction and assumes that contradiction can't be essential. And insofar as ultimately it believes the eternal to be beyond it and therefore doubts its own authority, a similarity seems to exist between the unhappy consciousness and the double alienation of oppression. Yet what makes the unhappy consciousness unhappy is not that its own authority is pitted against some larger objective authority that takes precedence over its own. It is not that the unhappy consciousness loses its own autonomy and agency to a social authority greater than itself—imperialist laws and colonization, for example. Rather, if anything, the unhappy consciousness is stuck between its own independence on a purely abstract level and the nonreflective level of its agency or actions. In other words, it "merely finds itself desiring and working" (Hegel 1977, 132, §218); it finds itself in the act. What makes it unhappy is that it cannot reconcile its autonomy, which it experiences only on an abstract level unrelated to its concrete actions, with its agency, which it experiences only on the most particular level as mere nonreflective doing. The problem for the unhappy consciousness is that its independence is too abstract and therefore becomes associated with a beyond, while its agency is too particular and therefore cannot be universalized. As a result, for Hegel, the unhappy consciousness attributes the universal and its own independence to some quasi-religious beyond for which it longs and to which it gives thanks. It attributes the authority and ground of both the universality of its actions and its autonomy with an autonomy and agency greater than itself. As with every stage in the *Phenomenology of Spirit*, however, ultimately the unhappy consciousness gives way to its own resolution in a third stage or position through which the universal and particular are reconciled in the individual, and the individual's autonomy and agency are reunited (128, §210).

Insofar as the colonial situation produces a double consciousness that locates authority, autonomy, and agency in a beyond in the face of which the individual loses authority, autonomy and agency, then its logic resembles the logic of Hegel's unhappy consciousness. In the colonial situation the most powerful forms of this beyond are God and nature. If the colonized are "inferior and less human" because it is ordained by God or nature, then the authority, autonomy, and agency of the oppressed are compromised by the absolute authority, autonomy and agency of God or nature. In the face of this absolute beyond, the colonized lose their individuality and freedom. Yet, unlike Hegel's unhappy consciousness, the double consciousness of debilitating alienation is not overcome by giving thanks to this great beyond or by finding itself therein. So while Hegel's description of the initial stage of the unhappy consciousness—"the first Unchangeable it knows only as the alien Being who passes judgment on the particular individual" (§210)—resonates with the debilitating alienation of oppression, the next two stages do not describe a necessary course to overcome that alienation, especially the third stage in which "consciousness becomes, thirdly, Spirit, and experiences the joy of finding itself therein, and becomes aware of the reconciliation of its individuality with the universal" (§210).

The double consciousness of debilitating alienation splits the authority of not only the subject but also the unchanging, essential, universal, objective beyond. So reauthorizing the subject requires more than reconciling it with the universal or the laws and values of the colonizers. The contradiction that undermines individual authority, autonomy, and agency does not stem from some opposition between autonomy and agency within the subject but rather from a contradiction within the beyond itself, within colonial values. As I have discussed elsewhere, colonial authority is founded on a contradiction between denying the internal life, mind, or soul to the colonized, on the one hand, and demanding that they internalize colonial values, on the other; the colonized status as human yet not human, agent yet not agent, is part and parcel of this contradictory logic (see Oliver 2001). So within the colonial logic the subject's debilitating alienation is caused by a split within what could be associated with the universal rather than a split between the universal and the particular. Or perhaps Hegel's system cannot truly account for concrete or particular universals. Overcoming alienation, then, is not simply a matter of reconciling universal and particular but rather a matter of resisting the particular universal forced on the colonies by the colonizers, which usually requires not only pointing out the contradictions in that universal but also fighting for a more universal Universal. Perhaps later stages in Hegel's dialectic of spirit—particularly the section on forgiveness and confession—speak to this struggle. My point, however, is not to justify Hegel but to explain oppression and resistance. To develop a politics of resistance to oppression, it is crucial to be able to distinguish between the alienation inherent in the development of consciousness or subjectivity itself and the alienation that results from oppression and domination. If there is no difference—if one is simply a necessary outgrowth of the other—then resistance is futile. Indeed, the alienation inherent in the development of consciousness turns out to be a privilege of the modern subject bought at the cost of another more insidious form of alienation—the alienation of being denied subjectivity and forced to occupy the place of Other or object for the modern privileged subject.

Estrangement from the Production of Value: Marx

Marx makes a distinction between alienated and estranged labor that comes close to diagnosing the inability to make meaning or the lack of the lack that makes self-reflection impossible. He distinguishes between *entfremdung*, estranged or foreign, and *verausserung*, alienated or outer.[4] *Entfremdung* distorts *verausserung* and thereby undermines human life and relationships. For Marx, human beings are unique in that they can act for the good of not only themselves but also other species and the earth. Human beings are in the fractured position of being both individual beings and social beings at once. Marx calls this unique position "species being" (e.g., 1975, 326–30, 347, 350–51, 369, 386–91). To realize our species being, we must first separate ourselves from the outside world. This requires alienation, which allows us to see ourselves as social beings; this separation, or alienation, is necessary for self-reflection. When this relationship is inverted and the separation of self from the world and others exists for the sake of covering over species being, then the relationship is one of estrangement (266–67, 326–27). Whereas alienation from the world allows us to see ourselves as beings among (and dependent on) others, estrangement from the world covers over our relation to others.

Marx's distinction between estrangement and alienation resonates with the difference between what I am calling debilitating alienation described by Fanon and the notion that alienation is inherent in subjectivity described by various philosophers of alienation. Marx's notion of estrangement addresses the alienation from the possibility of alienation in the sense of the distance necessary for self-reflection and meaning making. Estrangement is a type of debilitating alienation through which the human capacity for meaning and reflection are undermined by a situation that reduces people to objects or commodities. While Marx's identification of workers with commodities to be exchanged on the market within capitalism is in most cases a metaphor, all too often in the case of colonization, and certainly in the case of slavery, it is literal: people are bought and sold as chattel. In the history of colonization and slavery, the chains that bind workers are not Marx's invisible chains of capitalism but real ones.

The difference between alienated and estranged labor is the difference between production that actualizes the human capacities for self-reflection and social relations, and production that undermines those capacities and relations. Marx maintains that it is necessary for human beings to take that which they produce to be outside themselves; they are alienated from their products. But it is precisely this capacity to produce that is the effect of *verausserung* that makes us human. This type of alienation as the distance, or separation, that initiates reflection reveals the species being of human beings. In this relationship to labor, human beings eat, sleep, and procreate—stay alive—to maintain themselves so that they can actualize their uniquely human capacity to engage in social production, to be social. In the estranged relationship to labor, on the other hand, human beings work to stay alive; their social production is turned into the means to sleep, eat, and procreate rather than the other way around.

In "Economic and Philosophical Manuscripts," Marx (1975, 326–32) lists four characteristics of estranged labor: First, workers are estranged from nature and from their products. Second, workers are estranged from themselves and the process of production. Third, the work is estranged from the social aspect of work and life. Fourth, workers are estranged from other people. Workers are dependent on their products insofar as their livelihoods depend on their production. Workers do not see the product as a result of their "dialogue with nature" but rather as hostile (328). Workers' estrangement from the product and their relations with nature covers over the fact that nature is our "inorganic body." In estranged labor, we are estranged from our inorganic body, nature, which becomes a set of commodities on which we work in order to live. Life itself becomes a commodity, a means to live.

Marx (1977, 799) argues that capitalism turns workers into fragments, appendages of a machine. Workers are estranged from themselves insofar as they become one part among others of the machinery of production. The result of this estrangement is that workers feel free only when they are engaging in "animal pleasures"—eating, drinking, sex; when they are doing what animals cannot do, producing, they do not feel free. In estranged labor, workers feel human when engaging in animal pleasures and feel like animals when engaging in human production (Marx 1975, 327). This is how estrangement distorts the very being of human beings.

Human beings' unique capacity to interact with the world and others is turned into a way to maintain animal functions alone. And while "eating, drinking, procreating, etc., are also genuine human functions," Marx says that "when they are abstracted from other aspects of human activity and turned into the final and exclusive ends, they are animal" (327). This estranged relation to animal functions turns species life, and thereby the social life of human beings, into a means: "For in the first place labour, *life activity, productive life* itself appears to man only as a *means* for the satisfaction of a need, the need to preserve physical existence. But productive life is species-life. It is life-producing life. The whole character of a species, its species-character, resides in the nature of its life activity, and free conscious activity constitutes the species-character of man. [In estranged labor] Life itself appears only as *a means of life*" (328; emphasis in the original). Estranged labor conceals the social character of all human experience and reduces life to fulfilling animal needs. Consciousness of our sociality liberates human beings from purely animal functions—which is not to say that animal functions are not human or that humans are not animals. Rather, for Marx, how other animals perform their animal functions differs from how humans do; this difference is based on the human capacity for social exchange, which is denied in estranged labor.[5]

If estrangement is a type of debilitating alienation, an alienation from the possibility of alienation as self-reflection, then the alienation of colonization described by Fanon and the alienation experienced by slaves in the United States and Europe is yet another type of more crippling alienation. Slaves and, in many cases, the colonized cannot enjoy eating, drinking, and procreating. They are denied both the pleasures of production as an expression of humanity and creativity, and the animal pleasures. While they are reduced to animality, they are denied the pleasures that Marx associates with animal functions. They do not have enough to eat or drink, and their procreation is circumscribed. This is especially true of slavery, where family life was undermined and children were sold away from their parents. With slavery and colonization (which have not disappeared from the globe even if they may take different forms), even the so-called animal pleasures are denied, and life is not a means to one's own life but the means for the life of others.

The estranged relation to labor distorts not only the human as social being but also the human as individual being. On the one hand, the estranged exchange turns the social activity of work and exchange into a means for individual existence. Workers engage in social exchange to afford food and shelter to maintain individual existence. On the other hand, the estranged exchange reduces every individual to a substitutable equal or commodity that can be exchanged within the labor force. Through money, human beings and their products can be translated into exchangeable commodities that are no longer truly individuals. The estranged exchange not only turns the social activity of work into a means for individual subsistence but also turns each individual into a commodity to be exchanged on the market. Independence or freedom is an illusion: "The Roman slave was held by chains; the wage-labourer is bound to his owner by invisible threads. The appearance of independence is maintained by a constant change in the person of the individual employer, and by the legal fiction of a contract" (Marx 1977, 719). Finally, estranged laborers are estranged from other people because they take the estranged relation to nature, self, and species being to be the natural relation, for everyone like themselves is reduced to a commodity.

In the colonial situation, as in slavery, there is no fiction of a contract. The labor of workers is taken by force along with their lands and families. Women are raped, and children are not the result of the pleasures of procreation. All relations, not just the relations of production, are forced, including the so-called animal functions. And it is not just that individuals are exchangeable within the market economy, but within the colonial situation, as Fanon describes it, the colonized are no longer individuals at all, exchangeable or otherwise; rather, they are part of a group considered subhuman, barbaric, evil, or merely hopeless and therefore justifiably oppressed. So while Marx's distinction between estrangement and alienation goes further than most theories of alienation to address the double alienation of oppression, it does not reach the depths of the humiliation involved in colonial or racist alienation.

In *Frantz Fanon: Colonialism and Alienation* (1974), Renate Zahar takes a different tack in his argument that Marx's notion of capital does not capture colonial alienation. He suggests that, unlike the situation that Marx describes, in the colonial situation there is no true economic exchange between the colonizer and colonized. One important place where my analysis and that of Zahar differ is that his analysis of how Marx's theory does and does not apply to the colonies is based primarily on economic production, not on the production of value. Zahar (1974, 15) concludes, however, that "it would, therefore, not be justified to criticize Fanon for neglecting economic factors. His analysis specifically deals with psychological phenomena which no investigation of colonialism and neocolonialism along economic lines can afford to overlook. Furthermore, the phenomena of alienation caused by racism objectively take on a special relevance in view of the absence of exchange relations in the colonies." He sees two types of intimately linked alienation in the colonies, economic and psychological. Fanon's analysis of the psychological factors can be read, then, as a corrective or necessary supplement to Marx's account of economic alienation. Zahar also insists, with Fanon, that colonization operates through racism and that any theory of colonial alienation must account for racist alienation.

Howard McGary (1998, 268–69) continues this line of thought when he argues that Marx's notion of alienation cannot account for black alienation because for Marx, class and economy are primary, while race is secondary; Marx "fails to recognize that alienation occurs in relationships apart from the labor process." Fanon argues that all colonization involves racialization and racism; colonization is always justified through racialization and racism (see chapters 2 and 3 below). And while racism is related to the economy of colonization, it cannot be reduced to it. As McGary explains, the alienation particular to oppression is self-alienation and not just alienation from work or from life but from a positive sense of self (260).[6] Although Marx describes how estranged labor alienates workers even from themselves in terms of the capacities for reflection and meaning, he does not go far enough in describing how oppression, especially racist and sexist oppression, denigrates and abjects people in an attempt to deny a positive sense of self. It is not just that the sense of self is distorted from human to animal or base pleasures, but that the sense of self is abjected as bad, evil, or contaminated. It is this aspect of racialized alienation that even Marx's distinction between estrangement and alienation does not address.

If, with Gayatri Chakravorty Spivak, we read Marx's concern with production, especially in the two volumes of *Capital*, as primarily a concern with the production of value, both economic and cultural, then it is possible to reconsider the usefulness of Marx's notion of estrangement from the production of value in diagnosing alienation caused by oppression. As I show throughout the present volume, oppression operates by attempting to exclude those oppressed from the means of production of value, especially the value (or devaluation) of their own bodies. The alienation that results from this exclusion is different from not only the alienation necessary for subjectivity and self-consciousness but also what we usually consider estrangement from the means of production, the mechanisms of capitalism. This exclusion is not merely economic but also cultural and social, and it affects every aspect of life, which is not to say that it cannot be resisted or overcome. Oppression operates through a debilitating alienation based on estrangement from the production of value in a hierarchical system of values through which some bodies are valued and others are devalued or abjected. It is the colonial and racist production of values that creates the distinction that Fanon identifies between man and the black man.

Lack as White Privilege: Sartre

In *Black Skin, White Masks*, Fanon's distinction between man and the black man, and the implied distinction between being and meaning, in an important way is an engagement with Sartre's existential phenomenology. Against Sartre, who sees man as condemned to freedom because he confronts his own lack of being or nothingness, Fanon argues that the black man may be condemned but not free; within racist colonialism he is reduced to being and thereby denied the lack or confrontation with nothingness necessary for self-consciousness or humanity. In *Being and Nothingness*, Sartre (1956, 135, 136) maintains that "lack does not belong to the nature of the in-itself, which is all positivity. It appears in the world only with the upsurge of human reality. It is only in the human world that there can be lacks. . . . Human reality by which lack appears in the world must itself be a lack. . . . it is necessary that a being make itself its own lack; only a being which lacks can surpass being toward the lacked. The existence of desire as a human fact is sufficient to prove that human reality is a lack." As Fanon describes the separation between a man and a black man, it becomes clear that what the black man lacks is this very lack that makes subjectivity possible. The colonial values deny the black man not just individuality but also humanity. He is not considered fully rational or capable of subjectivity and agency. He is denied the transcendence that Sartre attributes to man. He is not allowed to make himself a lack of being to become self-conscious. Rather, he is chained to his being, to his body, more particularly to his skin, by colonial values.

In his critical engagement with Sartre's *Black Orpheus*, Fanon (1967, 134) responds that "in terms of consciousness, the black consciousness is held out as an absolute density, as filled with itself, a stage preceding any invasion, any abolition of the ego by desire." Contra man, within the colonial worldview, a black man represents a stage prior to desire, prior to the lack that initiates the desire and negativity necessary for self-consciousness, for being-for-itself. Within the colonial logic, the black man represents a pure positivity, an in-itself separated from the world of meaning as an object or animal. Fanon continues, "Still in terms of consciousness, black consciousness is immanent in its own eyes. I am not a potentiality of something, I am wholly what I am. I do not have to look for the universal. No probability has any place inside me. My Negro consciousness does not hold itself out as a lack" (135). Colonization makes the black man a lack of a lack, and through the process of what Fanon calls *disalienation,* he attempts to give the black man his lack back.

Fanon criticizes Sartre's claim that Negro poetry and negritude itself is a minor stage in history, which like all others will pass, that negritude is predetermined by the dialectic of history. Although Fanon suggests that negritude is defined by, and a reaction to, the white world, he objects to Sartre's idea of a preexisting meaning already determined because preexisting meanings are part of race alienation. In response to Sartre, he says, "And so it is not I who make a meaning for myself, but it is the meaning that was already there, pre-existing, waiting for me" (134). He rejects Sartre's suggestion that black poetry and black meaning do not come from their own suffering but have been waiting for a particular turn of history. This view of the black man's meaning as predetermined is the heart of the colonial logic, which maintains that the black man is determined in advance by history as subhuman and ripe for subservience, that he is subject to manifest destiny, that is, white destiny. Or, as Fanon says, "for the black man there is only one destiny and it is white" (10). The meaning of the black man is assigned by the white other. Fanon argues that even Sartre engages in naming the black man's meaning: "At the very moment when I was trying to grasp my own being, Sartre, who remained The Other, gave me a name and thus shattered my last illusion" (137). The struggle to liberate psychic space from colonization hinges on the black man's ability to make meaning for himself. He doesn't want recognition from the white colonists, an impossible recognition; rather, he wants to *recognize himself.* As I show in part II, creating meaning for oneself within the colonial situation, however, is always a dialectical operation between domination and resistance. Although the negritude movement is a reaction to whiteness in the sense that, as Fanon says, the black man is forced to secrete a race, it can be a form of resistance and revolt. It can be part of a psychic revolt in which the black man reasserts his agency as a meaning maker, which works against the alienated sense of arriving too late into the world.

It is precisely the sense of arriving too late to create one's own meaning that can make the colonization of psychic space so effective. Fanon describes going to films and waiting to see himself, his meaning already predetermined by racist stereotypes: "I wait for me" (140). He laments, "You come too late, much too late. There will always be a world—a white world—between you and us" (122). This sense of arriving too late is different from Lacan, Heidegger, or Sartre's sense of being thrown into a world that is not of your own making. The alienation of being thrown into the world differs dramatically from the debilitating alienation of being thrown there as one incapable of meaning making. For Heidegger, the connection between human beings and meaning is definitive. And, for Sartre, while we are thrown into a preexisting world of meaning, we are responsible for meaning making and for the meaning of the world. We become part of, and responsible for, that world of meaning. This is what makes us human beings, beings who mean. What Fanon describes is not simply arriving into a world of meaning that preexists us—that is true of everyone—but arriving too late into a white world in which one is defined as a brute being who does not mean and therefore is not fully human. Responsibility for meaning, and more particularly for the meaning of one's own body and self, has been usurped by the white Other. This is why Fanon says, "I came into the world with the will to find meaning but then I found that I was an object. Sealed into that crushing objecthood" (109); or, "All I wanted was to be a man among other men. I wanted to come lithe and young into a world that was ours and to help to build it together" (112). But "without responsibility, straddling Nothingness and Infinity, I began to weep" (140). Debilitating alienation is the result of being thrown into a world of preexisting meanings as one incapable of meaning making. And the greatest pain of this alienation comes from the fact that even the meaning of one's own body has been already defined.

Still, Fanon's phenomenology of the alienation of the black man within racist colonial society is arguably similar to the alienation inherent in an individual's relation to the social or to others described by Sartre or Heidegger. In *Being and Nothingness*, Sartre describes the alienation that results from the look of the Other that fixes him as an object and denies his transcendence.[7] Here, it seems that the Other can turn him into a thing and lock him into a crushing objecthood. Yet, as Sartre describes the encounter with the Other, not only is his own freedom always primary and therefore prevents assimilation by the Other, but also the conflict itself reaffirms his freedom. Sartre (1956, 473–75) describes a circle through which freedom guarantees itself both against and through the objectifying look of the Other. Although the look of the Other returns him to the world of being against the world of meaning, it does so in such a way that "I am revealed to myself as responsible for my being" and thereby restores him to the world of meaning through the world of being (475). This is possible because for Sartre, we are fundamentally beings who mean; the nature of our being is meaning.

Fanon's criticisms of the Hegelian dialectic of lord and bondsman could apply to Sartre's circle of conflict and freedom insofar as like Hegel, Sartre also assumes two equal and transcendent self-consciousnesses engaged in mutual recognition or at least in a necessarily and fortunately doomed attempt at mutual assimilation. Against Hegel, Fanon insists that colonialism does not allow any mutual recognition or assimilation. There is nothing reciprocal about the logic of colonialism. The black man within the colonial logic does not start from a place of transcendence and freedom; his freedom cannot be presupposed and therefore reaffirmed through colonial domination because there is no mutual conflict. Rather, within the logic of colonialism the one-sided "conflict" is justified precisely because the "native" is not free, human, and capable of transcendence. This conflict is not the metaphorical "pure 'possession' of myself by another" (475) described by Sartre but rather an exploitation of natives or possession of slaves circumscribed by colonial law. With colonialism and slavery, it is not just one's consciousness that is possessed by the Other, but one's body is property owned by the Other. Fanon (1967, 138) insists that "Jean-Paul Sartre had forgotten that the Negro suffers in his body quite differently from the white man." Within Fanon's analysis it is not just the body but also psychic space that is colonized by the white Other.

Beyond Fanon, and on a different tack, it could be argued that the look of the Other that causes Sartrean philosophy so much anxiety is in fact the look of those others who have been excluded from dominant cultural production by racism and sexism. It is the look of these concrete others whose exclusion and domination have served to shore up the borders of privileged subjectivity that causes anxiety and guilt. The free-floating guilt and anxiety that Sartre identifies with human self-consciousness and freedom can be read as a screen for concrete forms of exclusion, domination, and oppression. Sartre's metaphorical domination of the subject by the look of the Other can be read as the privileged subject's guilt and anxiety over racial and sexual difference and that subject's own racism and sexism. Moreover, Sartre's postulation that we are all alienated and dominated by the look of the Other covers over how specific forms of alienation and domination are literally beaten into the bodies and psyches of those excluded from, and oppressed by, dominant cultural productions of meaning.

On Fanon's analysis, existential phenomenology must be supplemented with psychoanalysis, and vice versa, to explain the effects of colonialism on the black man. The black man's alienation is neither merely ontological nor generated from his own existence. Within racist colonial culture, his existence is always only relative to the white man's. We cannot find the logic of colonial relations by examining the structure of human existence or by examining the world as it appears to us. Rather, we need to examine the structure of human relationships within particular social situations. As Sartre turns from setting out the conditions of possibility of human transcendence to analyzing the situation of freedom, he develops a more historical sense of alienation and begins to imagine restrictions on freedom that come from outside oneself or one's individual encounter with the Other, restrictions that come from society (cf. 1960, 1964). Yet, in light of Fanon's criticism of Sartre's analysis of the historical situation of black poets in *Black Orpheus*, there at least Sartre's notion of history is still too formal and dialetical to address Fanon's concerns with the liberation of psychic space through political action.

The Tranquillity of "the They" as White Privilege: Heidegger

Heidegger's notion of "the they" as an alienating force comes close to Fanon's description of the alienation of the black man. With *Being and Time*, alienation is no longer an individual's confrontation with the otherness of self-consciousness but, on the contrary, an *entanglement* with what Heidegger calls "the they," or public opinion. This social sense of alienation, however, still differs from the black man's alienation as described by Fanon. For Heidegger (1962, 178–79, 222–23), alienation (*entfremdung*) is the result of man's *falling* into "the they" and losing his individuality. This may sound similar to the loss of individuality experienced by the black man under colonial values and culture, but the effects of Heidegger's notion of alienation are dramatically different from the effects of racist alienation.

In an important way, Heidegger's "they" and its accompanying inauthenticity are the privilege of white (male) society. As Heidegger describes it, falling is the flip side of throwness. In the face of throwness, *Dasein* experiences anxiety because, as a result of its authentic confrontation with its own being-in-the-world and ultimately with its being there as meaning, it no longer feels at home in the world. Fleeing this anxious confrontation with the nothingness out of which human beings create the meaning of the world, and fleeing the fact that as human beings we already find ourselves thrown into a world of meaning, or into the world as *being there*, *Dasein* falls into inauthenticity and the security of "the they." Heidegger says that "in the face of its throwness Dasein flees to the relief which comes with the supposed freedom in the race of the uncanniness which is basically determinative for individualized Being-in-the-world" (277, 321). While in its individuality *Dasein* is not at home, with "the they" *Dasein* feels at home and tranquil. The tranquillity of "the they" becomes a temptation: "The supposition of the 'they' that one is leading and sustaining a full and genuine 'life,' brings Dasein a tranquility, for which everything is 'in the best of order' and all doors are open. Falling Being-in-the-world, which tempts itself, is at the same time tranquilizing" (178, 222). As Heidegger describes the human condition, it is more comfortable to live within a pregiven interpretation of the world from "the they" than to face the meaning of one's own life. Society presents us with the comfortable illusion that we can simply fall into a meaningful life already provided for us.

Certainly, no such happy illusion is available to the black man within racist culture. Society does not present him with an interpretation of the world that allows him to fall into the illusion that a meaningful life is already provided by colonial or racist society. And if he does accept the meaning of his life as it has been prescribed by colonial racist society, it does not provide him with a sense of tranquillity. Even the sense of a temptation to take the path of least resistance must be rethought for the black man within the colonial "they." The tranquillity of inauthenticity described by Heidegger in *Being and Time* is a white man's privilege.

Authenticity or asserting one's individuality against society, on the other hand, is not an option for the black man within the colonial logic. Fanon argues that the black man does not get the chance to face what Heidegger calls the alien voice of conscience inherent in becoming authentic *Dasein*, an individual against society, because within the colonial logic a black man is not distinguished from his group; he is not an individual. For Heidegger, one's individuality or authenticity is discovered through a sense of oneself as projected toward a future, the being-toward-death of *Being and Time*.

Yet, as Fanon describes the black man's experience, it is always one of coming too late. Within the colonial logic, the black man is not projected toward a future but always already predetermined by a past, a white past not his own. He is predetermined by white projections that deny rather than open up his future. Unlike Heidegger's authentic *Dasein*, he is neither ecstatic (standing outside being) nor a movement toward; rather, he is fixed and made static by the projections of his white colonizers.

Fanon (1967, 98) describes how the racist colonial values dehumanize and deindividuate the colonized: "I begin to suffer from not being white to the degree that the white man imposes discrimination on me, makes me a colonized native, robs me of all worth, all individuality, tells me that I am a parasite on the world, that I must bring myself as quickly as possible into step with the white world, 'that I am a brute beast, that my people and I are like a walking dung-heap that disgustingly fertilizes sweet sugar cane and silky cotton, that I have no use in the world.' Then I will quite simply try to make myself white: that is I will compel the white man to acknowledge that I am human." Fanon's analysis suggests that whereas white culture values individuality and the merits associated with this individualism, oppression works by denying individuality to the oppressed through stereotyping. The racialized other is seen as always and only a representative of a group, while the race "neutral," or "normal," dominant white is seen as an individual whose merit is self-determined. Insofar as the black man is deindividuated, he is not the man who struggles for his individuality against the social. Or, more precisely, he has to engage in a double struggle against the social to gain the privilege of struggling for his individuality.

If for Sartre and Heidegger the path of least resistance is to flee one's freedom and accept social norms without questioning them, and if facing one's freedom brings anguish and dread, then they can be describing only the white man's relation to both his own freedom and his own culture. For the black man, accepting the social norms of white society is not a way to *flee* his freedom even if it locks him into bondage. The idea that one *flees* his freedom assumes that one is in an active position in relation to that freedom; that one's culture gives one a choice to claim one's freedom. The individualism described by Sartre and Heidegger is also a value of Western culture. Within the racist colonial logic, however, the black man is given no such choice; he cannot choose to flee his freedom if it has been taken away from him. The dominant values of colonialism and racism assert authentic individuality for the privileged subject against the racialized other denied the privilege of authentic individuality. If Sartre's *bad faith* or Heidegger's *fall into "the they"* are the acceptance of social norms that bring a kind of naive tranquillity, for the black man the acceptance of racist social norms brings conflict and pain. Only the white man can find tranquillity within the norms of white society. And within racist colonial logic, only the white man has the freedom to flee his freedom. On the one hand, within the colonial situation, both authenticity and inauthenticity are the privilege of the white man and must be radically rethought to describe the world of the black man. On the other hand, Fanon's analysis shows that the white man's freedom is a deluded freedom insofar as it is based on the oppression of the black man. In fact, to take Fanon's analysis one step further, the privileged subject experiences anxiety or dread in the face of his freedom and the possibility of authentic individuality only because he can define himself against an inferior, devalued, disindividuated other. The privileged subject's anxiety and dread in the face of his freedom are symptoms of his anxiety and guilt over being forced by demands for freedom from those othered and excluded to confront the racism and sexism that have secured his privileged position as a subject who can choose his future.

The fact that Fanon's analysis of racist colonial oppression has been read as an application of Hegel or Sartre is also symptomatic of contemporary Western philosophy's attempts to substitute abstract accounts of the alienation inherent in the human condition for concrete accounts of specific forms of alienation. Moreover, leveling all forms of alienation as consequences of the human condition cover over the fact of racist and sexist oppression with their unique forms of debilitating alienation. If the alienation posited by Hegel, Sartre, and Heidegger are constitutive of Western freedom and subjectivity, the debilitating alienation of oppression undermines freedom and subjectivity. The alienation of oppression works against the "good" faith or authentic forms of alienation that supposedly make us human. If the modern world gives rise to the originary alienation that constitutes modern subjectivity described by contemporary philosophy, what emerges as the underside of this alienation is another treacherous and destructive form of alienation that undermines subjectivity and garners the psychic conditions for colonization, oppression, and social repression on which the modern subject gains its privilege.[8] The originary alienation enables the modern subject to emerge as an autonomous and creative source of its own meaning, while its debilitating underside brutally cancels that enabling power, leaving those othered by the first form of alienation excluded from the privileges of autonomy and creating their own meaning. Fanon's existential phenomenological psychology describes an experience left unthought within philosophies of alienation. Fanon's philosophy is original in its insistence on a type of alienation, a debilitating alienation, unique to those oppressed by racism that operates as the underside of privileged alienation.

The Colonial Mirror Image Is Reversed: Lacan

Comparing the effects of colonization on the ego of the oppressed to the effects of Lacan's mirror stage misrecognition further demonstrates how the alienation of oppression differs from an alienation postulated as inherent in subjectivity itself. For Lacan, the mirror stage offers a fiction that props up the ego in its struggle against others and its environment. The mirror stage reconciles the inner world of the ego with the outer world of the environment such that what Lacan calls its *fictional direction* gives the ego an illusory sense of agency in the world and control over itself and its environment. Fanon accepts Lacan's insistence on the fictional direction of the mirror stage when he argues that the mirror image or ideal ego for the black Antillean is neutral, or white. Following Lacan, Fanon (1967, 163) says that "perception always occurs on the level of the imaginary"; and this is how Antilleans *perceive* themselves and their fellows "in white terms." As I have argued elsewhere, however, the effects of the white mirror image for the black Antillean are the opposite of those of the Lacanian mirror stage.[9] Whereas the fictional direction of the Lacanian mirror stage operates as what Lacan (1977, 4, 2) calls an orthopedic image of the infant as a totality with agency in the world, the black man reflected in the white mirror of colonial racism experiences himself as fragmented and without agency. Whereas the infant in the Lacanian mirror misrecognizes its fragmented and out-of-control body as now unified and in control, Fanon (1967, 13) describes the effects of the white mirror as undermining any sense of unification and control, and returning the black body and psyche to a state of fragmentation and lack of control: "My body was given back to me sprawled out, distorted, recolored, clad in mourning in that white winter day."[10]

As Lacan describes the mirror stage, alienation is inherent in all subject formation because of the split between the inner and outer world. The subject's dependence on the outer world to shore up its sense of the unity and agency of its inner world makes it aggressive and hostile toward the Other on whom it depends. For Lacan, subjectivity is fundamentally an experience of alienation, and all human relationships are essentially aggressive and illusory. Fanon not only implicitly rejects Lacan's insistence on the necessity of alienation and hostility but also insists that the mirror stage is not an individual phenomenon but a social one.

Fanon claims that the Antillean mirror image is imagined as white or without color (162) and that ultimately while the white man can turn the black man into his Other, his negative that assures his positive identity, the black man cannot do the same with the white man. The white man is not the black man's Other in the same way that the black man is the white man's Other. Indeed, as Fanon describes it, blackness is also Other for the black man. In several places Fanon says that the Antillean considers the Senegalese black and associates them with violence (e.g., 161n).

Throughout *Black Skin, White Masks,* Fanon describes the debilitating alienation by which the black man identifies with white values that make blackness abject, but then he realizes that he is black and has to choose between denying his own blackness and identifying himself with the abject of white culture (197, 100). The onset of this debilitating alienation begins with the black man's contact with racist white culture. Fanon maintains that while in white culture the superego, or the assimilation of authority, begins in early childhood for the white child, for the black there is another, more sadistic, superego that he encounters only on contact with the white world: "A normal Negro child, having grown up within a normal family, will become abnormal on the slightest contact with the white world" (143).[11] Fanon describes the pathological effects of the internalization of the white sadistic superego as "the white man inject[ing] the black with extremely dangerous foreign bodies" (36). The black child is injected with the white superego that makes it abject itself. Fanon says that these dangerous white values are "secreted by his masters" (221), and he suggests that negritude, or the embrace of blackness, is a reaction against those white values through which the black man "secretes race" (122). As I show in chapter 3, the white man secretes values that force the black man to secrete a race in self-defense. Fanon muses that maybe the bodily fluids of blacks change when they encounter white society in the same way that the hormones of the husband change when the wife becomes pregnant (22). The white mirror image that brings with it the white superego is not just a visual perception but affects the bodily schema, the very bodily being of the black man.

These effects are the opposite of those on the white man of the black as mirror Other. In the passage about black children assimilating the white superego and becoming abnormal, Fanon also maintains that this is the "opposite" effect from a white child assimilating the white superego through which it abjects the black body and thereby fortifies its own identity (143). At another point, engaging with Anna Freud's theory of ego withdrawal as a defensive mechanism against failure, Fanon claims that while ego withdrawal may be a means of defense for whites, it is impossible for blacks, whose egos have been colonized by white values; withdrawing into the self is not a defense against failure when within the white values that black self is precisely the source of the failure. His analysis of the effects of colonization on the bodily schema of blacks led Fanon to the conclusion "that there is a dialectical substitution when one goes from the psychology of the white man to that of the black" (150).

While Lacan's later formulation of the gaze in relation to subject formation may be more akin to Fanon's thoroughly social ego, still, Lacan does not distinguish between the alienation inherent in all subject formation and the alienation unique to oppression or colonization in particular (cf. Lacan 1981, esp. 67–78). In his seminar 11, "The Four Fundamental Concepts of Psychoanalysis," Lacan maintains that alienation is fundamental to the subject (235). As he describes it, this is because man is born into a world that he did not create, a preexisting world, namely, the world of the Other: "We depend on the field of the Other, which was there long before we came into the world, and whose circulating structure determines us as subjects" (246). À la Heidegger, for Lacan, we are thrown into a world that we did not make.

The subject appears at the division between the world of being and the world of meaning, which is to say the world of the Other. It is this fundamental division between being and meaning inherent in subjectivity that Lacan calls alienation (210). As Lacan describes it, alienation is the either/or choice between being and meaning. The subject cannot have both at once. Lacan explains, "If we choose being, the subject disappears, it eludes us, it falls into non-meaning. If we choose meaning, the meaning survives only deprived of that part of non-meaning that is, strictly speaking, that which constitutes in the realization of the subject, the unconscious. In other words, it is of the nature of this meaning, as it emerges in the field of the Other, to be in a large part of its field, eclipsed by the disappearance of being, induced by the very function of the signifier" (211). The signifier is dependent on this division between being and meaning for its functioning. It operates only as a stand-in for an absent being. The word is not the thing and functions only by virtue of its separation from the thing. So, too, the subject is not being, but, to return to Sartre, a being who makes itself a lack of being. If the subject is reduced to being, then there is no subject, only some thing-in-itself. On the other hand, if the subject is placed solely in the realm of meaning, then it is just as much in jeopardy of disappearing as it is if it is placed solely in the realm of being. The subject must in some sense be a being first and foremost. For Lacan, this means that the subject must have an unconscious; its being is what he calls the real that resides within the unconscious. The split between being and meaning makes alienation the essence of the subject. It is neither and both at the same time. Yet it doesn't belong to either.[12]

For Lacan, whether it is the alienating gap between the mirror image and the body, between the ego ideal and the fragmented body in the mirror stage, or the split between being and meaning of seminar 11, alienation is inherent in the subject. (Within traditional psychoanalysis the ideal ego is the narcissistic relation to the maternal body; the ego ideal is the superego, or the prohibitions and standards instilled by parents and culture to which the individual tries to conform.) Several contemporary critics use Lacanian psychoanalytic theory to suggest that racist oppression is another version of this alienation at the heart of human subjectivity. For example, Homi K. Bhabha (1994, 45) says, "For Fanon, like Lacan, the primary moments of such a repetition of self [in the Other] lie in the desire of the look and the limits of language." Bhabha's reading of Fanon with Lacan suggests that there is no alienation specific to oppression or colonization; rather, the alienation described by Fanon is the same as the alienation described by Lacan as inherent in all subjectivity. On the contrary, the alienation of colonization and oppression is different from the alienation inherent in becoming a subject described in various ways by philosophers of alienation such as Hegel, Sartre, Heidegger, and Lacan. For Fanon, the alienation inherent in the subject, or what he calls man, does not capture the alienation of oppression, because within the colonial situation the black man is a black man and not a man. If man is alienated because he is thrown into a world not of his own making, the black man is doubly alienated because he is thrown there as one incapable of making meaning. For Fanon, the issue is not just that meaning preexists man but, rather, the particular types of meanings that preexist and determine the black man as subhuman or incapable of rationality or agency. It could also be argued that the privileged subject's ability to create meaning is constituted by and defined against animals and subhuman groups who do not create meaning. Certainly, imperialism rationalizes its right to colonize and dominate others through doctrines of manifest destiny dependent on distinctions between the civilized and barbarian, the rational and irrational, the human and subhuman. The privilege of autonomy and creative meaning making has been bought at a cost to those othered as inferior, dependent, and incapable of making meaning. This is true not only of colonization of other nations, lands, or peoples but also of oppression and repression in the forms of racism and sexism within a culture or nation.

Fanon's critical engagement with psychoanalysis continues to illustrate how the black man's alienation is unique. Another example is the section of *Black Skin, White Masks* devoted to Alfred Adler, in which Fanon rejects Adler's theory that neurosis, especially as it manifests itself in an inferiority complex, is a matter of character. Whereas Adler attributes the comparative logic of inferiority-superiority played out by the neurotic to an individual fiction and one's innate attitude toward the environment, Fanon insists that the inferiority complex of the Antillean is not an individual fiction but a social fiction that doesn't so much discolor the individual's interpretation of his environment (à la Adler) but comes from his environment to undermine his ego. Fanon (1967, 215) maintains that whereas "the Adlerian comparison embraces two terms; it is polarized by the ego," the "Antillean comparison is surmounted by a third term: Its governing fiction is not personal but social." Adler's neurotic suffering from an inferiority complex divides the world into self against other and inferior versus superior to prop up his own ego against the environment; those made "neurotic" by colonialism suffer their inferiority complex as an attack against the ego (cf. Fanon 1968b, 252). There is a fiction that causes the inferiority complex, but it is generated by the environment rather than generated against it and for the sake of diminishing the ego of the oppressed rather than for the sake of supporting it.

The effects of colonialism on the psyche of the colonized are social rather than individual neuroses. Colonial pathologies are social pathologies. There is an alienation particular to colonialism that goes beyond any notion of individual or existential alienation inherent in subject formation. Fanon (1967, 11) says, "The black man's alienation is not an individual question." He insists, "In the Weltanschauung of a colonized people there is an impurity, a flaw that outlaws any ontological explanation. Someone may object that this is the case with every individual, but such an objection merely conceals a basic problem. Ontology—once it is finally admitted as leaving existence by the wayside—does not permit us to understand the being of the black man. For not only must the black man be black; he must be black in relation to the white man. . . . The black man has no ontological resistance in the eyes of the white man" (109–10). It is impossible to answer the ontological question, what is the black man? since he exists only in relation to the white man. And while the same can be said of the white man, Fanon claims that in the colonial system of values the black man has no ontological resistance, that is, his being is determined in advance by the white man, which is not true of the latter. The alienation of oppression is not a universal phenomenon. It is not the alienation inherent in all subjectivity or in every individual. Rather, it is a social phenomenon that results from the privileged subject's attempt to define its autonomy and its privileged access to meaning against others whom it deems inferior.

Fanon continues to drive this point home in his discussion of how colonization forces black youth to choose between family and society.

Discussing the family, he says, "But, it will be objected, you are merely describing a universal phenomenon, the criterion of maturity being in fact adaptation to society. My answer is that such criticism goes off in the wrong direction, for I have just shown that for the Negro there is a myth to be faced. A solidly established myth. The Negro is unaware of it as long as his existence is limited to his own environment; but the first encounter with a white man oppresses him with the whole weight of his blackness" (149–50). Again, it is the fact that the colonized are oppressed by the preformed stereotypical image of themselves propagated by the colonizer that makes their alienation unique. They are not only thrown into a world of meaning not of their making, they are thrown there as those incapable of making meaning, as those whose meaning has already been defined as abject and less than fully human.

The notion that alienation, anxiety, and dread are inherent in the human condition, especially insofar as they are invoked through the look of the other, operates as a screen for a more treacherous form of alienation, the debilitating alienation of oppression on and against which the universal alienation of the privileged subject is conceived. The look that truly challenges the freedom of the privileged subject and makes it feel anxiety is not the look of any other, but the look of the concrete other who has been enslaved, oppressed, and dominated to secure the white European subject's privilege. Here I have analyzed some of the ways in which European notions of universal alienation cover over more concrete forms of alienation unique to colonization and oppression.

Fanon's writings also suggest a notion of debilitating alienation that functions almost in the opposite way from European notions of alienation. If European notions of alienation are inherent in the formation of subjectivity and agency, debilitating alienation undermines subjectivity and agency. If European notions of alienation are the result of human beings' ability to create their own meaning and project themselves into the future, debilitating alienation disables the ability to create meaning by tying those othered to a past that stereotypes them and projects them into a future in which they are disowned. In the next chapter, I continue with Fanon's suggestion of a debilitating form of alienation unique to colonization, now addressing its psychic manifestations. Fanon insists that colonization does not just operate on the land or the body but also and always on the psyche of those oppressed. The success of the colonization of a land, a nation, or a people can be measured through the success of the colonization of psychic space. Only through the colonization of psychic space can oppression be truly effective.

CHAPTER 2

Alienation's Double as Burden of the Othered Subject

Debilitating alienation can be described as the colonization of psychic space. If according to various twentieth-century theories, including existentialism and psychoanalysis, psychic space is the result of a primary alienation inherent in the human condition—finding ourselves in a world not of our making—then debilitating alienation turns alienation back against psychic space. If the alienation inherent in subjectivity is the subject turning back on itself to become self-conscious, then debilitating alienation is the subject being turned inside out to become an object for another. Debilitating alienation retroactively undermines originary alienation such that it debilitates the subject's sense of itself as an agent. If alienation instigates agency, then debilitating alienation breaks it down. Moreover, originary alienation is the privilege of the modern subject constituted against this dark underside of racist and sexist alienation that undermines subjectivity. Existential and psychoanalytic alienation and angst in the face of freedom and autonomy operate as a screen for a deeper anxiety and guilt that could be described as the return of the repressed. Confronting one's freedom as a privileged subject necessitates confronting the racist and sexist oppression and repression that shore up that privilege. The abstract anxiety and alienation inherent in subjectivity and humanity are symptoms of a concrete, if still unconscious, anxiety and guilt over racial difference and racism, and sexual difference and sexism. As Sartre makes so clear, with freedom comes responsibility; but can the privileged subject face its responsibility for proclaiming itself free and meaning full on the basis of excluding and dominating others?

The Colonization of Psychic Space and the Dynamics of Oppression: Fanon

In his criticisms of Sartre, Fanon (1967, 138) insists that Sartre forgets that the black man suffers in his body differently than the white man. As Fanon makes apparent, debilitating alienation manifests itself in the body of the colonized. The somatic symptoms of colonization are signs of the colonization of psychic space. As Fanon describes it, that colonization mobilizes an inferiority complex in the colonized. He insists that the inferiority complex of the oppressed is created by the colonial situation and is not a matter of character, as Adlerian psychoanalytic theory maintains: "The feeling of inferiority of the colonized is the correlative to the European's feeling of superiority. Let us have the courage to say it outright: It is the racist who creates his inferior" (1967, 93). "The black soul," says Fanon, "is a white man's artifact" (13). And in *A Dying Colonialism*, he says, "It is the white man who creates the Negro" (1965, 47).

To justify exploiting the colonized and taking their land, the colonizer makes them inferior. And, to make them inferior, the colonizer racializes them, that is, the colonizer, at least at first, makes their inferiority *natural* rather than, or in addition to, social or cultural—only later can more subtle forms of racism maintain domination (35, 37). As Fanon (1968a, 40) explains in *Toward the African Revolution*, "It is not possible to enslave men without logically making them inferior through and through. And racism is only the emotional, affective, sometimes intellectual explanation of this inferiorization. The racist in a culture with racism is therefore normal. He has achieved a perfect harmony of economic relations and ideology." In other words, the colonist justifies economic exploitation using racist ideology. Racism is normal or natural only because race is naturalized. Fanon continues, "Every colonialist group is racist. . . . Race prejudice in fact obeys a flawless logic. A country that lives, draws its substance from the exploitation of other peoples, makes those people inferior. Race prejudice applied to those peoples is normal" (41).

Yet Fanon maintains that colonization goes further than taking land or rendering the colonized inferior. While racism can provide the emotional and intellectual justification for colonization, the convolutions of guilt in the colonial identity formation and its production of values prepare the way for an even greater psychic justification. In *The Wretched of the Earth*, Fanon (1968b, 41) argues that:

> It is not enough for the settler to delimit physically, that is to say with the help of the army and the police force, the place of the native. As if to show the totalitarian character of colonial exploitation the settler paints the native as a sort of quintessence of evil. Native society is not simply described as a society lacking in values. It is not enough for the colonist to affirm that those values have disappeared from, or still better never existed in, the colonial world. The native is declared insensible to ethics; he represents not only the absence of values, but also the negation of values. He is, let us dare to admit, the enemy of values, and in this sense he is the absolute evil. He is the corrosive element, destroying all that comes near him; he is the deforming element, disfiguring all that has to do with beauty or morality; he is the depository of maleficent powers, the unconscious and irretrievable instrument of blind forces.

This notion that the native represents the very negation of the colonists' values resonates with Fanon's analysis of how colonialism and oppression enable the colonizer to project onto a racialized and inferior other all of the unwanted qualities in himself (190). The very identity of the colonizer is dependent on the oppression/repression of his projected fantasy of the colonized. The black man is forced to identify with the white superego that rules the colonial society, a sadistic superego that first projects evil and everything inhuman onto the colonized and then excludes them from proper civilization. The white man's violent attempts to expel his own otherness, which he has projected onto the bodies of those he oppresses, necessarily brings the return of the repressed in the form of both his own barbarism and guilt. Fanon's study of the effects of colonization on the colonizer suggests that it is the convolutions of guilt that initiate the move from making the colonized inferior to justify taking their lands and enslaving them, to making them the repressed unconscious Other against whom the white man defines his very identity by attempting an absolute exclusion of his own otherness projected onto the bodies of those he oppresses. The case studies of the neurotic symptoms of colonizers in Algeria in *The Wretched of the Earth* suggest that the psychic dynamics of projection and exclusion follow from economic exploitation and colonial domination as a type of reaction formation that aims (yet fails) to justify and solidify the ego boundaries of the colonizer.

On the other hand, in *Black Skin, White Masks*, Fanon (1967, 11) describes what he calls the "internalization" of inferiority by the colonized. As he describes it, the first stage is primarily economic; the second, psychic.

But the two are inherently connected. For Fanon, the social and the psyche are inseparable. Indeed, this is his criticism of traditional psychoanalysis, that it focuses on individuals out of the context of their social situations.[1]

It is through economic oppression that the colonizer also levels psychic oppression, an oppression that cuts to the quick of the individual psyche to create the "mass attack against the ego." Fanon says, "If his psychic structure is weak, one observes a collapse of the ego. The black man stops behaving as an actional person. The goal of his behavior will be The Other (in the guise of the white man), for The Other alone can give him worth. That is on the ethical level: self-esteem" (154). Conversely, psychic oppression is a crucial way for colonizers to not only attempt to render the colonized docile but also justify their own violence. This dialectic of social and psychic phenomena creates the oppressive situation of colonization. The colonized internalize the racist stereotypes and value system created by their white oppressors. When the colonists take over the economy, in a significant sense they also colonize the means of production of value in society, not only economic value but all values and meaning itself ("The Other alone can give him worth").[2] This double process of controlling both economic and psychic value is what makes colonization so effective. Through economic subordination and the technological propagation of images of inferiority, colonization and racism create the aberrations of affect that Fanon describes in *Black Skin, White Masks.* One of the most effective weapons of colonialism is its attempt to force the colonized to internalize a value system in which they are rendered subhuman, incapable of rational thought or morality. The morality of colonialism reduces the colonized to their bodies, which become emblems for everything evil within that morality. This identification of the colonized with their bodies, and more specifically within racist culture with their skin, leads Fanon (1967, 11) to call the internalization of inferiority a process of *epidermalization.* The black man is reduced to nothing but his skin, black skin, which becomes the emblem for everything hateful in white racist society.[3]

The logic of the internalization of colonial values, however, is a paradoxical logic, and, as such, it is destined to fail. The colonized are forced to internalize an image of themselves as subhumans lacking a soul, mind, psyche, or an ego as the seat of agency. In other words, the colonized internalize an image of themselves as lacking any internal life. Paradoxically, for the internalization of inferiority to be successful, they must internalize the lack of the ability to internalize. If they are merely bodies, subhuman animals unthinkingly reacting to stimuli, how can they internalize the racist colonial values? Although the logic of colonialism founders on its own paradox and ensures that colonization can never totally succeed—that even if you can colonize the land you can never completely colonize psychic space—the material dominance of colonial values is bound to adversely affect the psychic life of the colonized. Throughout his work, Fanon describes the radically disabling effects of racism and colonization of the psyche of the oppressed that must be counterbalanced by equally radical resistance to liberate not only physical and economic space but also the psychic space of the colonized.

As Fanon describes his project in *Black Skin, White Masks,* it is one of disalienation. The liberation of psychic space requires disalienation, perhaps even double disalienation, to counteract the debilitating alienation of colonization. If the thesis that alienation is inherent in subjectivity is implicated in Fanon's criticisms of colonialism that frame his engagement with Hegel, Sartre, and Lacan, then the "disalienation of the black man" may require not only overcoming the secondary alienation of colonization that denies the colonized that status of meaning maker in the world of meaning but also conceiving of subjectivity such that it does not require alienation, especially insofar as that alienation necessitates or instigates the exclusion of otherness. This means rejecting European notions that alienation is inherent in a subjectivity that requires a fight to the death or abjection of otherness. These notions of European alienation are symptoms of anxiety and guilt over the exclusions, enslavement, and abjection of concrete others to shore up subject privelege.

Racist Alienation in the Context of the United States

Fanon's account of alienation is unique in that it describes a secondary, or debilitating, alienation particular to colonialism and domination that retroactively has destabilized what European philosophers identify as an originary alienation inherent in subjectivity. In addition, Fanon argues that colonization operates through racialization and that all colonization brings with it racism. In this regard, Fanon's analysis of the racism of colonization speaks to racism in the North American context, where racism began with a type of colonization, the slave trade, and continued and continues with lynching, segregation, incarceration, and capital punishment for far more black men than white, with hate crimes, discrimination, and racial profiling.

What Fanon's texts suggest as the debilitating or double alienation of colonial racism resonates with what W. E. B. Du Bois calls double consciousness.[4] In *The Souls of Black Folk,* Du Bois (1969, 45) maintains that in racist America, blacks are not seen as real Americans, and yet they are Americans, as he describes in this famous passage: "This double-consciousness, this sense of always looking at one's self through the eyes of others, of measuring one's soul by the tape of a world that looks on in amused contempt and pity. One ever feels his twoness,—an American, a Negro; two souls, two thoughts, two unreconciled strivings; two warring ideals in one dark body, whose dogged strength alone keeps it from being torn asunder." What Du Bois describes, however, does not get to the heart of the colonization of psychic space inherent in racism as debilitating alienation. It is not just that the victims of racism (or sexism for that matter) are on both the inside and the outside—that they are and are not real or true Americans or citizens—and it is not just that dominant values exclude them from the world of meaning except as abject or inferior, but, moreover, it is that they are excluded from meaning making; they are excluded from making the meaning of even their own bodies and lives. In Marxian terms, they are excluded from the means of production of value, the value of their own lives. And it is this exclusion that produces debilitating alienation. Certainly, this form of alienation unique to oppression is about belonging to the community and the social sphere, but it is also about belonging as one who contributes to the meaning and value of that community. Once again, it is not just arriving too late into the world of meaning—that is, the human condition—rather, it is arriving there as one excluded from participation in the creation of meaning, especially the meaning of one's own body.

Fanon points to this alienation from his own body caused by coming too late into the white world of meaning with his famous description of his experience on the train when he is interpolated as Negro by a white child who says, "Look, a Negro. . . . Mama, see the Negro! I'm frightened!":

> In the train it was no longer a question of being aware of my body in the third person but in a triple person. In the train I was given not one but two, three places. . . . It was not that I was finding febrile coordinates in the world. I existed triply: I occupied space. I moved toward the other . . . and the evanescent other, hostile but not opaque, transparent, not there, disappeared. Nausea. I was responsible at the same time for my body, for my race, for my ancestors. . . . I discovered my blackness, my ethnic characteristics; and I was battered down by tom-toms, cannibalism, intellectual deficiency, fetishism, racial defects, slave-ships, and above all else, above all: "Sho' good eaten." . . . What else could it be for me but an amputation, an excision, a hemorrhage that spattered my whole body with black blood? . . . My body was given back to me sprawled out, distorted, recolored, clad in mourning in that white winter day. (1967, 112–13).

Racist values reduce his very being to his body, his skin, and then determine the meaning of that body and skin. Within the colonial economy, he is not free to actively participate in the creation of the meaning of his own body. This is why he must violently and by all means resist the colonial economy: not just to regain his land or resources, or his culture and traditions, but to reclaim his body and its psychic space.

The legal theorist Patricia Williams helps bring Fanon's description of his triple alienation from his own body and its value into a contemporary North American context when she describes how this debilitating alienation is both present in the United States and yet complicated by strivings for a color-blind society. Williams (1998, 27) maintains that concern with color-blindness can work to deny racial experiences and experiences of racism: "For black people, the systematic, often nonsensical denial of racial experiences engenders a sense of split identity attending that which is obviously inexpressible; an assimilative tyranny of neutrality as self-erasure. It creates an environment in which one cannot escape the clanging of symbolism of oneself. This is heightened by contrast to all the silent, shifty discomfort of suffering condescension. There's that clunky social box, larger than your body, taking up all that space. You need two chairs at the table, one for you, one for your blackness." Sensitivity about race is so intense that many whites feel that it isn't polite to mention race, that doing so in and of itself makes you a racist. The result, as Williams describes it, is that black people cannot discuss their racial experiences, let alone their experiences of racism; within this color-blind-obsessed world of white guilt, it is not polite to make white people aware of race. Race must remain the elephant in the room that everyone tries to go around. Race is that clunky social box that is always a stumbling block within contemporary race relations governed by the rhetoric of color-blindness.[5]

So while Fanon describes the overt and violent form of racism in colonization where Europeans (or Americans) invade the land or country of people whom they racialize and degrade to justify their occupation, Williams describes a more covert form of racism in the contemporary United States. Unfortunately, along with a more subtle racism, we still have violent and overt racism: in Brooklyn, an unarmed black man is gunned down by police as he reaches for his wallet; in Texas, a black man is dragged to death behind a pickup truck; in Queens, Arabs and Muslims are murdered after September 11. The physically violent acts of racism may not seem to be condoned by the U.S. government as they are in the situations of colonization described by Fanon, but they still exist with shocking frequency. What is invading Iraq but a form of colonization using the discourse of freedom? And isn't capital punishment, which for the most part only affects black men, a form of state-sanctioned violent racism? Certainly, rounding up over eight hundred Arabs and Muslims and holding them without legal representation, in harsh conditions with threatening guards, is state-sanctioned violent racial profiling in the name of patriotism. The more covert forms of racism, on the other hand, continue to colonize psychic space; and racist discrimination that leads to economic segregation continues to circumscribe physical space, as Williams points out so well in her discussions of the Howard Beach incident, where black men were killed merely for being in the wrong neighborhood. Freedom and patriotism have become a rallying cry for more overt racism than we have seen in the United States in decades. But, in addition to these violent forms of racism, there is the more covert racism that William describes with her clunky box metaphor. The effects of this racism are in some ways more insidious than the overt violence of the early-twentieth-century colonization because it even more effectively disguises itself with rhetoric of equality and color-blindness. Racism is passed off as democratic values of equality and freedom. More subtle even is the way that racism becomes a matter of denying racial differences that make a difference to the lives of people of color in the name of not only equality and color-blindness but also politeness or even attempts at not being seen as a racist. This kind of denial of difference that is construed as an attempt to treat all people equally by ignoring race or the idea that it isn't polite to bring up race is also implicit in Williams's example of the clunky box of race that is simultaneously there but not there.

The sociologist Ruth Frankenberg's study of white women's relations to race confirms Williams's speculations that race remains unspoken in polite conversation. Frankenberg (1993, 142) found that "for many white people in the United States, including a good number of the women I interviewed, 'color-blindness'—a mode of thinking about race organized around an effort not to 'see,' or at any rate not to acknowledge, race differences—continues to be the 'polite' language of race." On the other hand, for many of the women she interviewed, "to be caught in the act of seeing race was to be caught being 'prejudiced'" (145). Frankenberg concludes that what she calls the color- and power-evasive relation to race—color-blindness—is a response against earlier biological racism that operated by asserting a biological hierarchy of races: "White women who grew up before the 1960s came to adulthood well before the emergence and public visibility of the movements that emphasized cultural pride and renewal among people of color. During their formative years, there were only two ways of looking at race difference: either it connoted hierarchy or it did not (or should not) mean anything at all. Theirs was, then, a historically situated rejection of the salience of race difference" (145).

The double consciousness of Du Bois has become the consciousness that one is black and yet not supposed to be seen as black or speak as black, that black or racial experiences do and don't exist. Obviously, racial experiences and experiences of racism do exist, but within racist culture the meaning of those experiences is foreclosed, and the social resources for sublimating their concomitant affects are withheld. It is this lack of participation in, or belonging to, the meanings of dominant culture that turns double consciousness into debilitating alienation. As I show in part III, social support is necessary for sublimation of drives and affects that otherwise will manifest themselves in somatic symptoms and depression. Without the social space to create meaning for oneself from the culturally available symbols, it is impossible to gain a sense of individuality and of belonging to the community. As I show in part IV, the balance between individuality and community requires the social space of forgiveness that supports the revolt or trespass necessary for individuation in the context of community. One way that oppression operates is to withhold forgiveness from individuals or groups that have been abjected or excluded from, or devalued by, dominant values. A positive sense of self is unavailable within the values of oppression; agency depends on a positive sense of self. Subjectivity, agency, individuality, and community depend on the social space that supports sublimation of the individual's bodily drives and affects within available cultural meanings. Without supportive social spaces, the result is depression, shame, anger, and alienation. The colonization of psychic space through depression, shame, anger, and alienation is part and parcel of the dynamic of oppression. Conversely, resistance to oppression can restore agency, individuality, solidarity, and community. Despite a colonial or racist structure or logic that creates debilitating alienation and double consciousness, it is possible to transform the experience of alienation into resistance and agency. As McGary (1998, 270) and others point out, many black people do not experience their lives as alienated because black communities provide support against race alienation. And it may be that in the contemporary United States it is easier for people of color to find alternative communities, either with other people of color who share some of their experiences, or across color lines with various kinds of shared experiences at work or school. Some of these communities may be born out of struggles to resist racism and reform racist institutions. Fanon insists throughout his writings that resistance and revolt restore agency and become restorative means of disalienation. These are not just the major political revolutions of an Algeria or South Africa but also psychic revolts that can take place in the everyday lives of ordinary people who resist domination. Fanon, like the psychoanalyst Julia Kristeva, imagines the political and social space for everyday geniuses. In his vision of the

Algerian revolution, he insists not only that a new humanism is born from struggle but also that revolution can produce the space "in which every kind of genius may grow" (1965, 34). In part IV, I explore some possibilities for resistance, revolt, and genius that restore agency and community.

Alienation and Sexual Difference

In addition to considering some of the similarities and differences between the racism of colonization that Fanon describes and contemporary racism in the United States, it is also important to consider how notions of debilitating alienation and double consciousness, and resistance to them, may be inflected by gender; this is a consideration lacking in Fanon's analysis, which often appears sexist or insensitive to sexual difference.[6] By now, many feminist theorists have analyzed multiple sources of oppression and the intersection of racism and sexism in the lives of black women and other racialized women.[7] For example, Cynthia Willett (2001, 159, 162) points out that "Du Bois's romantic concept of the double consciousness of the black man does not address the [black] domestic worker's need to deal with incommensurate demands made by black men, white employees, and her own children, among others, in interlocking systems of power"; therefore, "male narratives staging confrontations outside the community may accommodate the more traditional romantic language of alienation and double consciousness than do the women's narratives." How do gender and sex affect how black women experience debilitating alienation? It seems reasonable to think that since men and women occupy different social positions within patriarchal culture, and since they have different options and restrictions, there will be differences in their experiences of, and reactions to, alienation, specifically the debilitating alienation of racism.

To see some of these gendered differences, I turn now to African American fiction and the possible differences between how male writers describe alienation and how female writers describe it. Although the fiction of writers like Ralph Ellison and Richard Wright resonates with that of the existentialist writers of alienation, the former present vivid and painful descriptions of the experience of racism and racist alienation through their outsider and underground characters. Black women writers, on the other hand, are less likely to present the loner, even macho, characters found in these men's writings. Rather, the women express (and experience) the debilitating alienation of racism as compounded by the restrictions on women in patriarchal society. While generalizations about the difference between black men's and black women's writing are by no means absolute and definitely do not apply across the board, they can illuminate the role of sexual difference in compounding the experience of debilitating alienation.

From her interviews with black women and a survey of their writing, Claudia Tate (1983, xix–xx) concludes that the American "quest theme—a character's personal search for meaningful identity and for self-sustaining dignity in a world of growing isolation and meaninglessness, and moral decay . . . assumes a special dimension when it is depicted by black American writers, inasmuch as their sense of isolation and moral hypocrisy has always been qualified by racial prejudice. Black women writers, of course, are confronted with the same racial climate as their male counterparts, but by virtue of their gender their depictions of it often reflect differences—sometimes subtle and sometimes obvious—in tone, in character selection, setting, and plot." What Tate calls the quest theme, the theme of isolation and meaninglessness in a hostile world, is complicated for black men, who experience isolation and hostility as a result of racism. In addition, meaninglessness is compounded by racism insofar as racialized subjects are thrown into a meaningless world not of their making and supposedly lacking the capacity to make meaning. Tate points out that for black women, gender oppression further complicates the situation, which has led some theorists to talk about multiple consciousness rather than double consciousness.[8]

One of the most striking differences that Tate finds is that the black heroine in women's writing "seldom elects to play the role of the alienated outsider or the lone adventurer in her quest for self-affirmation" and self-discovery in the way that male heroes in men's writing do. "She does not, for instance, journey across the Northeast like Richard Wright's Cross Damon in *The Outsider*, nor does she explore the underground regions of urban civilization like Ralph Ellison's invisible man. On the contrary, she is usually literally tied down to her children and thus to a particular place" (xx). While Wright and Ellison's heroes are more likely to characterize their alienation in terms of isolation and meaninglessness, and resist or overcome it through confrontations—sometimes macho confrontations—with other men, especially white men, the heroines of black women's fiction are more likely to characterize their alienation in terms of tensions or miscommunications in interpersonal relationships, and resist or overcome it through renegotiating those relationships with family and loved ones.

Like Tate, who figures the difference in terms of geography and terrain, the writer Alexis DeVeaux also describes the difference in terms of negotiating space, the space of the individual in relation to the community: "I see a greater and greater commitment among black women writers to understand self, multiplied in terms of the community, the community multiplied in terms of the nation, and the nation multiplied in terms of the world. You have to understand what your place as an individual is and the place of the person who is close to you. You have to understand the space between you before you can understand more complex or larger groups. Thus, the exploration of this space is a main focal point in our work" (Tate 1983, 55). Other black women writers describe the difference between their work and work by black men as a difference between the focus on psychic space and psychic violence (even if it is related to physical violence), on the one hand, and physical space and physical violence, on the other. For example, Kristin Hunter says that men emphasize "physical violence and actual brutal confrontations. . . . With the women there's more sense of personal relationships: family, home-centered dramatic scenes" (Tate 1983, 85). Hunter suggests that black women's writing might be more aggressive and violent than white women's writing, but unlike in black men's writing, the women characters are usually the victims of violence and not the perpetrators. Toni Morrison also identifies the difference as a difference not only between black men and black women's writing but between black women and white women's writing: "There's a male/female thing that's also different in the works of black and white women writers, and this difference is good. There's a special kind of domestic perception that has its own violence in writings by black women—not bloody violence, but violence nonetheless. Love, in the Western notion, is full of possession, distortion, and corruption. It's a slaughter without the blood" (Tate 1983, 123). Certainly, Morrison's work is notable for its violence by women; but this violence is usually a form of self-defense. Even Sethe in *Beloved* murders her daughter to save her from white domination.

According to these writers, black women's writing, more than either that of white women or black men, describes the violence of love and intimate relations. While black men describe relationships of confrontation, black women are more concerned with trust and loss of trust in family and love relations. Black men describe relations with the outside world; black women describe inner relations. And while black men primarily describe anger, alienation, and resentment, black women explore the emotional depths of love and intimacy. While they share the quest for self-affirmation and vivid descriptions of the violence of racism that undermine that quest, they articulate their visions in ways that, not surprisingly, correspond to the different social positions and expectations of men and women in patriarchal culture.

Gayl Jones, whose own writing so vividly portrays the violence of love and broken trust in the struggle for freedom, identifies the difference between black men and black women's writings already in slave narratives, where men are more likely to describe injustices in terms of outside relations, while women describe injustices in terms of inside relations: "With many women writers, relationships within family, community, between men and women, and among women—from slave narratives by black women writers on—are treated as complex and significant relationships, whereas with many men the significant relationships are those that involve confrontations—relationships outside the family and community. . . . If you compare the slave narratives written by men with those written by women, you see very delicate and complex interpersonal relationships in the latter, whether they be among members of the same race or between races. With men the focus is on social grievances, with little sense of intimate relationships among the slaves, precluding the desire for freedom" (Tate 1983, 93). Jones suggests that slave women's narratives reflect a desire for freedom complicated by connections to family and intimate relations in a way that men's narratives do not; slave men were more likely to describe struggles for freedom in terms of confrontations with those outside the family and were less likely to see intimate relations, especially with children, complicating their flight to freedom. Like Tate and DeVeaux, Jones figures this difference in terms of space: Women's characters move within the family and community, while men's characters move outside it; women develop intimate portraits of women characters' psychic spaces, while men develop confrontations in social space, which is not to say that both men's and women's literature cannot be read for the connections between social and psychic space. Tate reinforces this insight when in conversation with Jones she says, "A lot of stories, especially those by black males—I think of *Invisible Man*, I think of *Autobiography of an Excolored Man*—never tell you anything about the intimate self. They tell you about the self in conflict with external institutions. Your work [speaking to Jones], and also most of that by women, seems to be concerned with revealing the character's intimate sense of self through very complex relationships. Like those by many black women writers, your stories seem to focus on the revelation of inner character rather than on reporting head-on confrontation with social issues" (Tate 1983, 92).

Like many of the black writers in Tate's volume, the sociologist Patricia Hill Collins (1990, 105) concludes that black women's literature and music, especially blues, explore the "journey toward freedom in ways that are characteristically female." She maintains that "Black women's journeys, though at times embracing political and social issues, basically take personal and psychological forms and rarely reflect the freedom of movement of Black men who hop 'trains,' 'hit the road,' or in other ways physically travel in order to find that elusive sphere of freedom from racial oppression. Instead, Black women's journeys often involve [what Audre Lorde calls] 'the transformation of silence into language and action.' Typically tied to children and/or community, fictional Black women characters search for self-definition within close geographical boundaries" (105). Collins's analysis suggests that the difference in geography and physical space reflects or produces a difference in psychic space. Given the way that physical movement is circumscribed within patriarchal culture and institutions, it could be said that women's psychic space is deep and men's is vast. While cultural expectations based on race and gender may make it difficult for men to define themselves in terms of intimate relationships, those expectations may make it difficult for women to define themselves in terms of social or institutional relationships. At least since Carol Gilligan's groundbreaking work on the differences of moral perception of men and women, feminists have explored this possibility. Comments by black women writers suggest that this dynamic is complicated by race and racism, which not only further polarizes domestic and public spaces but also racializes them.

These women's comments on differences between the writing of black men and black women are meant to further complicate the notion of debilitating alienation with considerations of sex and gender. Obviously, an in-depth analysis of gender differences in African American literature is beyond the scope of this book. Still, it is worth noting that many of the writers from Tate's interviews who comment on gender differences compare more contemporary women's writing with earlier men's writing from the 1940s and 1950s, namely, Ralph Ellison and Richard Wright. This period in the middle of the twentieth century is perhaps not coincidentally the heyday of existentialism in Europe, including the writings of Fanon. In Europe and the United States, particularly black America, alienation was a central theme during this period. Indeed, it is possible that there are more similarities between alienation as it is articulated by men and women in this period than in more contemporary literature.

Ann Petry's *Street* (1946), for example, presents its female protagonist, Lutie Johnson, as isolated, alienated, and eventually on the road with a one-way ticket to Chicago. Even so, Lutie has to negotiate being black and being a woman. While most of her relationships are alienated and she does not define herself in relation to the kind of family community described by the women Tate interviews, Lutie's identity is very much defined by her struggle to raise her son in Harlem. The fact that she is a woman complicates her relationships in ways particular to gender politics of the 1940s and most of her relationships with men are abusive. Hers was a violent life, and in the end she kills the abusive Boots Smith by beating him with a heavy iron candlestick. In a fit of rage against the sexism and racism of her world, she continues to beat him even after he is dead. Like Wright's Bigger Thomas or Damon Cross's alienation, Lutie Johnson's alienation is articulated as violent isolation, but unlike theirs, it is the result not only of violent racism but also of violent sexism. In her last novel, *The Narrows* (1953), published the same year as Wright's *Outsider*, Petry develops a character, Link Williams, closely connected to his family and community. But Link could not be more different from *The Outsider*'s Damon Cross, especially in the connection between the former's self-identity and community. Link is not an outsider; he belongs to his community. Like Petry's other novels, *The Narrows* explores the complicated dynamics of racism and sexism in the affair between Link and a white woman, Camilo. Like Ellison and Wright, Petry presents the debilitating alienation of racism now complicated by sexism.

Even Nella Larsen's earlier "underground"-type character, Helga Crane, ends up married and oppressed by her role as wife and mother by the end of *Quicksand* (1928). Unlike most female heroines in novels by women, Helga Crane travels alone and makes her resentment, loneliness, and alienation known to the reader in terms as harsh as any of the great existential fictions, but now complicated by race. From Denmark, Helga laments returning to America: "Never could she recall the shames and often the absolute horrors of the black man's existence in America without the quickening of her heart's beating and a sensation of disturbing nausea. It was too awful. The sense of dread of it was almost a tangible thing in her throat" (82). Yet, by the end, Helga is pregnant with her fifth child and trapped in a life of oppression, but now not only as a black woman but also as a wife and mother: "Of the children Helga tried not to think. She wanted to leave them—if that were possible. . . . No. She couldn't desert them. How, then, was she to escape from the oppression, the degradation, that her life had become? It was terribly difficult. It was almost hopeless" (135). It is obvious that Helga's wandering days are over; she has a new sexist alienation, like quicksand, in which to sink.

The quicksand of sex roles and gender politics compounds the debilitating alienation of racism, which affects self-identity. As I further delineate in part III, just as the alienation unique to racist oppression is distinct from any alienation supposed to be inherent in subjectivity and subject formation, the alienation unique to sexist oppression is also distinct. To imagine resisting racism and sexism, it is necessary to distinguish the alienation of oppression from merely finding oneself in a world not of one's own making. Not only are those othered thrown into a world not of their own making, they are thrown there as incapable of making meaning. They are doubly alienated from the realm of meaning. They are estranged from the means of production of value, especially the value and meaning of their own bodies. It is crucial, then, that those othered within mainstream culture begin to take over the means of production of value of their own lives. But this is only one step in the decolonization of psychic space. If the true revolution is one of imagination, it requires not only the creation of positive values for those abjected by dominant culture but also the revaluation of values such that the very structure of valuation is opened up for transformation. It requires throwing off not only Marx's imaginary chains but also the chains that bind the imaginary and thereby restrict psychic space. These chains leave scars not only on the psyche and the sense of self-identity but also on the body, as the affects of oppression turn inward and are manifest as somatic symptoms. As Fanon so powerfully argues, decolonization requires disalienation, which is possible through a new valuation of what it means to be human. This new valuation and meaning must begin from the subject position of those othered. They, we, must articulate the meaning of our own bodies and lives and thereby transform the very means of production of value. Creating one's own meaning and community are possible through resistance and revolt against sexism and racism. Moreover, decolonizing psychic space begins with understanding the dynamics of the colonization of psychic space and how it invades the body and soul, which is the project of this book.

In the next chapter, I continue to explore how the colonization of psychic space that always accompanies colonization of land, or oppression or domination of a people within their own county, inflicts a debilitating alienation that goes beyond any notion that alienation is inherent in the human condition and suffered by all individuals. What I am calling the colonization of psychic space is in various ways common to colonization, oppression, domination, discrimination, and other forms of exclusion. Fanon's analysis of colonization offers a notion of the colonization of psychic space that can assist in a diagnosis of the effects of racism in the United States and elsewhere. The notion of the colonization of psychic space also helps delineate the effects of sexism and even the intersection of sexism and racism in black women writers' fiction. In the next chapter, again following Fanon, I analyze in greater detail how the debilitating alienation unique to the colonization of psyche space affects psychic life, particularly the affects of both colonizer and colonized. In subsequent chapters, I continue this analysis by diagnosing how the debilitating alienation of racism and sexism, what I am calling the colonization of psychic space, lead to depression, shame, and anger, which undermine subjectivity, identity, and agency.

Colonization is not just the invasion of foreigners who take over territory and natural resources. The traditional division between metropolis and colony, or foreigner and indigenous native, becomes complicated in light of the occupation of psychic space and identity formation that takes place *within* the culture of the metropolis. In the United States, for example, women, black men, homosexuals, and other marginalized groups are not considered colonial subjects, and yet they are subject to what I call the colonization of psychic space. Colonizing cultures and values can invade and occupy psychic space without establishing a colonial settlement on foreign territory. And physical movements can be restricted without colonial armies or even police presence. It is possible to talk of the colonization of psychic space of those oppressed who do not technically live in a colony.

The colonization of psychic space is the occupation or invasion of social forces—values, traditions, laws, mores, institutions, ideals, stereotypes, etc.—that restrict or undermine the movement of bodily drives into signification. The metaphor of psychic *space* helps delineate the intimate connection between bodies and culture. The psyche is the "place" where bodily drives intersect with social forces. Psychic space is robust when drives and their affective manifestations are discharged into signifying systems and thereby translated into meaning, which is inherently social. When the translation of bodily drives into meaning is disrupted or undermined by social forces, particularly oppression, psychic space is restricted and no longer open to the movement between drives and signification. Without the discharge of bodily drives into language and other signifying systems, we become cut off from the world of meaning on which we depend for meaningful lives. Oppression operates through social forces and institutions that work against the development and maintenance of open robust psychic space for particular groups or individuals. Diminished psychic space results in bodily drives and affects turned inward, which ultimately leads to depression and self-hatred unless these very affects can be turned or returned into resistance and fortifying strategies.

Part II

The Secretion of Race and Fluidity of Resistance

The "civilizing mission" of colonization could be said to turn on the repression, even foreclosure, of affect. Gayatri Chakravorty Spivak (1999, 5) says that "this rejection of affect served and serves as the energetic and successful defense of the civilizing mission." On Spivak's reading, the foreclosed affect is excluded from the "civilized West" through a projection onto what she calls the "native informant," the voiceless figure both excluded from, and necessary to, the civilizing mission (6, 49). Spivak argues that in the texts of Kant, Hegel, and Marx, autonomy, consciousness, and normativity are defined against their opposites projected onto the native informant, who is then denied a voice by virtue of that very projection. The native informant is constructed as heteronomous, unconscious, and abnormal, as dependent, irrational, and pathological. The civilizing mission, as Spivak describes it, relies on the rejection of affect as barbarous in the name of civilization, a name that she points out has its underside in the necessarily nameless native informant.

Many theorists have described the dynamics of projection and defensive identification that create a native Other. But perhaps none have described the other side of this projection—the effects of this "energetic and successful defense of the civilizing mission" on the oppressed—as well as Frantz

Fanon. Fanon describes the effects on the mind and body of taking on the colonizers' unwanted affects. His analysis in *Black Skin, White Masks* turns around the diagnosis of affective aberrations caused by the colonial situation. This analysis makes clear that psychic operations of projection are not self-enclosed within the ego but rather are related to economic, material, and bodily conditions that affect both the subject and object of projection; and affects are not purely mental phenomena or epiphenomena but, rather, energetic forces that link the mind and body in ways that challenge any presumptions of a neat separation between mind and body, psyche and soma, subject and object, self and other, black and white.

In *Black Skin, White Masks,* Fanon (1967, 10) diagnoses what he calls both the inferiority complex of the black man and the superiority complex of the white man as "the result of a series of aberrations of affect" (cf. 1967, 60). Fanon claims that in the black man "affect is exacerbated" by the inferiority complex (50), which leads to what he calls "affective erethism" (60). This affective oversensitivity is the counterpart to what Fanon calls the white man's "affective ankylosis" (122). As he describes it, negrophobia is the brittle and stiff "root affect" that shapes the world of the white man (155). It seems that the colonial situation causes hyperaffectivity in the colonized and desiccated affectivity in the colonizer. In psychoanalytic terms, Fanon describes the black man's neurosis as obsessional and the white man's as phobic. In both cases, these neuroses operate through a distortion of affect that can be linked to the transmission of affect or psychic energy suggested by Freud.

Chapter 3

Colonial Abjection and Transmission of Affect

Before I explore Fanon's analysis of the aberrations of affect inherent in the colonial situation, it might be helpful to return to theories that influenced Fanon's thinking, Freud's theories of cathexis (*Besetzung*) and repression (*Verdrängung*) in their relation to affect. In the context of discussing Fanon's psychoanalysis of oppression, it becomes striking that Freud uses the word *Besetzung*, which means occupation, particularly military occupation, to describe the investment of psychic energy in an idea, object, or body. And, in his early writings especially, Freud explains repression using the word *defense* (*Abwehr*). The psychic operations of cathexis and repression, then, are already charged with the metaphorics of colonization—occupation and defense. Freud (1915a, 152) develops his notion of cathexis by postulating that an idea and the "quota of affect" associated with the idea can be separated: "It [quota of affect] corresponds to the instinct in so far as the latter has become detached from the idea and finds expression, proportionate to its quantity, in processes which are sensed as affects." This explains why patients can report traumatic events with indifference even while they become upset by seemingly insignificant events or details. On Freud's theory, the psychic energy or affect associated with the traumatic idea becomes displaced onto another event, idea, body, or object. Psychic energy would seem to be what Freud (1915b, 177) describes as instinct (*Trieb*), or drive force, which expresses itself in ideas and affects. At some points, Freud suggests that the difference between the way that drives are expressed in ideas and the way that they are expressed in affects is the difference between the investment or occupation of unconscious drives in ideas (cathexes) and the discharge of drives into consciousness manifest as feelings (affects) (178). Yet, as Freud describes it, even when drives are invested in ideas, the affects associated with those drives can become detached from the idea and reattached and discharged elsewhere. Still, the relation between drives and affects in Freud's writings remains ambiguous. One thing is clear: both are related to psychic energy. If drives give rise to psychic energy, then affects are the charged by-products of that psychic energy.

Freud ([1894] 1962, 60) compares the investment, occupation, and discharge of psychic energy to an electric charge that flows over the body: "In mental functions something is to be distinguished—a quota of affect or sum of excitation—which possesses all the characteristics of a quantity (though we have no means of measuring it), which is capable of increase, diminution, displacement, and discharge, and which is spread over the memory-traces of ideas somewhat as an electric charge is spread over the surface of a body. This hypothesis . . . can be applied in the same sense as physicists apply the hypothesis of a flow of electric fluid." In this passage, Freud describes affect as a sum of excitation that can change in quantity, direction, and location; and, he describes affective energy as mobile and as powerful as electricity.

In most of his discussions, it seems as if Freud is thinking of drive or psychic energy as mobile yet contained within one body. Where he diagnoses cultures and civilization itself, however, his analysis suggests that psychic energy can be a group or societal phenomenon moving between and among bodies.[1] Whereas Freud saw only the effects of projection on the ego of the agent, Fanon focuses on the effects on the recipient. For Fanon, if not Freud, the transmission of affect is a significant force in colonization. Unwanted affects are not so much projected onto another person but transferred onto or injected into another person such that the recipient's own affects are transformed. Along with economic imperialism that divides the world into "haves" and "have nots," colonization brings with it affective imperialism that divides the world into the civilized, those who have control over emotions, and the barbaric, those who don't.

Psychic Fluids

Fanon often uses bodily metaphors, especially biological and medical metaphors, to describe mental and social phenomena. For example, in *The*

Wretched of the Earth, he explains that "in the colonial world, the emotional sensitivity of the native is kept on the surface of the skin like an *open sore* which flinches from the caustic agent; and *the psyche shrinks back*, obliterates itself and finds outlet in *muscular* demonstrations which have caused certain very wise men to say that the native is a hysterical type" (1968b, 56; my emphasis). Here Fanon both uses physical embodied metaphors to describe the emotions and the psyche, and suggests that the native converts emotions and psychic tension into somatic symptoms; the native's muscles, which remain tense and paralyzed during the day, run free only in dreams at night (52). The affects of the colonized are on the racialized skin like an open sore, while the white man's values are caustic agents that cause pain that can no longer be divided into neat categories of the physical, emotional, psychological. The caustic agent burns through the skin to the psyche itself, which shrinks back, obliterates itself, and becomes somatized as hysterical symptoms lodged in the muscles. The circular—or perhaps dialectical—movement between skin, emotions, psyche, muscles, sores, and values undermines any "black and white" distinctions between mind and body or between economic and psychological oppression, and suggests that the colonization of the body and of the material world is also always the colonization of psychic space.

Even the breathing of the colonized is an "occupied breathing": "It is not the soil that is occupied. It is not the ports or the airdromes. French colonialism has settled itself in the very center of the Algerian individual and has undertaken a sustained work of cleanup, of expulsion of self, of rationally pursued mutilation. There is not occupation of territory, on the one hand, and independence of persons on the other. It is the country as a whole, its history, its daily pulsation that are contested, disfigured, in the hope of a final destruction. Under these conditions, the individual's breathing is an observed, an occupied breathing. It is a combat breathing" (Fanon 1965, 65). Colonialism affects the economy, the infrastructure, the physical environment, but it also affects the psyche, the sense of self, the bodies, and the very being of the colonized. Even their breathing is occupied breathing. Colonialism attacks the bodily schema of the colonized.[2]

In *Black Skin, White Masks*, Fanon (1967, 110) says that "in the white world the man of color encounters difficulties in the development of his bodily schema." He defines bodily schema as "a slow composition of my *self* as a body in the middle of a spatial and temporal world—such seems to be the schema. It does not impose itself on me; it is, rather, a definitive structuring of the self and of the world—definitive because it creates a real dialectic between my body and the world" (111). The bodily schema, then, is the sense of self in the world; it is not imposed on the self but constitutes the very sense of embodied subjectivity. Body images are not what I experience but what I experience with; they are not objects of my perception or consciousness, but the agents of perception and consciousness.[3] But for the man of color the corporeal schema is "ahistorico-racial schema" sketched "not by 'residual sensations and perceptions primarily of a tactile, vestibular, kinesthetic, and visual character' [Jean Lhermitte's definition of bodily schema in *L'image de notre corps*] but by the other, the white man, who had woven me out of a thousand details, anecdotes, stories" (111). The black man is the white man's creation, and race is merely a by-product.

Fanon sees race as part of a system of values and therefore akin to bodily fluids or, perhaps more accurately, to bodily waste. This is not to say that race is biological or in the blood in the way that the early-twentieth-century eugenicists believed. Rather, for Fanon, race is a by-product like a bodily waste product *secreted* in response to colonial occupation: "The other's total inability to liquidate the past once and for all. In the face of this affective ankylosis of the white man, it is understandable that I could have made up my mind to utter my Negro cry. Little by little, putting out pseydopodia here and there, I secreted a race" (122). This passage appears in the chapter titled "L'expérience vécue du Noir" (The Lived Experience of the Black) in which Fanon critically engages the negritude movement. He suggests that the negritude movement and the acceptance of "the lived experience of blackness" are themselves responses to the fixity and rigidity of the white man's values, particularly as they are manifest in the white man's affects. In response to the white man's affective ankylosis, the black man secretes a race. Throughout *Black Skin, White Masks*, Fanon describes race in relational terms: there is no black man without the white man and vice versa. Here, the relation is described in terms of bodily fluids. In response to the white man's lack of fluidity, the black man is forced to secrete a race. This passage suggests that the black man is forced to secrete the white man's waste, something that the white man can't (or won't) do on his own because of his affective ankylosis.

Fanon's work suggests that there is a transfer of affect in the colonial situation, that the white colonizers *inject* or *deposit* their anger into the colonized, who are then forced to expel it in self-destructive ways, secreting the waste-product *race* that perpetuates and justifies racism, or doing violence against themselves either individually or in tribal or gang wars. In *The Wretched of the Earth*, Fanon (1968b, 52) describes how aggressiveness and violence against the colonized's own people and himself are "deposited" in "the bones" of the colonized. He says that "the settler keeps alive in the native an anger which he deprives of outlet; the native is trapped in the tight links of the chains of colonialism. But we have seen that inwardly the settler can only achieve a pseudo petrification. The native's muscular tension finds outlet regularly in the bloodthirsty explosions—in tribal warfare, in feuds between sects, and in quarrels between individuals" (54). And later he explains that this violence against each other, this self-violence, is the result of colonialism, which turns the oppressed against each other in competition for the colonizer's recognition and material means for survival (307–9). As Fanon describes the dynamics of colonization, the colonizer deposits anger into the bones of the colonized and then keeps this anger alive through oppression. This anger is expressed as muscular tension, which in turn is discharged as self-violence. It is not so much that the colonizer's violence against the colonized is internalized as it is deposited or injected into the colonized by the colonizer in the form of a cruel superego.

With his notion of epidermalization, Fanon revises the notion of internalization of inferiority. He insists that the colonized do not internalize but rather epidermalize racist ideology. The values of racist imperialism enter the colonized through the skin. He describes the process as the injection of white values, which he refers to as dangerous foreign bodies, into native culture. For Fanon, values are secreted, injected, born of the blood, amputated, and hemorrhaging; they are analogous to bodily fluids. As such, they are dynamic and mobile; and, more important, they move from body to body and can infect entire populations. Fanon uses the discourse of contamination and infection so effective in the "civilizing mission" against itself.

Fanon even suggests that when the black man encounters a racist culture, this causes changes in his bodily fluids/psyche: "In married couples a biochemical alteration takes place in the partners, and, it seems, they have discovered the presence of certain hormones in the husband of a pregnant woman. It would be equally interesting—and there are plenty of subjects for study—to investigate the modifications of body fluids that occur in Negroes when they arrive in France. Or simply to study through tests the psychic changes both before they leave home and after they have spent a month in France" (22). This passage, like others analyzed here, compares affects and values to hormones or bodily fluids that are capable of dynamic movement between people and groups of people.

Fanon's work suggests that we cannot separate affects and values; we cannot separate colonial values from the affective aberrations of colonialism. On his analysis, the specific affective aberrations of colonialism express themselves as obsessional and phobic neuroses. The colonized are obsessed with gaining the white man's love and recognition even while becoming infected with the white man's superego that designates the colonized black and evil. Conversely, the white man's projection of evil onto, or abjection of, the black man is a symptom of white phobia, a phobia that Fanon (1967, 165) describes as sexual: "The civilized white man retains an irrational longing for unusual eras of sexual license, of orgiastic scenes, of unpunished rapes, of unrepressed incest. . . . Projecting his own desires onto the Negro, the white man behaves 'as if' the Negro really had them."

In traditional Freudian psychoanalytic theory, both obsession and phobia are considered affective disorders insofar as they operate on the affective level. Freud ([1895] 1962, 74–75) distinguishes obsession from phobia according to their affective operations: "Two constituents are found in every obsession: 1) an idea that forces itself upon the patient; 2) an associated emotional state. Now, in the group of phobias this emotional state is always one of 'anxiety,' while in true obsessions other emotional states, such as doubt, remorse, or anger, may occur just as well as anxiety." For Freud, whereas in obsession the extreme affect associated with an original troubling idea—an idea that can have its source in a traumatic experience—moves to a substitute idea, in phobia the anxiety or fear remains attached to the original idea, which can be what he calls either a "common" phobia or an individual one (see [1895] 1962, [1894] 1962). In obsession, "any idea can be made use of which is either able, from its nature, to be united with an affect of the quality in question, or which has certain relations to the incompatible idea which make it seem as though it could serve as a surrogate for it" (Freud [1894] 1962, 54). Furthermore, obsessional neurosis is associated with the "internalization of a sado-masochistic relation in the shape of tension between the ego and a particularly cruel superego" (Laplanche and Pontalis 1973, 281).

Freud, at least in his early writings, is more interested in obsessions that do not originate in traumatic experience and phobias that are not "common." Fanon's diagnosis of colonial obsessions and phobias not only complicates Freud's focus, which is more often than not on individual traumatic experiences, but also interrogates what are considered "common" phobic objects, particularly what he calls "negrophobia." Colonization produces obsessional relations in the colonized through social trauma that is repeated daily on almost all levels of social life. On Fanon's analysis, the idea that forces itself on the colonized is the idea of their own inferiority and the white man's superiority. The affects associated with these ideas are a complex of anger and shame. The self-reproach typical of obsessional neurosis is the result of the internalization of—or, more accurately, the infection with—the particularly cruel super-ego of the colonized, a superego that abjects the colonized as racialized others. Fanon suggests that the strong affects engaged by the inferiority complex of colonization become associated with gaining the recognition and love of the colonizer. Anger directed toward the colonizer turns inward and becomes anger and shame directed toward the self, which in turn flips over into the desire for recognition and love from those very same people who have rejected the colonized as barbaric in the first place. Elsewhere, I have argued that the need for recognition from the colonizer is a symptom of the pathology of colonization.[4] The colonizer's violent and cruel superego is forced onto the colonized to produce an inferiority complex, which in turn leads to the obsessive need for recognition from the "superior" white colonizer. The colonized's anger at the violence and degradation leveled against them by the colonizer is transferred to the idea of their own inferiority. The colonized suffer from an obsession with gaining love and recognition from their harsh dominators.

Insofar as the superego of racist imperialist ideology takes over culture, the phobia or fear of racialized others becomes what Freud calls a common phobia, a phobia accepted by dominant society. Fanon insists on investigating for whom the black body, especially the body of the black man, is a phobic object and why. Within the colonial ideology, the black body is abjected, which affects not only the treatment of black "natives" by white colonizers but also the psyche of the colonized, who are forced to negotiate their own abjection within the dominant culture. The phobia is "common" if it is a socially prescribed phobia. Here Julia Kristeva's theory of abjection may be more useful than Freud's theory of phobia precisely because Kristeva emphasizes the social aspects of phobia, particularly what Freud calls common phobias. In *Powers of Horror*, Kristeva (1982, 2) says, "To each ego its object to each super-ego its abject." For her, the abject is not yet an object but rather that which calls into question boundaries. The abject is the in-between that challenges all categorization. She maintains that on the social level the abject and abjection are ways of negotiating our relationship to, or separation from, other animals and animality; on the personal individual level abjection is a way of negotiating separation from the maternal body (4). Phobias always take us back to the abject with its questionable borders. In other words, it is ambiguity itself that is the phobic "not-yet-object." Phobia is a type of defense against this ambiguity. What we exclude as abject recalls our own ambigious borders in relation to animality and maternal origins. Phobia, then, is the result of the subject's own fear and aggressivity that come back to it from outside: "I am not the one that devours, I am being devoured by him" (39). This is precisely what Fanon describes when he discusses what he calls the white man's negrophobia.

Although Fanon's analysis of negrophobia is provocative (e.g., when he suggests that negrophobic white women fantasize about being raped by black men in what turns out to be their desire for sexual fulfillment), it points to the threat of ambiguity associated with the abject. Fanon proposes that negrophobia is the affect at the root of the white man's world (1967, 155); and all evil and malefic powers are associated with the abjected black body. The white man's bodily schema is determined by this abjected black body (160). In this sense, the white man's sense of himself as good and civilized is defined against the black body, which he abjects as evil and animal. This abjection follows the logic of shoring up borders as a defense against ambiguity. Recall Spivak's analysis of the foreclosure of affect on which the civilizing mission operates. Fanon's text suggests that there is a fear of ambiguous borders—borders of animality and racial borders—behind negrophobia, which is primarily a fear of the black man's imagined sexual powers. Fanon says, parodying phobic stereotypes of Negro animality and miscegenation, "As for the Negroes, they have tremendous sexual powers. What do you expect, with all the freedom they have in their jungles! They copulate at all times and in all places. They are really genital. They have so many children that they cannot even count them. Be careful, or they will flood us with little mulattoes" (157). This passage suggests that the real fear is of the breakdown of borders between civilized and barbaric, human and animal, white and black.

Fanon describes the white man's phobia as the correlate, even the cause, of the black man's obsession and inferiority complex. He also diagnoses a "sensitizing" and "collapse of the ego" as a result of the interiorization of the white man's phobia that leads to the black man's obsession with gaining recognition from his oppressors (154). Moving away from Freud, he insists that the neurosis of the colonized is the result of the cultural or social situation rather than individual psychology (152). Phobia and obsession make up the pathology of the colonial situation rather than a few neurotic individuals.

Colonization attempts to force the colonized to take on the white man's anxiety over his uncertain and ambiguous borders (both physical and psychological). This anxiety is manifest in the white man's phobia, which acts as a defense against unwanted affects that are projected onto racialized others. The success of the colonization of psychic space can be measured by the extent to which the colonized internalize—or become infected by—the cruel superego that abjects them and substitutes anger against their oppressors with an obsessive need to gain their approval. In other words, the colonization of psychic space depends on the colonized internalizing the inferiority-superiority dichotomy that sustains the colonizer's self-identity.

However, this logic is full of self-contradictions that ensure its failure.[5] Indeed, as I have argued elsewhere, the logic of colonization is paradoxical because it requires the colonized to internalize the lack of an interior, soul, or mind (Oliver 2001).

Psychic Infection

The literary critics Kalpana Seshadri-Crooks and Juliet Flower MacCannell in different ways address the relationship between race, affect, and colonization using the vocabulary of Lacanian theory. Following Fanon, both theorists describe the racialization of colonization as the result of phobia and a cruel superego. Seshadri-Crooks (2000, 45) argues that "the paradox is that Whiteness attempts to signify the unsignifiable, i.e. humanness, in order to preserve our subjective investment in race." In this Lacanian train of thought, whiteness attempts to signify the unsignifiable intersection of being and meaning in human beings. For Lacan, there is always a fundamental split between being and meaning. How can we signify our being as beings who mean? On Lacan's analysis, either we signify and—to use Sartre's phrase—make ourselves a lack of being, or we simply are (being), in which case we do not mean. As Seshadri-Crooks explains, "Whiteness is merely a signifier that masquerades as being and thereby blocks access to lack" (45). On her analysis, whiteness operates as a transcendental signifier, itself outside the realm of signification. Whiteness poses as nature or being, or more precisely as the essence of human being. The paradox is that whiteness both signifies nature or being—the lack of lack—and the lack of being that makes meaning, that is, human existence, possible. As Seshadri-Crooks describes it, this encounter with the lack of lack or being produces anxiety in the raced subject, and this anxiety in turn produces a phobic object, namely, the surface of the body, the skin, and other surface traits (45–46). On her analysis, all of us are raced subjects trying to live up to the impossible ideal of whiteness. Within the colonial logic, whiteness becomes an ethical good impossible to attain; and the phobic object must be excluded to sustain the good or clean and proper body image (37).

For MacCannell, like Seshadri-Crooks, whiteness is related to the real beyond signification. But, whereas for Seshadri-Crooks, whiteness or race is not in the real but poses as nature as a defense against the anxiety of confronting the contingency, even arbitrariness, of our own nature, for MacCannell race is the result of the white man's real, which infects the colonized. Like Fanon, MacCannell is concerned to diagnose how it is that colonization affects the psyches as well as the material conditions of those colonized. Reading Fanon's *Black Skin, White Masks*, MacCannell (2000, 65) maintains that colonization is effective because it infects the colonized with what she calls the "White Man's Thing": "The colonized body is one that has been exposed or invaded by drives other than its own. The colonization of the subject arrives through the White Man's Thing. The signifier that had granted one person his humanity is displaced by a dehumanizing Thing not his own. The signifier *white* carried its own traumatic Thing in its wake and invaded the colonized with it." MacCannell argues that the dehumanization of colonization takes place through a kind of advertising campaign that infects the colonized with the white man's desire ultimately fueled by the death drive, a death drive that does not properly belong to the colonized. Resonant with my analysis so far, MacCannell maintains that the colonized are infected with the colonizer's sadistic superego, a superego that protects its own humanity by dehumanizing the other as foreclosed phobic "object."

MacCannell says that "the proper name of the White Man's Thing is 'the Good'" (66). The white man's fantasy of the good displaces the colonized's own fantasies; and the white man's unconscious invades the unconscious of the colonized. Colonization is not just an invasion of physical space but also an invasion of psychic space. The ideology of colonization centers on the notion that the civilizing mission is driven by an ethical imperative to bring the good to the "barbarians." As MacCannell describes this operation, it turns on the contradictory function of the good in the psyche of the white man. The white man is caught between the social pressure to sacrifice pleasure for the common good and the perverse demand of the superego to enjoy without regard for others. She argues that "colonialism provided the perfect outlet for both the guilt of enjoyment and the imperative to enjoy the colonizer's own superego imposed" (72). The bad good (enjoyment, bodily pleasure, affect) is projected onto the colonized, who are seen to laugh and dance without regard for the common good, while the good (civilized restraint over pleasure and affect) is reserved for the white man.

Resonant with Seshadri-Crooks's notion that the surface of the body is the most immediate place where the anxiety produced by the transcendental signifier whiteness attaches its phobia, MacCannell claims that "race was the weak point or lesion where the alien's Good was inserted" (73). Because the body seems to inhabit the realm of nature or the real, it is supremely susceptible to a good that divides the world into nature versus culture, barbaric versus civilized, animal versus human. Within the logic of this civilized good, the body always falls to the other side. And insofar as this good must insist that it is universal, all differences, including different notions of good, become nothing more than justification for the civilizing mission and evidence of the need for colonization; all other goods become lesser goods in need of the lesson of the universal good. Nothing short of an alternative universal good can compete; anything "less" is at a disadvantage when faced with the white man's claim to the truth and the good. The construction and maintenance of this universal good is further complicated by the operations of the Western civilizing mission to cover over its abjection and exclusion of the black body as bad or evil. As Lewis Gordon (2000, 4) points out, "Fanon realized that the more he asserted his membership in Western civilization the more he was pathologized, for the system's affirmation depends on its denial of ever having illegitimately excluded him; he is, as in theodicy, a reminder of injustice in a system that is supposed to have been wholly good."

Fanon demonstrates that the effectiveness of colonization and its inherent racism are not merely epistemological but also psychological. Taking her lead from Fanon, MacCannell argues that the psychic consequence of colonialism is that the white man's desire becomes the only desire; it displaces the colonized's own desires and takes root as a perverse desire for the white man's thing. This desire is not only the desire for the white man's goods (material goods and moral goods) but also for the thing that lies behind them. MacCannell (2000, 63, 79, 87) variously describes this thing as first, the place where your nature and its sacrifice meet—that is, the place where culture, meaning, or humanity require the sacrifice of nature, being, or animality; second, *das Ding*, the inaccessible and unknowable thing-in-itself or unconscious that lies behind the world as it appears to "us," that is, the colonizers; and third, the original lost object, the maternal breast. As she describes it, "the deepest nature of the White man's Thing" is "the white woman's breast" (89). What white men, the colonizers, desire is the impossible return to the mother's pure, nourishing breast. This is the desire that infects the colonized, for whom it is all the more impossible because it is not their own desire or their own mother. MacCannell describes this desire for the white maternal breast as "a pure *commodity*. A commodity of an ultimate sort: one that (so the scenario is written) if the Indian or Malagasy or Congolese has even had a whiff of it, he must simultaneously pursue and forsake if he is to *be* any good. Always just below the possibility of attaining, doing, and being good himself. He has contracted the superego disease of the Westerner" (91). Colonization, then, contains a powerful ad campaign that substitutes the white man's desire for that of the colonized. The pure white, yet eroticized, maternal breast is desired by, and yet forbidden to, the white man, and it is doubly forbidden to the black man. But this prohibition, as Fanon sees very well, fuels, and is fueled by, perverse fantasies of miscegenation and white women defiled by black men.

If, as Julia Kristeva maintains, all social prohibitions are prohibitions against ambiguity most powerfully evoked by the maternal body, then the white maternal breast is itself an eroticized phobic object, whose fascination and horror is increased by imagining it nourishing the black man. In other words, if the maternal breast itself evokes the fear of ambiguity and lost boundaries for the clean and proper white man, then the fear of the black man possessing that breast excites and incites even more anxiety. The white man's anxiety over the loss of the clean and proper boundaries of himself and his defensive subject formation find a powerful reaction formation in the fantasy of the black man possessing the white woman. His anxieties over sexual ambiguity, the ambiguity of maternal origin, and racial ambiguity come together to produce the ultimate phobic fantasy that both threatens and protects the clean and proper borders of his own subjectivity. The white man displaces the prohibition against, and incestuous desire for, the maternal breast onto the colonized to maintain his notion of the good despite the contradiction at its heart.[6]

The colonized, on the other hand, are infected with the cruel superego that sets up an impossible desire by both demanding and prohibiting it at the same time. Whereas this perverse superego constructs and protects the white man's subjectivity and defines the place of his ego, Fanon (1968b, 252; 1967, 143) maintains that in the colonized it becomes a mass attack against the ego. As Fanon points out, the effects on the colonized are the opposite of the effects on the colonizer. Most simply, this is because while the perverse operations of the cruel superego make the white man, they can never make the black man over (fully) into the white man. The black man is denied the desired (eroticized phobic) object—the good and the white maternal breast (good and bad)—as well as the place of the subject, the white man.

The pathology of colonialism takes place on the level of deepest desire and affect, the very construction of the psyche with its unconscious and conscious desires. The colonizer infects the colonies with his perverse and paradoxical desires and affects, which attach to the surface of the bodies of the colonized, in whom they often appear as somatic and psychic symptoms or what Fanon (1967, 52) calls "the emotional sensitivity" . . . "kept on the surface of the skin like an open sore."

Given this analysis of the colonization of psychic space and the transmission of affect, Fanon's insistence on the healing power of violence in his later works can be seen in a new light. Fanon prescribes violent resistance to colonialism to regain not just territory and physical freedoms but also a sense of agency, which is undermined through the colonization of psychic space. As Fanon (1968b, 295) says in *The Wretched of the Earth*,

"From the moment that you and your like are liquidated like so many dogs, you have no other resource but to use all and every means to regain your importance as a man. You must therefore weigh as heavily as you can upon the body of your torturer in order that his soul, lost in some byway, may finally find once more its universal dimension." Note, too, that Fanon insists that you must pressure the body to get to the soul. Violent resistance restores the sense of agency or action lost through oppression. Fanon says, "At the level of individuals, violence is a cleansing force. It frees the native from his inferiority complex and from his despair and inaction; it makes him fearless and restores his self-respect" (94, cf. 293; cf. 1968a, 121). For Fanon, violence plays an important function for nation building and collective history; collective violence creates a sense of collectivity and collective history and restores the sense of agency undermined by colonialism. If the colonizer attempts to render the colonized as subhuman objects incapable of rational thought and subjective agency, then active resistance serves to restore a sense of agency to the oppressed. For Fanon (1968b, 252), violence is one effective means (along with love and understanding) to address what he calls the "mass attack against the ego" leveled against the colonized by the colonialism.

In addition, it could be that violence is necessary to redirect the colonizer's affects, particularly anger, outward. Violence directed inward by colonialism is now redirected outward. Recall that on Fanon's analysis the colonizer deposits anger into the bones of the colonized. This anger becomes directed inward and leads the colonized to violence against themselves. The struggle against colonialism must include a struggle to free psychic space from this domination by the cruel superego of the colonizer.[7] That anger must be excised; it must be redirected outward. If colonial affects are deposited in the bodies of the colonized at the same time that colonial prohibitions against affect infect them, then those affects must be sent back. How this is possible is another story, a story that Fanon envisions as violent resistance accompanied by various forms of working through that might someday lead to a new humanism that overcomes race and thereby racism.

CHAPTER 4

Humanism beyond the Economy of Property

To suggest that projection onto, or abjection of, some other is necessary to fortify the boundaries of the proper self, Fanon insists that both the superiority complex of the colonizer and the inferiority complex of the colonized are pathological.[1] As I suggested in part I, for Fanon, alienation is not inherent in the human condition; it is the result of colonization and oppression. Just because European privilege is built on imperialism and colonialism does not mean that subjectivity is necessarily bought on the backs of others. European privileged subjectivity is pathological, and there are alternative models for subject formation. Fanon (1967, 60) says that "the Negro enslaved by his inferiority, the white man enslaved by his superiority alike behave in accordance with a neurotic orientation." This pathological relation between inferiority and superiority perverts humanity. It is not just the black man who is dehumanized in the colonial situation; the white man also loses his humanity. This is why Fanon insists on the need for a new humanity to put an end to colonization and oppression. The philosopher Robert Bernasconi (1996, 116) argues that this is the central difference between Fanon's vision of humanism and European humanism: "Whereas European humanism is differential and survives only so long as the non-European is defined as subhuman, the new humanism liberates both colonized and colonizer." He also points out that for Fanon it is through the colonized's struggle against their oppression that this new humanity will be born, a new humanity that necessarily remains an open question (118–21).

Contra European humanism, in Fanon's vision of humanism it is not the case that identity, personal or national, necessitates excluding otherness or difference. Instead, the projection onto others of one's own unwanted affects, the abjection of what is undesirable in one's self by identifying it with difference, or the brutal insistence that others are barbaric to prove one's own civility, are for Fanon symptoms of colonial neurosis. Insofar as it is based on oppositions between human and animal, civilized and barbaric, proper and abject, reason and affect, European humanism is itself a symptom of colonial pathology. Humanity—at least the future humanity envisioned by Fanon—is not established by excluding the animal or projecting animality onto others to justify their enslavement and one's own superiority. The future humanity will not operate according to this kind of relative or exclusive logic, the logic of noncontradiction by virtue of which if I am human, then you are not; or, more precisely, if you are not human, then I am. The future humanity will not be based on property, sovereignty, and ownership but rather on the body's responsive agency unfettered from notions of self-enclosed ego or sovereign subject. The new human is an acting and reacting body connected to others at its very heart; and the new humanism is based on agency without sovereignty, investment without ownership, and bodies without properties.

Agency without Sovereignty

With the notion of the transmission of affect and Fanon's suggestive descriptions of bodies interacting on the level of muscle, secretions, and bones, bodies without properties begin to emerge as bodies without fixed borders. Bodies without properties and without proper borders also challenge the notion of a sovereign subject. If bodies are as interrelational as this analysis suggests and if a unified body no longer exists, then how can a unified sovereign will direct that body? Don't we need to conceive of the agency of that body apart from a sovereign will? Indeed, isn't the notion of sovereignty both in terms of notions, states, and individuals part of the pathology of colonialism? If so, to think beyond the logic of colonialism, we need to think agency beyond sovereignty.

To develop a theory of agency without sovereignty may require a theory of action without authorship (cf. Arendt 1959, 164).[2] Actors have agency, but their agency does not necessarily imply sovereignty or authorship. Indeed, assumptions about the authorship or sovereignty of agents are part of the economy of property in which everything is a product made by a maker—the world is made by God, our lives and culture are man-made, our actions are made by us. But actions and lives are not made. As Hannah Arendt (1959, 166) says, "The real story in which we are engaged as long as we live has no visible or invisible maker because it is not made." The *who* of the story becomes manifest through action and speech, and can be reduced neither to an object-product nor to a substantial or essential subject maker. To see them as such is a fundamental category mistake. As I have argued elsewhere, we are subjectivities without subjects.

If, as Arendt argues, we conceive of ourselves as primarily homo faber, or producers, then we reduce all action to production and the results of action to products (204).[3] In this world of producers and products, the violent manipulation of the world and its resources is justified in the name of production. The discourse of production sustains the economy of property that turns even human beings into objects that can be owned and exchanged. Everything becomes fungible. Seeing the world in terms of producers and products, that is, within the economy of property, renders human beings fundamentally violent, and the earth and environment nothing more than raw materials to be violently transformed for human purposes. This form of humanism takes man as the measure and maker of all things (except perhaps nature, which is made by the super producer, God).

This worldview also leads to instrumental reason through which human beings and their actions become objects to be produced and manipulated along with other raw materials. Politics becomes a matter of instrumental means justified by the end of producing a better product whatever the cost to the environment or human laborers. All of human experience and agency is reduced to a sphere of fabrication whose output can be quantified and calculated.[4] In the natural world, too, we have fallen under the spell of fabrication and see ourselves as makers rather than as actors reacting to our environment as its dependents. Even the world of human artifice is more interactive than the notion of humanism, as *homo faber* suggests.

Our actions are not transparent to us and we are never fully in control of them, because they always take place within an interactive context or environment that we cannot absolutely control. Moreover, if we take into account the psychic dimension of action and add the unconscious, then we are always to some extent unaware of the motives for our own actions. We are not the authors of those actions in any fully conscious sense. Rather, sovereignty becomes what psychoanalysts might call a reaction formation created as a defense against the very indeterminacy of our authorship. As I show in part IV, the sense of individual sovereignty is the effect of unconscious and social processes always beyond any individual's control;

sovereignty does not precede action but is produced through it insofar as it engages unconscious processes of transference between individuals and groups. In part IV, I identify this process with a form of social forgiveness necessary to shore up the sense of agency. There I argue that colonization, domination, and oppression foreclose the social forgiveness necessary for the sense of agency with its sovereignty effect.

Investment without Ownership

One hallmark of colonial capitalist logic is that everything, including one's own actions and body, become property. And property is always controlled or made by someone. But rather than think of authority or power in terms of possessions and ownership, if we think of authority and power in terms of investments in the world and others, then we can come to see ourselves through that investment; and self-identity becomes the interest or excess generated through investment as gift or donation. This is an investment not as a bet on a future return or profit but rather in the very possibility of living, which means living together; it is an interest in or caring about others, an investment in others that yields what phenomenologists call interest as intentionality or care that is definitive of self-conscious subjectivity. We are empowered not by enslaving, owning, or disempowering others; to the contrary, by empowering others we also invest in ourselves. This notion of investment is based on an acknowledgment of, and appreciation for, our fundamental relatedness and dependence on each other. If we think through the premise that we are constitutionally dependent and relational beings in terms not only of our physical bodies but also of our subjectivity and all that this entails, then investment is necessarily circular: to invest in others is to invest in myself and to invest in myself is to invest in others. But without the premise that we are fundamentally related and all that this entails, the circularity of investment can become either an apology for not investing in others (by investing in myself only, I invest in others) or entirely self-motivated (I invest in others only for the payoff to myself). Thinking our dependence and relationality to its logical conclusion requires rethinking our notions of self and other such that we cannot simply import discussions of dependence into existing frameworks without turning relationality into something else, for example, by reinserting it into the economy of property.

Patricia Williams (1998, 16) imagines the possibility of thinking of investment without ownership: "What a world it would be if we could all wake up and see all of ourselves reflected in the world, not merely in a territorial sense but with a kind of nonexclusive entitlement that grants not so much possession as investment. A peculiarly anachronistic notion of investment, I suppose, at once both ancient and futuristic. An investment that envisions each of us in each other." As Williams suggests, we have to go back to more archaic meanings of investment that work against the modern sense of investment as money deposited for the sake of making a profit, which is part of the very essence of the economy of property. The 1985 *Oxford English Dictionary* defines *investment* as the means to clothe, robe, or envelop, an outer covering or envelope of any kind, to clothe with dignity, to endow or furnish with power, authority, or privilege. We can imagine investment as clothing, enveloping and thereby protecting the body of another. We can imagine investment as empowering or authorizing another. Investment means clothing with the dignity of individuality and agency, empowering others to act by respecting rather than denying or denigrating our dependence on one another. By looking for an alternative past for the sake of an alternative future (what Foucault might call a subjugated discourse, a part of the past that has been ignored or disgarded), perhaps we can begin to imagine investment outside the economy of property, investment without ownership.

Exchange becomes nourishment rather than property; giving becomes giving provisions, clothing each other, giving life.[5] The value of oneself or others is not fungible, but the result of an investment in each other without ownership. This investment provides an envelope of protective power, the fragile power of belonging that supports creativity and meaning. This investment authorizes individuals to act within the supportive structure of forgiveness and promise without which agency is compromised or underdeveloped. Human beings can thrive on investments that enable agency, creativity, and meaning only when these investments exceed the economy of property in which every investment is made in the expectation of some payoff. Humanity can prosper only when we attempt to think outside the economy of property. This prosperity cannot be quantified or reduced to exchange value on the global market. Rather, this prosperity can be measured only in terms of the meaning of life itself.

Bodies without Properties

Against those who would claim that Western civilization is the intellectual property of the white man, Fanon (1967, 225) argues that "I am a man, and in this sense the Peloponnesian War is as much mine as the invention of the compass." He challenges the economy of property by virtue of which one culture or race can claim to possess or own civilization. He insists, "There is no white world, there is no white ethic, any more than there is a white intelligence" (229). Outside the economy of property, it no longer makes sense to talk about a white world or a white good. Outside the economy of property not only material goods but also values—moral goods—cannot be possessed. For the West to maintain that the ideals of democracy, freedom, and justice are its own creations is racist arrogance.[6] In challenging the economy of property, Fanon challenges—even as he employs it—the black-white opposition to point up the presumption that *man* is always white and a black man is some*thing* else; only by virtue of the economy of property can men become things or animals who can be owned or disowned by others.

Like Fanon, Williams fastens onto the problem of property and ownership in relation to race in ways that promise to open up new possibilities for thinking through and beyond the economy of property, that is, the economy that makes slavery, colonization, and disowning others possible. Williams (1995, 232) insists that we must continue to look for the legacies of slavery not only in contemporary culture and its institutions but also in our conceptions of ourselves and others: "It is with great care, therefore, that we should look for its [slavery's] echoing repercussions in our world today, for 1856 is not very long ago at all." The economy of property pervades our conceptions of self, individual, and citizen. Williams's work is full of compelling examples and analyses of how individuals are considered citizens with rights in connection to property and ownership. She shows how seemingly outdated conceptions of propertied citizens continue in more subterranean forms today. Her analysis moves from consideration of the lack of rights extended to homeless and propertyless people to communities where public space is owned in order to keep others out.

In addition, Williams (1995) criticizes how our conceptions of ourselves as having bodies that can be divided into parts, cloned, transplanted, fertilized, and even sold turns bodies into property. Human blood, semen, and eggs are all legal commodities. Babies and organs are illegal commodities that are nevertheless exchanged both legally and illegally in connection to property and economic status. Even characteristics such as ethnicities, genders, and races are considered properties that individuals possess, properties that are more or less fungible with greater or lesser exchange value on the market. Williams (1991, 124) argues that "'black,' 'female,' 'male,' and 'white' are every bit as much properties as the buses, private clubs, neighborhoods, and schools that provide the extracorporeal battlegrounds of their expression. . . . possessions become the description of who we are and the reflection of our worth. . . ." Difference itself has become a marketable commodity (212).

Against the colonial economy of property that makes race and difference a commodity, Fanon (1967, 231) reminds us that race and even skin color are not properties in themselves, but rather they are manufactured by colonial pathology; there is no "black man" or "white man." Rather, black and white exist by virtue of their relationship. More specifically, black exists always in relation to a standard or norm that is white (110). Although Fanon's writings on the status of race have been interpreted in different ways, he consistently maintains that *white* and *black* are relative terms that refer more to social standing than to some natural skin color in itself; there is no skin color in itself.[7] In the Antillean (and the European) whom Fanon describes, whiteness is primarily associated with an idea of civilization and culture, and only secondarily attached to skin color. Whiteness and blackness are part of an ideology created to justify exploitation, which becomes a psychological justification for a sense of superiority. Skin color, or its significance, is created by a racist colonial logic.

Fanon's insistence that there is no white world, that no one owns civilization, and that race is not a property suggests that humanity must think and be thought outside the economy of ownership that renders values and concepts, as well as bodies and skin, property. Fanon's metaphors for subjectivity and intellect are not primarily those of minds, souls, and egos that he inherits from philosophy and psychology—he says that the black soul is a white man's artifact (13) and that the white soul is reached through the body (295). Rather, his texts are full of bones, tissues, muscles, and epidermis acting and reacting in relation to other bodies; and minds, souls, and egos become the by-products secreted from these interacting bodies. The future humans/bodies are fluid moving skeletons, muscles, tissues, and skin. These bodies have not been hollowed out by a colonial past that creates interior spaces, minds, souls, or egos. These bodies act and react to one another without being reduced to mere possessions or objects for corresponding possessors or subjects. These are subjectivities without subjects, bodies that move without any sovereign prime mover. Fanon's future humans are bodies without properties.

The colonization of psychic space not only turns psychic phenomena and their bodily manifestations into properties/property but also turns the past into property: Just as conceiving of bodies without properties—outside the economy of property—requires imagining the past outside linear genealogies, conceiving of agency without sovereignty requires imagining action outside the instrumental notion of cause and effect. This is a challenge to the traditional view that the future is predetermined by the past or the effect is predetermined by the cause. The past is not a stable or unified property or commodity inherited by bodies or determined by actor or agents.

Fanon argues that white men think they own Western civilization, while black men are reduced to cannibalism (cf. Fanon 1967, 224). Within this economy, the past becomes a possession, a piece of property, that justifies colonization, exploitation, and the civilizing mission; and the black man is chained to the past invented by the white man. Fanon describes the experience of being defined by a past created by the colonizers: "I discovered by blackness, my ethnic characteristics; and I was battered down by tom-toms, cannibalism, intellectual deficiency, fetishism, racial defects, slave-ships, and above all else, above all: 'sho' good eatin'" (112).

Within the colonial logic, which cannot be separated from the economy of property, the past has become a fortress in which time is defended against change and different possible futures. Fanon insists that any new humanism must begin both by loosening the chains of the past and by giving up the notion that the past is a possession or inheritance. He proclaims, "I am not the slave of the Slavery that dehumanized my ancestors. . . . The body of history does not determine a single one of my actions" (230–31). More than delineations of the experience of the black man—which has been described in painful detail throughout *Black Skin, White Masks* as the products of racist and colonial culture—these are prescriptions for a future beyond black and white. The future requires what Friedrich Nietzsche in *On the Genealogy of Morals* calls an active forgetting of the past of slavery and colonization for the sake of a different future beyond domination. What Fanon calls the disalienation of all humanity, white and black, requires imagining a future that is not like the past: "Those Negroes and white men will be disalienated who refuse to let themselves be sealed away in the materialized Tower of the Past" (226).

Even if history and the past are our inheritance, and our social and subject positions are framed by them, Fanon insists that we are not determined by them. For if the future is determined—in the strong sense of determinism—by the past, then there is no hope of change or transformation: once a slave, always a slave. Against this determinism, Fanon imagines a future in which "the Negro is not. Any more than the white man" because "both must turn their backs on the inhuman voices which were those of their respective ancestors in order that authentic communication be possible" (231). Within Fanon's account, the inhuman voice is not animal but child—"The tragedy of the man is that he was once a child" (231). And man's is not a happy childhood but a cruel one. The voice of the inhuman is the voice of this cruel past, a voice that cannot be silenced but must be vigilantly scrutinized, resisted, and worked through for the sake of future communication, for the sake of what Fanon calls "the ideal conditions for a human world" (231). For Fanon, it is this communication and questioning based on the body, touch, and affect that will be human. Against the economy of property, in a utopian moment he asks, "Why not the quite simple attempt to touch the other, to feel the other, to explain the other to myself? . . . O my body, make of me always a man who questions!" (231–32). Not the mind, ego, or sovereign subject, but the body in relation to other bodies, touching other bodies, engenders thoughtful reflection and critical questioning.

If we can imagine bodies authorized to act without having or possessing particular properties that legitimate them, then we can begin to live without reducing our bodies and actions to commodities with or without exchange value on the market within the global economy of property. This may seem a utopian goal, but the necessity of psychic revolt gives hope that the authority of the economy of property contains the seeds of its own transformation and that imagining the past differently can open up the possibility of alternative futures. This hope is based on the notion that the economy of property is itself fundamentally dependent on another logic, a time outside time, a past that cannot be contained within lineage, the unconscious. To realize this hope, we need to rethink our relation to time, history, and the past. And to do that, we need to conceive of bodies without properties, agency without sovereignty, and investment without ownership.

We not only need to imagine the fluidity of bodies, agency, and investment in the abstract but also need to consider how this fluidity really operates in both monumental and everyday forms of resistance to oppression and domination. I have shown how colonization infects the colonized with the cruel and punishing superego of the colonizer in ways that undermine the colonized subject's sense of agency and self-worth. I have also shown how that infection operates through a kind of affective fluidity through which affects are transferred from the colonizer onto the colonized, who carry the affective burden for the privileged white subject. The privileged subject shores up its subject position as dominant, and its active agency and subjectivity, by projecting unwanted affects onto the colonized in an attempt to render them subordinate and passive. But, as I show in the next chapter, this fluidity between subjects and subject positions serves not only domination, oppression, and colonization but also resistance and the restoration of agency to colonized or oppressed subjects. Only by imagining this more positive side of the fluidity of bodies, agency, and investment can we begin to think outside the economy of property, sovereignty, and ownership that justify the colonial and imperialist mission, that unfortunately is still operating today within the so-called global market.

Chapter 5

Fluidity of Power

Fanon's writings display a tension over the notion of sovereignty, a tension between his vision of a future beyond the economy of property and his diagnoses of the damaging effects of that economy of the colonized. This tension shows up as a demand for self-possession and self-ownership for the oppressed, on the one hand, and criticisms of the economy of property that enables their dispossession and exploitation/enslavement, on the other. This conflict can be read as the tension at the heart of subjectivity between the conditions of possibility for subjectivity and agency, and for subject position and social context. Subjectivity is fostered by values and relations that cannot be reduced to an economy of property or self-possession. Subjectivity and the agency that comes with it should not be confused with illusory ideals of unified egos and autonomous sovereign subjects. Rather, subjectivity and agency are engendered by relationships that belie the supposed unity and sovereignty of the subject. Fanon's vision of a new humanity points beyond the illusions of sovereignty even as his diagnoses of the effects of colonization employ the rhetoric of sovereignty and self-possession. This rhetoric speaks to the undeniable relation between subjectivity and subject position. Subjectivity does not exist in the abstract apart from real-world situations. Rather, subjectivity and its agency are empowered or disempowered by the context in which they are fostered or impaired. Colonization affects people at the deepest levels of their sense of themselves as agents and desiring subjects. The antidote to the colonization of psychic space is resistance that restores a sense of agency and perhaps even the illusion of sovereignty and self-possession that have been stripped from the colonized by the logic of colonialism. It may be possible, then, to read Fanon's use of the rhetoric of sovereignty, which is the rhetoric of colonization, against itself.

Foreshadowing Foucault's analysis of biopower as both discipline and resistance, Fanon's writings, particularly in his essays on the roles of the radio and the veil in resistance and revolution in Algeria, delineate how disciplinary practices can move between domination and resistance. He diagnoses how the forces of domination can be turned into forces of resistance and the disciplinary practices of one culture can be turned against the disciplinary practices of another. Anticipating not only the Foucauldian analysis of shifting power relations but also recent attempts to combine discursive analysis and psychoanalysis, Fanon works between social and psychoanalytic theory.[1] He describes a material, embodied psyche inseparable from its social context; his is a psychoanalytic social theory that moves out of Freud and toward Foucault. Fanon's version of biopower is a biopsychic power insofar as bio and psyche cannot be separated. While the body is determined by its subject position in its sociohistorical context, the psyche is dependent on the structures of subjectivity that always exceed that context even as they are governed by it. Subject position and subjectivity are bound together such that to talk about one requires talk about the other.

Any theory of subjectivity must also consider subject position. Subjects, subjectivity, and agency always exist only in a political and social context that affects them at the foundation of their constitution. One's social position and history profoundly influence one's very sense of oneself as an active agent in the world. Yet the contradictions and inconsistencies in historical and social circumstances guarantee that one is never completely determined by one's subject position. It is possible to develop a sense of agency despite, or in resistance to, an oppressive social situation.

By *subjectivity* I mean one's sense of oneself as an "I," as an agent. By *subject position* I mean one's position in society and history as developed through various social relationships. The structure of subjectivity is the structure that makes taking oneself as an agent or a self possible. The structure of subjectivity is what I have called a witnessing structure founded on the possibility of address and response; it is a fundamentally dialogic structure. Subject position, on the other hand, is not the very possibility of one's sense of oneself as an agent or an "I" per se, but the particular sense of one's kind of agency, so to speak, that comes through one's social position and historical context. While distinct, subject position and subjectivity are also intimately related. For example, if you are a black woman within a racist and sexist culture, then your subject position as oppressed could undermine your subjectivity, your sense of yourself as an agent. If you are a white man within a racist and sexist culture, then your subject position as privileged could shore up your subjectivity and promote your sense of yourself as an agent.

The play between subject position and subjectivity can lead to the colonization of psychic space when subjectivity and its agency are undermined by subject position in an oppressive or repressive social context. Yet the play between the two also opens up the possibility that the resistance to domination and oppression within one's social context can restore subjectivity and particularly a sense of agency. By resisting oppression, one regains a sense of oneself as an agent. When the power relations of social contexts, especially oppressive social contexts, are added to the equation of subjectivity, the fluidity of both subject position and subjectivity in relation to the fluidity of power becomes apparent.

Fanon's Analysis of the Radio and the Veil

Fanon's analysis of shifting power relations in his essays on the radio and the veil vividly illustrates the shifting positions of resistance and domination and their effects on the psyche, particularly the sense of agency of the oppressed. This analysis of particular struggles to overcome oppression that indeed restore a sense of agency and thereby shore up subjectivity makes my discussion of the relationship between subject position and agency more concrete. Moreover, Fanon points up some of the contradictions and complications in the relation between power, resistance, and subjectivity that theoretical discussions can only approximate in the abstract. His essays demonstrate that resistance empowers the oppressed, but it does so in some unexpected ways.

These two essays demonstrate that because power is fluid, so are subjectivity and agency. Techniques used to dominate can become means of resistance that empower oppressed subjects and restore their sense of agency. The moments that Fanon describes exemplify what he calls disalienation insofar as they are forms of resistance that reverse the debilitating effects and affects of racist alienation. If racist alienation undermines subjectivity and agency by turning the colonizer's violence and hatred inward against the oppressed self, then resistance can return that violence and hatred to the colonizer in ways that act as an antidote to the psychic infection and pathological subjectivity formed within the colonial context by reauthorizing and empowering colonized subjectivity.

In "This Is the Voice of Algeria," Fanon analyzes shifting power relations mediated by the colonizer's technology.[2] He describes the complex ways in which materiality, bodies, traditions, and perception are caught up in circuits of biopsychic power that can be a means of resistance or domination. As he describes the role of radio in the Algerian revolution, in the beginning the radio represented the technological superiority of the French colonizers, which for them confirmed their right to settle Algeria as manifest destiny (Fanon 1965, 71). The radio broadcast in French was a voice of the colonizer, a voice that haunted the colonized in dreams and in hallucinations (87). Refusing and destroying radios was a way to resist foreign domination. After 1954, with the introduction of radio broadcasts supporting the Algerian revolution such as *Free Radio Algeria, The Voice of Algeria, The Voice of Fighting Algeria,* and *Voice of the Combatants,* the colonized's relation to the radio changed. Even the relation to the French language changed, since some of these sympathetic broadcasts were in French: "Used by the Voice of the Combatants, conveying in a positive way the message of the Revolution, the French language also becomes an instrument of liberation" and unification against the enemy (90).

Having a radio and listening to these broadcasts became an act of resistance; and resistance had a powerful voice constituted through these broadcasts. The radio gave hope to Algerians that they could overthrow their oppressors. According to Fanon, the broadcasts brought Algerians together for the cause of revolution like nothing before: "*The Voice of Algeria,* created out of nothing, brought the nation to life and endowed every citizen with a new status, *telling him so explicitly*" (96; emphasis in the original). Fanon calls these broadcasts the voice of a new nation; the unified Algeria was hearing itself for the first time (cf. 92–93). Significantly, the radio provided more than information on revolutionary victories and resistance; it provided a new authority for the revolution through voice, a voice that also challenged the authority of the voice of the colonizer (cf. 95). Fanon describes how Algerians would listen to interrupted and nearly inaudible broadcasts and still hear the truth of the revolutionary cause; they would reconstruct the truth of the revolution and of their independence and nation from what little they heard on the radio: "This voice, often absent, physically inaudible, which each one felt welling up within himself, founded on an inner perception of the Fatherland, became materialized in an irrefutable way. Every Algerian, for his part, broadcast and transmitted the new language. The nature of this voice recalled in more than one way that of the Revolution: present 'in the air' in isolated pieces, but not objectively. The radio receiver guaranteed this true lie" (87). Although not necessarily an accurate historical truth, this truth creates the possibility of resistance, which opens psychic space and restores a sense of agency to the oppressed.[3] Now, the radio gave voice to a resistant subjectivity constituted through its imaginary voice.

The radio is a mobile site of both domination and resistance that can change the perception of reality and one's self in moving from one to the other. The radio as a means of resistance gave Algerians a sense of common struggle and unity; it created a sense of nation and of a people as it gave them hope of victory. Fanon describes how radio changed Algerians: "The national struggle and the creation of Free Radio Algeria have produced a fundamental change in the people. The radio has appeared in a massive way at once and not in progressive stages. What we have witnessed is a radical transformation of the means of perception, of the very world of perception" (96). What was at first technology used to dominate became used to resist domination and thereby de- and reterritorialized the psychic space of the colonized. Resistance reauthorizes individuals and returns a sense of agency and, at bottom, a sense of humanity: "Challenging of the very principles of foreign domination brings about essential mutations in the consciousness of the colonized, in the manner in which he perceives the colonizer, in his human status in the world" (69). Fanon suggests that resistance can produce a new humanity beyond the economy of property. The radio, or technology generally, is not the possession or property of one culture or another; rather, it operates within networks and circuits of agency and investment that shapes and reshapes bodies and power.

In "Algeria Unveiled," Fanon continues to analyze the mobile and shifting role of cultural "capital."[4] There he vividly describes the effects of colonization on the bodily schema of Algerian women, as the veil becomes overdetermined within both colonial domination and Algerian resistance: "Removed and reassumed again and again, the veil has been manipulated, transformed into a technique of camouflage, into a means of struggle" (Fanon 1965, 61). Like the radio, the veil becomes a mobile site of both resistance and domination in the circuits of biopsychic power that circumscribe women's bodies. Even as the veil disciplines the bodies of Algerian women, Fanon describes how the veil becomes the site of resistance against the preying eyes of the West. The more that French colonizers insist on unveiling Algerian women in the name of progress and women's rights, the more the veil becomes a symbol of resistance; when convenient for imperialist justifications, women's rights become a standard by which the West measures the progress of the so-called third world.

Discursive practices from one culture move into the other, and what seems like a symbol of patriarchal control, like the veil, becomes a symbol of resistance against colonization. Traditions from both cultures are strategically adopted, discarded, or combined to resist. For example, Fanon notes that the traditional white veil was replaced by a black veil as a symbol of protest against, and mourning of, the exile of the king of Morocco, even though in Arab society black was not an expression of mourning. And, on the other hand, as families and fathers in particular discover their daughters unveiled and involved in the revolution, they no longer fear their dishonor but see their daughters' commitment to the cause, which in turn converts the fathers to the revolution. Fanon describes how the daughter's unyielding commitment to liberation demonstrated by her Western clothes displaces patriarchal authority: "From the young girl's look of firmness the father would have understood that her commitment was of long standing. The old fear of dishonor was swept away by a new fear, fresh and cold—that of death in battle or of torture of the girl. Behind the girl, the whole family—even the Algerian father, the authority for all things, the founder of every value—following in her footsteps, becomes committed to the new Algeria" (60). The daughter usurps patriarchal power in the name of the revolution. Resistance to colonization becomes the grounds for resistance to patriarchy. Fanon emphasizes that this shift in power is itself revolutionary.

Fanon (1965) calls the shifting role of the veil—how it was taken up, abandoned, and then taken up again in the struggle against colonization—"a historic dynamism." In the first phase, the Algerian woman wears the veil and affirms a tradition that may in effect discipline her and restrict her freedom as a protest against the colonizers who demand that she remove it: "The veil was a mechanism of resistance, but its value for the social group remained very strong. The veil was worn because tradition demanded a rigid separation of the sexes, but also because the occupier was bent on unveiling Algeria" (63). In the second phase, revolutionaries discover that women passing as European or unveiled can move freely in the city to deliver messages and arms; women remove the veil to fight against the occupation: "The mutation occurred in connection with the Revolution and under special circumstances. The veil was abandoned in the course of revolutionary action" (63). But once this strategy becomes less effective and more dangerous, women again don the veil to hide ammunition and guns and again pass freely through the occupied streets. The veil is a mobile site of discipline and resistance; its significance changes with shifting power relations: "What had been used to block the psychological or political offensives of the occupier became a means, an instrument. The veil helped the Algerian woman to meet the new problems created by the struggle" (63). The veil's relation to both Western and Arab cultures becomes complicated by colonization. It becomes caught up in the circuits of biopsychic power that can be at once both resistant and dominating.

Here, Algerian women's sense of themselves and their bodies is constituted in relation to their changing social circumstance. Fanon describes the effects of the shifting biopsychic power on the bodies of Algerian women: "Without the veil she has an impression of her body being cut up into bits, put adrift; the limbs seem to lengthen indefinitely. When the Algerian woman has to cross the street, for a long time she commits errors of judgment as to the exact distance to be negotiated. The unveiled body seems to escape, to dissolve. . . . The absence of the veil distorts the Algerian woman's corporeal pattern. She quickly has to invent new dimensions for her body, new means of muscular control. [She] relearns her body, re-establishes it in a totally revolutionary fashion" (59). This dialectic between body and world, between body and psyche, creates what Fanon calls the "revolutionary woman." Her body and her sense of herself are in a dialectical relationship with her world and the colonial situation. As resistance requires that she lose the veil and pass as a Western woman, she renegotiates both her physical and psychic space. As resistance requires that she use the veil to hide the new revolutionary woman whom she has become, she again renegotiates the relationship between her clothes, traditions, the artillery of resistance, and men, both colonizers and colonized. Fanon describes "the Algerian woman's body, which in an initial phase was pared down [without the veil], now swelled [with the veil full of armaments]" (62). Along with the veil, her body and psyche are caught up in the circuits of biopsychic power, which open pathways for resistance and liberation even as they discipline.

Fanon's remarks about Algerian women also reveal his own traditional attitudes toward women.[5] For example, he argues that Algerian women become revolutionaries by "instinct," while European women do it by imitation and through education (50). He identifies Algerian women with "childish fears" (52) and talks about their "inability to measure the gravity of events" that leads to their "constant smile" (66). And his descriptions of the European man's fantasies about Algerian women are suspiciously vivid and graphic.

Shifting Power Relations in Julia Alvarez's Fiction

If, as Fanon's analysis suggests, colonization and oppression have an essentially affective dimension, to begin to understand the affective effects of domination it may be useful to turn to literature to speak to the affective level of experience in a way that theory cannot. In addition, given Fanon's own limitations in describing the gendered effects of oppression, again it is necessary to supplement his analysis with the writings of women of color. For a more subtle description of how shifting power relations are gendered, I turn to Julia Alvarez's fiction. Literature not only helps illustrate the theoretical discussion of the fluidity of subject position in relation to power and domination but also suggests that perhaps literature can show what theory still struggles to describe: the contradictions and complications in the relationship between subject position and subjectivity, between the social and the psyche, between oppression and desire.

One central theme in Alvarez's novels is how power dynamics shift according to race, class, and gender. Alvarez's reflections on these shifts in *How the García Girls Lost Their Accents* and *In the Time of the Butterflies* reveal how resistance is gendered. Alvarez's descriptions of the use of the conventions of domestic femininity, womanhood, and motherhood to resist patriarchal authority both at the level of private family life and in public institutions, including government, at once demonstrate that resistance to domination involves shifting power dynamics and at the same time make all the more striking sexual difference in relation to power. Alvarez's first novel, *How the García Girls Lost Their Accents* (1991), is in one sense a study in mobile and transitory points of resistance and shifting power dynamics that fracture unity and effect regroupings. The first chapter opens with the narrator describing the color coding of class hierarchy: old aunts in the grays and blacks of widowhood, cousins in bright colors, nursemaids in white uniforms, and kitchen help in black uniforms (3). This chapter, and the book as a whole, repeatedly recounts the deferential gestures that signal power relations among race, class, and gender. When scolded for not having matches on hand to light the candles on the cake, one of the maids, Iluminada, makes a pleading gesture with her hands clasped against her breast (4). When another maid, Altagracia, is asked to explain the word *antojo* to Yolanda, one of the García sisters, she "puts her brown hands away in her uniform pockets" and "says in a small voice, you're the one to know" (8). These deferential gestures signal class and race hierarchy and the differential power relation in terms of class and race privilege.

Later in the chapter however, when Yolanda, who has returned to the Dominican Republic after a five-year absence, gets a flat tire, gender hierarchy displaces class hierarchy, and the power dynamics shift. Alone with her car, Yolanda is terrified when two men appear out of the grove with machetes hanging from their belts. She considers running, but she is paralyzed with fear and rendered speechless (19). The narrator describes her repeating the same pleading gesture of Iluminada, hands clasped on her chest (20). Yolanda's class privilege in relation to the maid, and in relation to the young boy, Jose, who has taken her to pick guavas, shifts in relation to these two men whose gender privilege is threatening to Yolanda. Now she is the one using deferential gestures.

The power dynamics again suddenly shift in this scene when she begins speaking in English, and the two men conclude that she is American. At this point, they are "rendered docile by her gibberish," and when she mentions the name of her aunt's rich friends, the Mirandas, "their eyes light up with respect" (20–21). The relation between gender hierarchy and class hierarchy is reversed again. In the end, when Yolanda tries to confirm her class privilege and express her gratitude by paying the men, they refuse and look at the ground, as the narrator tells us, with the same deferential gestures of Iluminada and Jose (22). The chapter ends with Jose returning from the Miranda's slapped, shamed, and accused of lying when he tells the guard that a woman is out picking guavas alone. Even Yolanda's dollar bills can't cheer him. The collusion of rigid gender and class structures results in Jose's punishment, which is only intensified when Yolanda offers him money. Even in her attempts to make Jose happy, Yolanda reaffirms her class dominance over him.

Although the novel is full of such reversals, I mention just one more example from the tenth chapter, "Floor Show." As the novel moves back in time, this chapter takes place in New York when the García girls are young, shortly after their family has fled the Trujillo dictatorship. Here, the García's have been invited to join Dr. Fanning and his wife for dinner at a restaurant. Dr. Fanning arranged the fellowship that allowed "papi" García to take his family to New York and was trying to help papi get a job. For days, "mami" gave the girls instructions on how to behave, and the evening of the dinner she dressed them in binding braids and tights in the hopes of disciplining not only their behavior but also their bodies. The dinner scene is tense because the Garcías, used to having class privileges in the Dominican Republic, in New York are financially beholden to the Fannings. In their presence both mami and papi García display deferential gestures and repeatedly look down at the floor.

This chapter displays several reversals among race, class, and gender hierarchies. First, because mami studied in the United States as a girl, her English is better than papi's, and this gives her more power in social situations: "Mami was the leader now that they lived in the States. She had gone to school in the States. *She* spoke English without a heavy accent" (176). The power dynamics between mother and father are reversed by linguistic access. Class dynamics shift when the Garcías, struggling to make ends meet in the United States, no longer have class privilege. Papi no longer has the honor of paying for dinner. The Fannings, who appeared in the Dominican Republic as silly-looking tourists speaking bad Spanish, now make the Garcías look small (184). Gender dynamics shift when on the way to the bathroom Mrs. Fanning kisses papi García. In this context, his class and race deference to Mrs. Fanning make him powerless to object to her flirtations. Power dynamics shift again when one of the girls, Sandi, who witnessed the kiss, uses what she saw to blackmail her father into allowing her to get a doll that they cannot afford and for which the Fannings end up paying. In this chapter, Sandi recognizes the value of passing as a white American when she studies her fair skin and blue-eyed beauty in the mirror after she has seen the power Mrs. Fanning exercised over her father with the kiss.

Shifting power dynamics are also central to Alvarez's second novel, *In the Time of the Butterflies.* In a scene similar to "Floor Show," a daughter becomes more powerful than her father when he wants her to keep a secret from her mother. When Minerva Mirabal discovers that her father has a secret second family, she gains power over her father; gender and generation power relations shift. In the end, it is this second illegitimate family, much poorer and less powerful than the first, that smuggles letters and care packages back and forth between the girls in prison and their family at home; the power dynamics of class shift when the lower-class family has access to the guards in a way unavailable to the upper-class family. Alvarez's fiction brings to life various ways in which women and girls resist domination by turning patriarchal restrictions to their advantage by using one form of domination against another.

Like Fanon's account of the radio and the veil, Alvarez's fictional account of shifting power relations exemplifies mobile and transitory sites of resistance that reconfigure those relations. Individuals are furrowed by intersecting axes of power, cut up and remolded and marked by their various positions in shifting power relations that constantly regroup them in terms of race, class, and gender, among other alliances. Alvarez's novels make clear that the differential norms for masculinity and femininity within patriarchal cultures circumscribe power relations differently for men and women. Alvarez is sensitive to how women's subject positions within patriarchal cultures affect their sense of their own agency both in terms of their subjection to patriarchal restrictions and in terms of their resistance to those restrictions.

Moreover, like Fanon, Alvarez attends to the effects of the colonization of psychic space on the affects of her characters. Like Fanon, in and with her fiction Alvarez insists on the relationship between body and psyche or soul. Indeed, in the postscript to *In the Time of the Butterflies*, Alvarez (1994, 324) tells us that "a novel is not, after all, a historical document, but a way to travel through the human heart"; and that an epoch of life "can only be understood by fiction, only finally be redeemed by the imagination." For Alvarez, fiction speaks to the heart in a way that "immerses" readers in an epoch and helps them "understand" it. This understanding is not intellectual but affective. Fiction helps us understand the effects of colonization, domination, and oppression on the affects of those oppressed. Alvarez's fiction gives us especially powerful portraits of the effects of domination on women's psyches and affects and how anger and pain can be transformed into resistance.

Fanon's analysis of the radio and the veil and Alvarez's fiction give hope that even debilitating alienation can be turned against itself in ways that empower the oppressed subject and restore a sense of agency even within the restrictions of colonization or patriarchy. The playfulness of Alvarez's fiction, resonant with Fanon's insistence on a new humanism, suggests that subjectivity and identity do not have to be bought on the backs of others. Contra European philosophies of alienation, subjectivity need not be born in opposition to the hostile look of the other. Both Fanon and Alvarez imagine a powerful vision in which identity is not necessarily built on exclusion. Yet, as they so poignantly show, exclusion can be turned into a means of resistance that restores subjectivity. This does not mean, however, that subjectivity is necessarily the product of conflict and aggression. Rather, within contexts of domination, colonization, oppression, and exclusion, subjectivity can be a product of conflict.

As Fanon so eloquently explains, within these contexts both privileged subjectivity and othered subjectivity are formed as pathological symptoms of superiority and inferiority complexes inherent in situations of domination. Fanon, Spivak, and others have argued that one of the primary forces of domination is that the Western subject's privilege is secured by forcing those oppressed to carry their affective burden—guilt, shame, anger, depression. The philosopher Teresa Brennan applies this argument to patriarchy when in *The Interpretation of the Flesh* (1992), she develops a theory of active attention to explain what many feminists have described, how the male ego is sustained and supported by female caregiving that forces women to do the emotional labor.

In the next part, I continue to explore how debilitating alienation operates in different contexts, specifically in the context of women's oppression within Western culture. Just as an exploration of the affective and psychological effects of colonization can help diagnose racism, so too can they help diagnose sexism, which is in many ways even more invisible and institutionalized than racism. Sexism exists not only in covert or subtle forms that have a debilitating effect on the psyche and lead to what I am calling the colonization of psychic space but also in overt, violent forms—rape, incest, and domestic violence—that pose a constant threat for women. In the next part, I turn to how the colonization of psychic space affects women, specifically in the affects of oppression. Resonant with Fanon's analysis of the effects of colonization on the psyche, I consider how depression, shame, anger, and alienation result from pathological social situations rather than individual pathologies. In part IV, I again turn to how resistance, female genius, and forgiveness transform these affects into ways for restoring agency, individuality, and community.

Part III

Social Melancholy and Psychic Space

Love has become the modern obscenity, it's more obscene than sex, you can talk about sex and violence; everybody knows that it exists, but love is too strange.
—Julia Kristeva, *The Portable Kristeva*

Thus far, I have focused on the dynamics of debilitating, or double, alienation unique to oppression and how that alienation shapes the psychic lives of colonized peoples through the transmission of negative affects from colonizer to colonized. More specifically, I considered how European notions of alienation become screens that cover over concrete forms of racist oppression. I postulated that the look of the other causes anxiety not just because that look threatens the freedom of the self but more specifically because that look from those who have been oppressed or repressed so that the Western (male) subject becomes the beneficiary of privilege causes guilt, anxiety, and dread in that privileged subject. And I have diagnosed how colonization perverts affects and turns the negative affects of the colonizers against the colonized through the workings of a cruel superego. In addition, I have considered alternatives to the conception of humanity inherent in the notion of manifest destiny, a conception that necessitates oppression of one group or groups to shore up the privilege of others. With Fanon, I began to imagine a humanism beyond the economy of property which turns people into property and commodities to be exploited and dominated or even enslaved. Finally, I considered how the privilege and agency of power are fluid and can be regained by those oppressed or othered using the very means of their oppression against their oppressors—Julia Alvarez's notion that one nail takes out the other.

While in the first half of this volume I was primarily concerned with the racism inherent in colonization and how the dynamics of the colonization of psychic space also operate in the metropolis, specifically in the United States, in the chapters that follow, I turn to how debilitating alienation and the colonization of psychic space affect women within sexist cultures, specifically Western cultures. I have already touched on how debilitating alienation affects black women in different ways than black men or white women. Now I again turn to how sexism compounds alienation and leads to particular somatic symptoms in women.

The first chapter in part III, "The Affects of Oppression," merely outlines the themes and particular affects that I analyze in much greater detail in chapters 7 and 8. "The Affects of Oppression" presents an overview of how the debilitating alienation of oppression translates into the negative affects of oppression suffered in silence by women in cultures that devalue them and deny the existence of sexism or even sexual difference, thereby silencing them. Using Marleen Gorris's film *A Question of Silence*, I attempt to give life to these negative affects—melancholy, shame, anger, and alienation—through her characters. Again, I show how literature and film not only animate theory but also embody the contradictions inherent in oppression with which theory continues to struggle.

Chapter 7 considers why depression is reportedly so widespread among women and mothers. My analysis in this chapter suggests that the medical and psychological discourses around women's depression not only pathologize the stereotype of women, white women in particular, as passive and emotional but also cover over the social causes of women's depression. In place of depression, I develop a theory of *social melancholy* to explain how the debilitating alienation of oppression and everyday sorts of sexism lead to melancholy and depression. Against traditional psychoanalytic theory, I argue that social melancholy is not the internalization of a lost love as refusal to mourn the loss but rather the refusal to mourn the loss of a loved and lovable self-image, an image missing in mainstream culture.

I continue my analysis of social melancholy by linking it to sublimation in chapter 8. There, I argue that just as we need a theory of social melancholy, we need a theory of *social sublimation.* Oppression and the colonization of psychic space operate through undermining the ability to sublimate; this is why Freud can conclude that women are less able to sublimate than men. But if women are less able to sublimate than men, it is not because of women's anatomy, psychology, or individual pathologies but rather because of social repression and the lack of social support required for sublimation. I argue that if sublimation is the hallmark of subjectivity, then an impaired ability to sublimate undermines agency and ultimately leads to depression and melancholy. Finally, using, revising, and expanding Kristeva's theory of intimate revolt, I associate sublimation with the ability to revolt against the authority of the social in order to authorize oneself as a legitimate subject with agency, a form of revolt denied to those othered within mainstream culture but at the same time a powerful potential site of resistance to domination.

Chapter 6

The Affects of Oppression

Although countercultures and resistance are possible, within mainstream culture the affects of oppression—depression, shame, anger, and alienation—are pathologized as individual or group sickness or even as evil. As the result of institutional and systematic oppression, exclusion, and marginalization, which prohibits even speaking of their existence, these affects cannot be fully articulated until the experiences of women and men of color are valued. Women, and racialized or sexualized others, are denied full participation in mainstream cultural and social institutions; and the affects that result from the experience of that exclusion are also denied social space for articulation. It is not just that those othered are excluded from positions of power and not accepted as fully rational autonomous subjects, but also that their very experiences of exclusion are rarely allowed articulation or signification within mainstream culture. In seemingly more "progressive" societies like that of the United States, this double exclusion, like the debilitating double alienation discussed in part I, makes oppression more effective in colonizing psychic space. When those oppressed are denied the cultural or social authority to articulate the experience of their oppression, then their exclusion is compounded. By discounting or pathologizing the affects of oppression, the dynamics of oppression all the more effectively prevent politicization of experiences of humiliation and pain that result from discrimination. Sexism, racism, and homophobia are covered over and denied within dominant culture through the double movement of the colonization of psychic space, which operates first as a form of social abjection and exclusion and second as a form of silencing. Both operations undermine the ability of those othered to create their own meaning, especially that of their own bodies and experiences. As Fanon says, they arrive too late into a world that already has constructed their meaning as abject and debased. They are doubly alienated and doubly excluded through the absences of supportive social space within mainstream culture to express painful and angry affects. This is why resistance strategies are essential to restore the ability to sublimate and thereby express the affects of oppression.

Suffering, pain, depression, shame, anger, or alienation are not seen as the results of oppression because within the United States today supposedly there is no sexism and no racism. If such feelings exist, then they are seen as products of individual pathology and mental imbalance. Anyone who feels discriminated against is considered crazy—paranoid, hysterical, or oversensitive. Politicization of experience becomes pathological: feminists and activists become oversensitive paranoid hysterics who overreact; and sexism and racism become all in their heads.[1] Within this world, to articulate the affects of oppression and their concomitant experiences is to be crazy, to suffer from paranoid delusions. Unless resistance strategies are developed, oppression becomes a question of silence.

The colonization of psychic spaces works through silencing the effects and affects of oppression. First, those othered within mainstream culture are excluded from the world of meaning except as abject or inferior. Then their exclusion is silenced. Moreover, they are excluded from meaning making, even, or perhaps especially, creating the meaning of their own lives and bodies. They are excluded from the means of production of value, especially that of their own value. The meaning of their own lives and bodies has already been defined as inferior, deficient, or sick; but more than this, they have been defined as incapable of defining themselves. It is this double movement that creates the double alienation of oppression. This alienation is not merely the alienation that results from being born into a world of meaning not of one's making, but rather of being born into that world as one who is seen as incapable of fully making meaning, especially the meaning of one's own body. The alienation of oppression goes beyond constitutive alienation or violence supposedly inherent in the human condition. In fact, double alienation undermines what some theorists identify as the alienation constitutive of subjectivity. While the debilitating alienation of oppression may seem necessary to sustain the lifestyles of the beneficiaries of domination, it is not necessary to subjectivity or humanity. As I have argued elsewhere, it runs counter to an ethics of responsibility and witnessing at the core of subjectivity and thereby humanity (Oliver 2001). As I have shown in chapter 1, notions of originary alienation and originary violence cover over very concrete forms of alienation and violence specific to oppression. Here, I show that the affects of oppression—depression, melancholy, shame, and anger—are diagnosed as individual pathologies, which cover over their institutional and social causes. This chapter presents an overview of the affects of oppression, and the chapters that follow develop a more sustained theoretical analysis of alternative accounts of depression, shame, and sublimation.

Melancholy

Unlike classic melancholy, as described in psychoanalytic theory, which is the incorporation of a lost loved other to avoid losing her or him, what I call *social melancholy* is the loss of a positive or lovable image of oneself and the incorporation of abject or denigrated self-images widely circulating in mainstream culture. With social melancholy, it is not the loss of a loved other but the loss of a loved self that causes melancholy; and it is not the incorporation of the loved other but the incorporation of the denigrated self that leads to self-abnegation. It is not only the lack of positive self-images that leads to social melancholy but also the absence of social acceptance. Social acceptance and support are necessary for psychic life, specifically sublimation, which is essential not only for creativity but also for meaning, both the meaning of language and the meaning of life.

Here, sublimation is conceived more broadly than it was by Freud, who identifies sublimation with artistic and intellectual activities into which sexual drives are diverted from their sexual aim into a nonsexual aim. There is neither reason to limit sublimation to sexual drives nor reason to limit nonsexual aims to artistic and intellectual activities. Rather, all drives make their way into signification—artistic, intellectual, linguistic—through sublimation. Sublimation is the socialization of drives. Through sublimation, bodily drives and their attenuating affects become discharged in signifying practices; and insofar as signification depends on the discharge of drives, through sublimation drives become signs. Most basically, drives are bodily needs, where the body is always a biopsychic-social being. The goal of sublimation is connection or communion with others. Even aggressive drives become socialized when they are sublimated into art or language. Freud ([1923] 1955, 45) describes this need for communion and communication as eros; and he concludes that sublimation is a form of eros: "If this displaceable energy is desexualised libido, it may also be described as sublimated energy; for it would still retain the main purpose of Eros—that of uniting and binding—in so far as it helps towards establishing unity, or tendency to unity, which is particularly characteristic of the ego."

The meaning of language depends on the sublimation of drives and affects into words. Affects and emotions are the experiential representatives of bodily needs, fluid, embodied sociopsychic dynamics that can be discharged in signification. Infants enter language by virtue of sublimating their drives or bodily needs into forms of communication; their early means of communication—cries, jibberish, smiles—can be seen as primordial modes of sublimation. At the other end of the spectrum, the depressive gives up on words because of a breakdown in the process of sublimation such that drives and affects are no longer discharged in language. When bodily needs and affects become cut off from words, the result is depression. In its most severe forms, depression is the inability to sublimate, or more generally the loss of eros—the ability to connect with others. At the extreme, the depressive becomes cut off from others and enters a catatonic state. This catatonia is not necessarily the result of individual pathology but rather often the result of social melancholy caused by the devaluation of women and their emotional and physical labor. In a sense, the depressive has given up on words and society because they have given up on her.

Shame

Unlike classic melancholy, in which self-beratement is the result of guilt over ill will or bad thoughts toward the lost loved one, with social melancholy self-beratement is the result of shame over the loss of a lovable self. The distinction between shame and guilt is crucial to understanding the theory of social melancholy. Whereas guilt is associated with particular actions, thoughts, or desires, shame is associated with the very being of the subject. Guilt is the feeling of wrongdoing, while shame is the feeling of inferiority and defect. If guilt is associated with moral evil, shame is associated with bad in the sense of defective. The melancholic, suffering from social melancholy, experiences the shame assigned to her by culture as her own inferiority or defective being. In addition to feeling guilty, she is made to feel flawed in her very sense of self. The self-beratement caused by shame can be more painful than that caused by guilt because it attacks the core of identity and self-esteem. While we can make amends or reparations for wrongs done, we cannot make amends or reparations for wrong being. We can apologize or ask forgiveness for bad acts, but what does it mean to apologize or ask forgiveness for *being* bad?

Sublimation requires not only social acceptance and support but also social forgiveness. The process of individuation necessitates the sublimation of one's own particular bodily needs and affects into social codes and signifying systems. This sublimation is at once a trespass against those codes and systems and an assimilation of them. Individuation requires trespassing social codes to assert one's singularity. But this trespass is possible only with the presupposition of forgiveness. Forgiveness allows the individual to trespass the social order and thereby possess it and yet be accepted back into the order as one who belongs. As Hannah Arendt (1959, 213) says, without forgiveness we would all be capable of one and only one act after which we would be paralyzed by its consequences. This first "act" is the assertion of our individuality by questioning or trespassing the social authority into which we are born. It is only by questioning that authority that we can authorize ourselves as social agents.

The child's why? is one of the first linguistic acts of revolt against, and assimilation of, social authority. It is through this questioning that we become individuals who belong to the community. The child's why? asked repeatedly not only discharges the negativity of bodily drives into signification but also transforms it into communication. Questioning can also reconnect word and affects by negating the depressive resignation that words cannot express pain, trauma, or anything else. If the depressive gives up on words because they seem to negate the very experiences that she is trying to express, especially insofar as those experiences are excluded from the social or even from polite society, then questioning is a type of revolt against restrictive prohibitions and can reauthorize the subject. The negativity inherent in questioning represents a negation of signification's negation of things, bodies, or experiences. If we despair because the word is not, and can never be, the thing, that it always falls short of articulating our experience, questioning whether we have said or can say what we mean opens up the possibility of infinite rearticulation and creativity. By questioning meaning, we play on meaning's fluidity and thereby tenuously reconnect fluid words and fluid bodies. Questioning discharges the fluidity of the negativity of bodily drives into language.

At both ends of the spectrum, the child's entrance into language and the depressive's renunciation of language, questioning is essential to bring the negativity of drive force into signification and transform it into creativity and meaning. The negativity of bodily drive force becomes positive creative sublimation through repetition and response from others. Repetition and response usher the child into society with its linguistic codes and support the renewal of meaning for all of us. To restore the ability to sublimate meaning and make it our own and thereby belong to the community, it is necessary to restore the ability to question, trespass, and revolt against that very meaning and community; but to question, trespass, or revolt presupposes forgiveness. Without positive, supportive, accepting, forgiving response from others, we feel ashamed of ourselves for being defective or inferior, which prevents us from meaningful communication. We blame ourselves for lack of meaning, and shame leads to depression, which in turn can make us ashamed. This is the vicious circle of the colonization of psychic space.

Asserting our individuality or difference is a trespass against the social that requires social forgiveness to forge belonging. But it is not trespass but forgiveness that is definitive of both individuality and community. This is not to say that there is any sovereign agent of forgiveness. On the contrary, the agency of social forgiveness is meaning itself, which produces the effect of sovereignty. It is not that social forgiveness presupposes a sovereign agent, but rather that forgiveness is a prerequisite for sovereignty. Only the possibility of forgiveness allows us to assert our individuality and difference with the assurance that we will be accepted back into the community. Without this assurance, we cannot become individuals. It is precisely this assurance that is denied to those oppressed by, or excluded from, the values of mainstream culture. And it is only through asserting our difference by sublimating social codes or meanings that we take ourselves to be sovereign agents. Our sense of ourselves as agents capable of action depends on the dynamic of social forgiveness through which we belong to the community as individuals. By withholding social forgiveness, oppression undermines the sense of agency and the very subjectivity of those othered.

Freud and his followers maintain that if we can acknowledge our aggressive feelings, then we won't need to act on them. If we confess our desire to kill, then we won't need to kill. But this acknowledgment and confession require, even presuppose, forgiveness. Without the support of social forgiveness, sublimated revolt is impossible. Oppression operates through a double movement that undermines the possibility of sublimation for women and others excluded from dominant values: it withholds or forecloses positive and accepting meanings for the subject that support the transfer of affects into signification, on the one hand; and it withholds or forecloses the forgiveness necessary to support psychic revolt against the authority of culture through which we become individuals who belong to the community, on the other. Those who benefit from dominant values are forgiven their individuality, their difference. But those excluded and disowned by dominant values are not forgiven; they are shamed, ridiculed, abjected, and abused for their difference. They are not allowed to become individuals who belong to the community. Rather, they are excluded as inferior beings who do not belong or belong only as abjected beings who serve the needs of others.

Anger

Even anger as a normal response to oppression and repression becomes pathologized. Those who feel this anger come to blame themselves or each other for aggressive or hostile emotions pathologized within mainstream culture. They are expected to carry this affect without expressing it. Indeed, they are expected to carry the affective burdens of the culture. They are not only made ashamed of their very being but also forced to carry the shame of culture. As I have shown in chapter 3, unwanted affects are projected onto those othered to shore up the privilege of the rational autonomous subject.

Feminists have argued that women bear the affective or emotional burdens for men in an unequal affective division of labor.[2] As the philosopher Sandra Bartky (1990) puts it, women feed egos and tend emotional wounds. Like Bartky, Teresa Brennan (1992) describes this emotional labor as feeding the masculine ego and self-esteem by directing attention toward it and away from oneself. And recall that Gayatri Chakravorty Spivak (1999) claims that the civilizing mission rests on the foreclosure of affects, which are then projected onto the oppressed, who are expected to carry the affective burden for dominant culture. This denial of unwanted affects is not so much a projection as a transfer or injection of affects into those othered within dominant society. As we know, philosophers have long associated lack of control over emotions with a lack of reason, and lack of reason with a lack of humanity. Affects are associated with the irrational and barbaric in a complicated movement through which they are transferred onto the abjected other and at once become signs or symptoms of that abjection. They are further disavowed by the foreclosure of their articulation by those forced to carry them. Even mainstream culture's rage over difference, which should be met with anger by those whose difference is abjected, is transferred to those othered who are forced to carry it. Resistance, then, is seen as a symptom of irrational monstrous rage, while the domination, oppression, and abuse against which it was directed (perhaps misdirected) are normalized and naturalized as a rational self-defense against monstrous evil or disease to maintain proper order.

In terms of psychoanalytic theory, those othered within culture are subject to, and interiorize, a punishing superego that excludes them as abject. The superego of dominant culture judges them inferior and defective. This harsh superego maintains the good on which dominant values rest by projecting its opposite onto those marginalized and excluded; they become evil. They are expected to carry the burden of evil, sickness, weakness, and dejection for the entire culture. They become the scapegoats of the dominant superego. But this superego and its good are not only self-contradictory but also self-destructive and therefore necessarily leave open the possibility of resistance.

Ironically, those marginalized seek love and recognition from the very culture that rejects them as inferior. The dominant values with which they are raised cannot but affect them; they cannot but internalize those values as valuable. The contradiction of valuing that which devalues oneself can lead to feelings of inferiority, shame, and depression, or it can lead to reflection, resistance, and revolt. Anger and aggression redirected outward or sublimated into creative expression can renew agency and self-esteem. Feelings of shame and discrimination can become the basis for alternative communities and modes of expression. But the very restrictions of oppressive cultures can be turned back against those cultures; as Alvarez's character, Minerva Mirabal, says, "One nail takes out another." Turning again to art, this time film, not only brings to life the theory of social melancholy but also reveals the contradictions within patriarchy that both undermine agency and constitute the othered subject as abject even while denying the existence of sexism or sexual difference.

A Question of Silence

> A housewife, a waitress, and a secretary walk into an upscale boutique.
> The well-dressed owner condescendingly asks, "Can I help you . . . *ladies*?"
> The secretary replies, "No thank you, I'm just looking."
> The waitress answers, "No thank you, I'm just looking."
> The housewife just kills him.

This is the gist of the crime scene in Marleen Gorris's 1982 film *De Stilte rond Christine M.*(The Silence around Christine M.; released in the United States as *A Question of Silence*). Gorris's film poignantly exemplifies some of the central dynamics of the colonization of psychic space outlined in the last section. Although everyone in the film is convinced that the three women must be insane to kill the boutique owner without motive, the psychiatrist assigned to the case comes to realize that the murder was in some sense a response to the everyday humiliations and oppression suffered by these women in a culture that devalues women. *A Question of Silence* presents the depression, shame, anger, and alienation associated with the humiliation that these women face daily as women. In the context of diagnosing the effects of oppression on the psyche and self-identity, I continue to delineate the connection between oppression and affect established in chapter 3, there in relation to colonization, here in relation to the colonization of psychic space more generally. Gorris's film makes vivid how sexist oppression colonizes women's psychic lives. Her film shows how the affects of oppression are the consequence of the debilitating alienation of sexist oppression. Moreover, the film shows what theory can only describe, the relationship between the colonization of psychic space and the lack of social space within which to discharge the negative affects that infect women within patriarchal cultures. The film shows how women are silenced to the point that they give up on words; in the end, their laughter, which cannot be contained by the patriarchal institution and must be forced out, is their only form of rebellion.

Flashbacks show that before the murder the secretary had just come from work, where at a meeting a board member claimed one of her ideas as his own and grabbed her hand to stop her from making noise with her coffee spoon. The waitress also had just come from work, where customers continually harassed her. And the housewife had just come from "work," where her husband yelled at her to take care of *her* three kids and the house, and claimed that she didn't do anything all day. In the boutique, the housewife is caught stuffing a blouse into her bag by the boutique owner, who arrogantly and condescendingly chastises her with his eyes as he takes her bag from her hands and removes the garment. The housewife defiantly stuffs another garment into her bag, and the waitress and secretary join in. The three women circle the man, and soon they are beating him to death with hangers, clothes racks, and other objects in the shop. Obviously, this brutal murder is not funny. The real joke in the film, as it turns out, is to think that the housewife, the waitress, and the secretary could just as well have been men.

The psychiatrist assigned by the court cannot explain this crime except by virtue of the insanity of its perpetrators. They must be crazy; why else would three women beat a man and complete stranger to death? But could all three of these women, who are strangers to each other, be insane? After trying to discover a motive for the murder, the psychiatrist comes to understand that the everyday oppression silently suffered by these women explains their outburst of rage. She concludes that they are not insane, they are women. And, as women, they are oppressed in virtually every facet of their lives. The psychiatrist tries without success to explain this to the (male) judges. But her attempts to understand and explain the heinous crime are interpreted as her condoning it. To entertain the idea that these women could have a motive and that this motive could be born out of their everyday experience in a sexist society is seen as complicity with the murder itself. Despite her insistence that it is not her place to judge the women guilty or innocent but rather to judge them mentally competent, the psychiatrist's conclusion that they are rational women rather than insane monsters is seen as her justifying the crime or exonerating the perpetrators.

When one judge asks what difference it makes that they are women, since it could just as well have been three men killing a woman, the psychiatrist, the defendants, and the women witnesses break out laughing and are expelled from the courtroom. Again, the judges seem to interpret their laughter as insensitivity to the crime rather than as a response to the judges' disregard for sexual difference. Ironically, even as the judges dismiss the women from the courtroom and declare that the trial will continue in the defendants' absence, the judges cannot be made to understand the experiences of these women, who remain silent and silenced within a sexist culture.[3] They don't understand why it is funny to think that the housewife, the waitress and the secretary could have been three men. They don't get the joke. In fact, in their eyes, the women's laughter merely confirms that they are all insane, including now the psychiatrist. Their laughter and their rage are beyond what can be recognized, let alone understood or accepted within patriarchal institutions.

It is not just the judges in Gorris's film but Western culture in general that cannot recognize or understand the rage of the oppressed as anything other than pathology. Think of how any attempt to explain or understand the terrorist attack on the World Trade Center as rage at U.S. imperialism was seen as unpatriotic and as justifying the act or as exonerating the perpetrators; even seeing the perpetrators as rational cold-blooded criminals and not insane monsters was suspect. It is not just that the anger and rage of those excluded are silenced but also that the depression, shame, and alienation of oppression are denied social space for signification. The affects of oppression are out of bounds.

The Housewife (Melancholy)

Even before the psychiatrist's evaluation, it is clear that the film's protagonist, Christine M., a housewife with three kids, suffers from depression. She lives without affect or words, except when caressing her infant. The film suggests that her depression is the result of her social situation rather than individual pathology. It becomes clear that Christine is expected to stay home with the kids and take care of them and the house while her husband is at work. Her husband is verbally abusive and does not appreciate Christine or her domestic and child-care work, which in themselves become oppressive through their monotony and lack of adult interaction. In response to, perhaps as a protection against, the screaming of her children and the yelling of her husband, Christine withdraws to a world of silence. She has given up on words to express her affects, which have become shut up in some psychical closet at the corner of an otherwise empty space. Christine lacks the social support to structure or bridge the empty space between words and affects because her life as wife and mother is not valued by either those close to her or society at large. Why put words to affects if there is no one who can hear them or understand? With no available social support, Christine suffers from what I am calling social melancholy.

Perhaps if the culture around the three women in Gorris's film had been more supportive and forgiving of these women's small gestures of revolt through which they attempted to assert their individuality and sexual difference, they would not have killed the boutique owner. Their lives, especially the housewife and secretary, were full of silent resistance that went unacknowledged and unheard by those around them. It is a question of silence, a silence imposed by a culture that does not support or accept the transfer to meaning of the affective lives of women and other marginalized peoples. It is not just that individual men or others are insensitive and cruel, but rather that mainstream culture and dominant values are oppressive. This is why the suffering of these women is ordinary. As the psychiatrist concludes, these are ordinary women suffering ordinary humiliations. Yet even the psychiatrist was slow to understand the everyday humiliations that continually shamed these women to the core of their beings without an end in sight. She herself goes unheard and is in the end denigrated and demoted by the court to the status of "woman" rather than expert witness and psychiatrist. Even with her professional training, she too lacks the words with which to explain the humiliation of ordinary women in a way that it can be heard and understood.

The Waitress (Shame)

The waitress, Anna, is the most vocal of the three, but her chatter only thinly veils her depression and shame. She is also the most easily embarrassed. It is obvious that she is lonely and does not enjoy living alone, yet she tells the psychiatrist that she is happy to be rid of her husband and daughter, and refuses to admit to her sadness. Only the viewer sees her sorrow as she stands alone in her apartment imagining the times she shared with her family. She is embarrassed—ashamed—to admit that she cooked herself a big gourmet dinner the evening after the murder. Despite her laughter, like Christine, she often averts her eyes when questioned, adopting the posture and gaze of someone flustered and ashamed. It is not so much that she is ashamed of the murder, but rather she is ashamed of her pleasure, especially her pleasure in food. She pleads for chocolates but is embarrassed when receiving them. At the diner where she works, she is ridiculed by customers about her weight and joins in making jokes when the police arrive, claiming that she murdered someone by sitting on him. Her laughter and jokes are made with averted gaze as a defense against her shame, shame at being divorced, at being fat, at being old, at being a waitress, ultimately at being a woman; these are the things that she jokes about to hide the many ways in which she has interiorized the humiliations she has suffered that affect how she conceives of herself and her world—without power and without hope . . . without acceptance or forgiveness.

The Secretary (Anger)

Along with shame, the secretary, Andrea, is full of muted anger and contempt for her boss, for the board members, for the society that led the young housewife to commit murder, and for the psychiatrist. Her anger is palpable yet restrained. When her boss praises the board member who takes her investment advice as his own, she stirs her coffee in resistance. When he grabs her hand to make her stop, she silently glares into space. When the police come to her office to take her away, she silently leaves her boss in midsentence. With men, her protests and resistance are silent, muted, and ultimately ignored. With the psychiatrist, her words are laden with anger as she tells the psychiatrist that she doesn't understand women and that her questions are ridiculous. Although Andrea had never met Christine before, Andrea explains why the housewife's life might lead her to murder. She is cynical about the psychiatrist's insistence that her report can influence the court. Andrea knows better. She knows that women won't be heard. But despite her reflections on the plight of women in sexist culture and her anger, she, like the other women, feels powerless. She realizes that she will be sentenced to a life in prison where she will slowly go mad. Her anger cannot prevent the system from driving her mad. Rather, her muted rage becomes shame, self-disgust, and resignation, evidenced by her conclusion that all women are stupid.

Her anger against the culture and men who oppress her is turned against other women, especially the psychiatrist. While she never says anything to resist the domination of the men for whom she works, she is constantly challenging the psychiatrist and her class privilege. She is not in a position to resist the men who have authority over her. When Andrea says that women are stupid, she turns her hostility toward her oppressors back onto the oppressed. This turn inward of aggression is another classic operation of oppression. In a culture that forecloses the affects of oppression, especially anger and hostility, these affects are translated into feelings of inferiority. Again, in the complicated movements of oppression, domination is normalized and any response to it, especially angry responses, are foreclosed, ignored, or pathologized.

On the other hand, although extreme in its form, *A Question of Silence* offers a sense of how resistance and redirecting anger outward can renew agency and self-esteem. In Gorris's film, this renewal is short-lived and ultimately self-destructive insofar as the women's anger reaches homicidal levels before it is redirected against the boutique owner. Still, despite the brutality of their act—which cannot be condoned—the redirection of their aggression and anger outward does give them all a sense of freedom, evidenced by the pleasures they experience directly after the crime (Christine rides a ferris wheel, Anna cooks a gourmet dinner, and Andrea has ice cream).

The Psychiatrist (Alienation)

The psychiatrist, Janine, does not so much display depression, shame, or anger as frustration. From the opening scene in which she is trying to seduce her husband and he continues reading until she playfully threatens his genitals with a pen, to her struggle to understand the three women, and finally to the lack of sympathy and understanding she receives from her husband and other men around her, she is frustrated. Throughout the film, her husband and other men—the attorneys, the judges—insist that the three women must be insane, that it is an open-and-shut case, and that "you can spot women like that a mile away." But Janine is not convinced. She is bewildered precisely because they are ordinary women. The three women know that because they are women, Janine's report will not make any difference. The film proves them right when in the end the judges reject Janine's expert testimony, and she leaves the courtroom with the other women. But this is not first time that men do not listen to her. In one scene at a dinner party at her home, Janine and the wife of a visiting couple are nearly silent while the two husbands converse. But there is nothing extraordinary about this scene. There is nothing extraordinary about the lives of the three women or Janine's life or how any of them are humiliated and ignored because they are women. In the final scene, as she leaves the courtroom, a man bumps into Janine and calls her a "cunt" while her husband honks incessantly for her to get in the car. Even this is not unusual; rather, these are the everyday ways in which women are alienated from themselves and the meaning of their own lives.

It seems that Janine is a "liberated" woman, with a career and a husband who cooks. But it becomes clear that despite her class privilege and her education, ultimately she is not considered capable of creating meaning because she is a woman. Her testimony in court as an expert witness is dismissed because she is a woman attempting to give meaning to women's experiences of oppression. And, in everyday situations, the film shows Janine being silenced, ignored, or patronized. Even the space of the film suggests that the physical restrictions on women's lives become metaphors for the restrictions on psychic space. The women are seen in restrictive spaces, confined to prison cells, walking through narrow corridors, descending stairways, locked behind door after door.[4] These doors become the barriers that contain and restrain the affects of oppression, behind which the women go quietly mad.

Chapter 7

The Depressed Sex

In the nineteenth century, hysteria was the name of the disease associated with white women.[1] Hysteria produced and reproduced stereotypes or ideals of white bourgeois femininity as passive, emotional, irrational, and incapable of serious thought or work.[2] In the twentieth century, hysteria has been replaced by depression, again a disease associated with women that produces and reproduces the meanings of feminine, woman, and mother. Depression is diagnosed as a pathological condition that, according to most studies, affects women at rates two or three times the rates of men affected worldwide. Why is depression disproportionately a female disease? Some studies, never conclusive, link depression to hormonal changes and other physical differences between women and men. Few studies, however, consider lifestyle, behavioral, and attitudinal differences imposed by patriarchal culture and the historical value placed on men over women. Is it a coincidence that many of the characteristics of stereotypical femininity are also the characteristics of clinical depression? In various ways, lack of activity, passivity, silence, moodiness, irritability, excessive crying, lack of sexual appetite, and nervousness—the very description of the symptoms of depression given by the National Mental Health Association—have been part of our ideas and even ideals of femininity for centuries.[3] So is it a surprise that doctors would look for, and find, these characteristics in women more often than in men?

In a sense, the female subject is constructed as passive and emotional, then pathologized as depressed, diagnosed as depressed, and finally treated with drugs and electroshock therapies for mental illness.[4] This resembles what Friedrich Nietzsche describes as the philosopher or scientist who hides truth behind a bush and then praises himself when he finds it. I am not arguing that there is some type of *Stepford Wives* or *The Handmaid's Tale* science fiction conspiracy to keep women docile through drugs. Nor am I denying that there are physiological aspects of depression that should be treated. Rather, I am suggesting a critical analysis of the very studies that so powerfully document women's depression and of the social conditions that render women passive, lacking appetites, moody, in order to diagnose the dynamics of culture's pathology and the relation between social and psychic space. In this chapter, I argue that the pathologization of women's depression covers over the institutional causes for that symptomology. Patriarchal culture continues to devalue and debase women and mothers. Depression becomes a cover for what I call social melancholy, which is not the melancholy of traditional psychoanalysis but a form of melancholy that results from oppression, domination, and the colonization of psychic space. Debilitating double alienation manifests itself in women in the form of depression.

In various ways, the discourses of medicine and disease continue to produce and reproduce the meaning of sexual difference.[5] Throughout the history of medicine, women's bodies have been pathologized to circumscribe, even control, their behavior. Several contemporary theorists have analyzed how medical discourses and clinical practices reinforce, even create, racial and gendered identities, and legitimate disciplinary and regulatory controls.[6] Particular diseases like anemia, yellow fever, hysteria, depression, schizophrenia, and AIDS are distinguished not only epidemiologically but also by linking them to specific races, genders, sexualities, or places.[7] Identifying these epidemics legitimates intervention and management of these groups in particular. Medical categorizing, surveillance, reporting, regulation, and treatment not only construct diseased racial and gendered subjects but also legitimate continued research and treatment that objectifies those subjects and keeps them dependent on the medical establishment, whose superior knowledge and stature is reinforced against the racialized and sexualized "others" whom they study and treat.

Depression is certainly a gendered disease. The pathologization and treatment of depression affects women more than men. And, through a complex of biosocial factors, depression and its treatment renders women diseased and unable to *perform* as well as men. Several studies conclude that women's depression affects performance, especially on the job.[8] This conclusion is in keeping with stereotypes of emotional women who can't do the job as well as men can. Some studies have tried to correlate women's depression and "poor performance" to biological changes such as menstruation, pregnancy, and menopause, but none of the studies are conclusive in their attempts to find a purely biological or hormonal basis for the high rates of depression in women. It is important to be vigilant in our critical analysis of studies that suggest in ever more subtle ways that women are biologically or psychologically inferior to men. Moreover, it is crucial that we diagnose the culture that produces not only these studies but also women susceptible to symptoms of the pathology of that culture. For my purposes here, I merely raise the first concern with the studies themselves and concentrate on the second concern with how the culture reproduces depressed women. The tension between challenging studies that pathologize women as depressed and diagnosing that depression as social melancholy may be relieved by considering that the studies and the indicators of depression as they are found or appear in women are symptoms of the same cultural phenomena that devalue women and their experiences, especially as mothers.

Numerous examples from popular culture, legal discourse, and medical discourse "explain" poor performance by women and racially and ethnically marked groups with appeals to biological or mental inferiority. One seemingly innocent example comes from the *Seattle Times* newspaper, which ran a story on October 23, 1998, that began: "Biology keeping women awake, study concludes." The article said that "a study released . . . by the National Sleep Foundation shows that three specific biological events—menstruation, pregnancy and menopause—disrupt the sleep of a majority of women and interfere with how well they function during the day." The implication of this study is that women's inferior performance during the day is the result of a biological fact; this kind of study harkens back to the idea that women are naturally inferior to men, that they just can't cut it in the professional and public world of men. Socially charged issues like menstruation, pregnancy, and menopause are reduced to mere biological facts that make women function poorly. The *Times* article says that the study was based on interviews with women, that is, women's own perceptions of themselves, their sleep patterns, and how well they perform during the day. In a culture where women internalize sexist ideas about their own inadequacy, it should be no surprise that women perceive themselves as unable to function. The irony is that the article also says that married women report that their husbands' snoring keeps them awake, which suggests that biology may not be the cause of their sleeplessness and resulting poor performance after all.

It is also curious that some studies find links between depression and race, ethnicity, and social class.[9] Using data from various National Institutes of Health studies, recent research at the University of Texas Medical Center concludes that the highest rates of major depression are in the lowest social classes and that rates of psychiatric disorders are higher among blacks and Hispanics.[10] And the National Mental Health Association reports that "the depression rate among African American women is *estimated* to be almost 50 percent higher than the rate among Caucasian women."[11] The reason why this is only an "estimate" is that most statistics from various health organizations are based on the number of cases diagnosed and reported as depression by doctors, a diagnosis that is highest among white women and much higher for whites generally than for blacks. It is interesting that the number of cases diagnosed as schizophrenia, on the other hand, is significantly higher among blacks than whites.[12] While none of these studies address how cultural prejudices inform diagnosis, we need to ask why some categories of mental illness are diagnosed and reported more frequently among women than men and why other categories of mental illness are diagnosed and reported more frequently among blacks than whites. Why are so many women diagnosed as depressed? And why are blacks disproportionately diagnosed as schizophrenic? In what ways are these diagnoses made through the lens of cultural prejudice?

Just as the link between depression and women can be diagnosed as a symptom of the patriarchal construction of a passive female body, the link between schizophrenia and blacks can be diagnosed as a symptom of the racist construction of a schizo black body. In *The Souls of Black Folk* W. E. B. Du Bois poignantly describes the double consciousness forced on those marked by race in a racist culture. As we know, fifty years later, Frantz Fanon (1967, 110, 112) describes a similar fragmented experience on a train when a child's exclamation, "Mama, see the Negro! I'm frightened!" forces him to see himself not only in "a third-person consciousness" but also in triplicate, and therefore in need of three places: one for his body, one for his race, and one for his ancestors.

Forty-five years after Fanon, and almost a century after Du Bois, recall how Patricia Williams (1998, 27) describes the double consciousness endemic to the fragmented subject of racism: "For black people, the systematic, often nonsensical denial of racial experiences engenders a sense of split identity attending that which is obviously inexpressible; an assimilative tyranny of neutrality as self-erasure. It creates an environment in which one cannot escape the clanging of symbolism of oneself. This is heightened by contrast to all the silent, shifty discomfort of suffering condescension. There's that clunky social box, larger than your body, taking up all that space. You need two chairs at the table, one for you, one for your blackness."

There is a connection between this sense of fragmentation or alienation and the imposition of dominant values on those oppressed. Domination infects those oppressed with the punishing superego that excludes and abjects them. The result is that desire itself becomes split and fragmented, and those oppressed are forced to identify with the fascinating and terrifying abject excluded by the dominant superego. The introjection of this superego necessarily creates a sense of debilitating double alienation, which at its extreme can be akin to voices heard by schizophrenics. Like those voices, this perverse superego commands self-destruction and undermines the seat of agency.[13]

Fanon's analysis of the role of the radio in the Algerian revolution speaks to how the voices of the colonizers become schizophrenic voices that haunt those oppressed. Recall that as Fanon describes it, when the radio was introduced into Algeria, most of the broadcasts proclaimed French victories and the defeat of the rebels. These voices were the voices of the enemy, violent and condemning. Fanon (1965, 88–89) notes that, as a result, in hallucinatory psychoses the voices heard were those of the colonizers, hostile voices. After the introduction of the Voice of Algeria radio broadcasts that focused on accounts of victorious revolutionaries, the voices become reassuring and friendly. Fanon's essay, "This Is the Voice of Algeria," suggests the complex ways in which the white superego of the colonizers becomes a hostile voice that haunts the colonized even to the point of hallucinatory voices. In addition, he suggests that black resistance to colonization and oppression is interpreted as madness.[14]

It stands to reason, then, that the haunting white superego of racist culture with its hostile voices is diagnosed as schizophrenia in blacks. And, after racist culture constructs the black subject as fragmented and schizo, it also finds higher rates of schizophrenia among blacks. If oppression causes depression and schizophrenia, it not only creates pathological subjects who internalize the conditions of their oppression and become more like cultural stereotypes but also reinforces racial and gendered identities and hierarchies through these very categories of disease by linking particular diseases to specific races or genders and thereby legitimating various types of invasive, regulatory practices to manage epidemics. To echo the language of the social sciences, it could be said that oppression *is a factor* in depression. Therefore, a social analysis of depression is necessary to analyze how oppression affects the psychic space of women and leads to the symptoms diagnosed as depression.

Maternal Depression

In the 2000 presidential election, Americans witnessed the return of the rhetoric of family values and the conservative diagnosis that the health of the nation depends on the moral fiber of its families and communities. For feminists, this appeal to morality in the political sphere sets off some alarms. First, such rhetoric only thinly masks the patriarchal assumption that the morality of our children and therefore of our nation depends on strong paternal authority, and that youth crime, drugs, and gangs are signs that single mothers cannot instill proper values in their kids. Underlying this rhetoric is the presumption that mothers are ineffective in disciplining their children, especially their boys, and what we need is the return of a strong patriarch. In a postelection issue of *Talk* magazine in 2001, when asked "what was the big innovation of the 2000 election," Mark McKinnon, George Bush's media liaison, said: "Values. What people are looking for in a president is a head of the family—a paternal figure to take care of us . . . President Dad." Second, the use of the rhetoric of values and morality in the political sphere turns social and political problems into individual moral and psychological problems. Crime, drugs, and gangs are not considered institutional problems but rather the fault of some "bad" or "sick" individuals. By rendering social and political problems as individual problems, governmental and social institutions pass off any responsibility for addressing issues of poverty, housing, child care, health care. This is the all too familiar strategy of pathologizing and blaming the very people disadvantaged by institutional sexism and racism; for example, inner-city single moms, especially blacks and Hispanics, are held responsible for drugs and violence.

Blaming the mother for everything from maladjustment and disease to drugs and violence is nothing new. Literature, medicine, and popular culture are full of images of bad mothers. Whether they are blamed for loving too much or too little, mothers are held responsible when something goes wrong. In films (and the novels on which they were based) like *Now, Voyager* (1942), *Carrie* (1976), and *The Virgin Suicides* (1999), overprotective and controlling mothers are represented as the cause of mental breakdown, violence, mayhem, and death. In early Hollywood films such as *The Blue Dahlia* (1946) and *Leave Her to Heaven* (1945), and the more recent *The Ice Storm* (1997) and *Caught* (1996), sexualized mothers are represented as the indifferent cause of violence and death. In *White Heat* (1949), *Bloody Mama* (1970), *Sybil* (1976), *Citizen Kane* (1941), *Throw Mama from the Train* (1987), and *Artificial Intelligence: AI* (2001), popular culture gives us mothers whose cruelty and abuse cause violence, death, or mental illness in their children.[15] And the question of the representation of mothers in popular culture is complicated by race in films such as *Imitation of Life* (1936, 1959) where the mother, presented as a mammy figure, is blamed for her mixed-race daughter's blackness and therefore her subjugated social status.

Popular images of bad mothers are fueled by medical discourses, in which mothers are held responsible from conception for the health of their children. The recent emphasis on prenatal care makes the expectant mother anxious about the effects of all of her actions on her unborn child. Civil and criminal law make it possible for mothers to be held responsible for harm done to their "unborn children." A 2001 article in the *New York Times* described how in South Carolina, Regina McKnight was sentenced to twelve years in prison after she was convicted of homicide by child abuse for "killing her unborn fetus" by smoking crack cocaine. Legal precedent even makes it possible for children or others to sue mothers in civil court for their actions while pregnant. Mothers are held responsible not only for any and all harms suffered by the children whom they raise but also for any harms suffered by their "children" not yet born. While raising their children, mothers can be blamed for any and all ailments, both mental and physical, suffered by their children.[16]

For example, in the literature on ADD (Attention Deficit Disorder; also called Attention-Deficit/Hyperactivity Disorder, ADHD), many of the studies test for "maternal pathology," while none of them specifically test for paternal pathology (even when they test for sexual abuse and incest as factors in ADD, these studies identify "parental" or "family" factors or pathology, but never paternal pathology).[17] One study suggests that maternal depression is a factor in children developing ADD (Faraone and Beiderman 1997). More generally, many of these studies suggest that maternal pathology gives rise to pathology in children. Medicine and popular culture work together to trace children's problems back to maternal pathology, specifically maternal depression. Rather than blame mothers for their children's problems, traditional notions of maternity can be seen as the source of a cycle of violence and oppression. Again, to echo the language of the social sciences, it could be said that maternal oppression *is a factor* in maternal depression.

Recent literature is overflowing with narratives that in various ways attempt to articulate maternal depression and its social context. Many of these literary works testify to the effects of daughters identifying with maternal depression, a depression caused by a social context that forces women to "choose" motherhood and then devalues it: "The body of a poor woman still obeyed its own laws; there was no alternative but to 'choose' motherhood . . . or infanticide" (Vilar 1996, 71). For example, novels like

Amy Tan's *Joy Luck Club* and Toni Morrison's *Beloved* depict the consequences of repressed and guilt-ridden maternal loss for mothers and their daughters. In *Ladies Gallery*, Irene Vilar vividly recounts her melancholy identification with her depressed and suicidal mother and grandmother.[18] As I show in the last section of this chapter, Julia Alvarez's *In the Name of Salomé* gives a moving portrait of a woman whose poetic voice is stifled by the conventions of motherhood and of her daughter's lonely search to recover a lost mother. Jamaica Kincaid also describes a search for, and identification with, a lost mother in *The Autobiography of My Mother*. Amy Tan's *Bonesetter's Daughter* tells the story of a daughter in search of her true mother's name and life. And in *Hanna's Daughters*, Marianne Fredriksson tries to give three generations of mothers and daughters back their voices buried within cultural norms and taboos.

There is more than a coincidence between this upsurge in women writing about mothers, particularly depressed mothers, and women's struggles with depression. In *A Feather on the Breath of God*, Sigrid Nunez (1995, 72–73) describes a daughter's troubled negotiations with a depressed mother: "At her lowest she would say, 'I feel like a bug crushed under someone's heel.' I believe that, in spite of all her railing against her lot, she never really expected anything different. You made your own bed, now you have to lie in it. I don't believe my mother made her own bed." Many of these novels can be read as social criticism of how patriarchal restrictions lead to women's depression, which in turn affects their daughters (and sons). The novels tell stories of mothers, whose "beds were made" for them, so to speak, and who were forced to lie in those beds. More than that, these stories depict what has and continues to be so difficult for theory to articulate, the complicated relationship between the social and the psyche, between oppression and desire.

As a practicing psychoanalyst, Julia Kristeva often uses examples from her case studies. After decades of reading case after case of neurotics who identify with their depressed mother's suffering, I began to wonder why Kristeva focuses only on the children and not on their mothers. Although, as I argued in *Reading Kristeva*, Kristeva replaces Freud's question "What does Woman want?" with "What does Mother want?" her analysis of feminine sexuality as depressive doesn't fully account for the relationship between maternal depression and women's depression (cf. Oliver 1993, 48–68; see also Hansen 1999). Why doesn't she formulate an explanation for this maternal depression that lies behind the sorrow of so many of her patients? Specifically, why doesn't she mention the social circumstances that might contribute to, if not cause, maternal depression and its consequences for children? Without some theory of social melancholy, doesn't psychoanalysis risk becoming another blame-the-mother discourse? Why are there so many depressed mothers, whose pain is then internalized by their daughters and sons alike?

Although in her female genius trilogy Kristeva gives us a new conception of maternity as genius, her account of feminine sexuality in *Black Sun* only gives us recourse to an infinite regress of depressed mothers to account for any particular case of depression: we can diagnose the mother's depression as a result of her own identification with her mother, that is, with what Kristeva calls the maternal thing that traps her in an unrepresentable realm of buried affects. This infinite regress of depression either begs the question of the depressive mother or leaves us wondering if depression is a natural or essential part of the female or maternal psyche, neither of which adequately explains maternal depression. It is more productive to read maternal depression as a form of social melancholia. If we reformulate Kristeva's psychoanalytic description as social analysis, we can diagnose maternal depression and women's depression more generally as a social melancholia through which the subject mourns not the loss of the object per se but the loss of a lovable and loved self-image.

Discussing several cases of obsessional neurosis in men, Kristeva (1995, 53) claims that "a veritable 'buried mother' resides at the core of their psyche." Describing hysteria in women, she says that "the mother is also a counterpart to that other aspect of the hysterical psyche: its signless sensuality, its inaccessible and sublime want-to-be. Thus repulsion with the mother coincides with submission to her, which results in a desirable, and abject replica" (75). In the cases of both obsessional and hysterical neuroses, Kristeva diagnoses an identification with a silent depressed mother and an eroticization of her suffering. As she says in *Black Sun: Depression and Melancholy* (1989), these children, especially daughters, carry their mother's silent suffering body in the crypt of their own psyches.

Depressed mothers have given up on words to discharge their suffering because there is no social space available within which to express affects denied by patriarchal stereotypes. In the case of the obsessional neurotic, his problem is that he identifies with his depressed mother's disavowal of words; like her, he acts instead of feeling (Kristeva 1995, 53–54). The hysteric, on the other hand, can't act but can only feel; torn between an identification with paternal words and buried unrepresentable maternal affects, the hysteric is split in two (71). In both cases, the neurotic identifies with a depressive mother, who has given up on words to express her pain. At the core of both of these neuroses, despite their different symptoms, is a mute, buried maternal affect.

Kristeva diagnoses female sexuality as a depressive sexuality. Following

Freud, she maintains that females cannot completely disassociate themselves from their mothers and that they end up identifying with a lost maternal *thing* that remains "locked in the crypt" of their psyches. She calls it a maternal "thing" rather than an object because, unlike an object, this lost maternal is not yet specified, or separated from the subject (1997, 200 n7). In this regard, the maternal thing resonates with what Kristeva calls the abject, the indeterminate in-between that she also associates with the maternal body (239). As she describes psychic development, the infant must abject the maternal body in order to separate from it and become a subject and take it as a proper object. To do so, the infant needs the support of what she calls the *imaginary father*. If this accepting third party is lacking, then the subject ends up melancholy or depressed, unable to mourn an abject thing that it can never completely lose. For Kristeva, the imaginary father is a necessary counterbalance for the abject mother.

In her diagnosis of female sexuality as a melancholic sexuality, Kristeva applies Freud's theory of melancholia to the lost maternal body. In "Mourning and Melancholia," Freud ([1917] 1989, 586–87) describes melancholia as an identification with a lost object; the subject holds onto love for the lost object through identification with it. On Kristeva's theory, insofar as female sexuality is an identification with the maternal body to avoid losing it, it is melancholic. Unlike Freud's melancholic, however, Kristeva's depressive does not turn hostility toward the other back onto itself or torture itself with guilt for that hostility (Kristeva, 1998, 186). In fact, the depressive's sorrow is the result of a primary narcissistic wound that leaves the depressive feeling empty, incomplete, or flawed (186). This primary narcissistic wound is the result of an identification with the maternal body, which has been made abject not only by the infant during weaning but also by the culture at large, which devalues maternity by reducing it to repellent or asocial animality. Insofar as the girl is expected to identify with her mother and with motherhood, the girl cannot leave the abject maternal body behind, but drags this abjection with her like a festering wound at the core of her psyche. In her case studies, Kristeva finds sons and daughters not only identifying with depressed mothers but also eroticizing their sorrow and suffering as the secret, silent pain that binds mother and child.

Social melancholy is neither the Freudian inability to mourn the loss of a loved object nor the Kristevean inability to mourn the loss of the maternal body but the inability to mourn the loss of a loved or lovable self. On this account, maternal melancholy is the result of the unavailability of positive representations of motherhood. Freud describes the mother's desire for the child as a desire for the father's penis: the child is a penis substitute that satisfies the woman's penis envy. Although Freud's theory seems objectionable to most feminists, there is a sense in which it is telling. If within patriarchal culture women are valued only or primarily as mothers, then their relation to the social order is through the child. The child is a substitute for access to culture and positions of power; in this sense, the child is a substitute for phallic power. To the depressed mother, the child becomes a substitute for symbols, for words. The mother, who has been denied full access to the symbolic, gives up on the symbolic and turns to the child as substitute, the only compensation available within patriarchal culture. This is too much responsibility for most children to bear. They cannot be responsible for their mother's psychic life and link to sociality.

Moreover, insofar as the mother is required to sacrifice the child to the social order, to wean the child and even help it become independent, she sacrifices her own identification with the child. For the depressed mother, then, the wounded narcissistic identification works both ways: not only is the child identified with a wounded and depressed mother who is exiled from the realm of words but also the mother is identified with the child as substitute symbolic destined to sacrifice. This narcissistic wound is related to the shame that accompanies depression, a shame aimed at the very core of the self; unlike the guilt that Freud describes that can be correlated with certain bad thoughts or actions, shame is not associated with any particular thoughts or actions but attaches itself to the subject's own self.

Effectively combining psychoanalysis and social analysis, Frances Restuccia, in *Melancholics in Love* (2000), presents a compelling account of abused women as the daughters of depressed mothers. Using Kristeva's theory of female melancholia, Restuccia argues that women caught in abusive relationships form masochistic identifications with an abject depressive mother and unconsciously believe that they deserve abuse. Revising Kristeva's theory of the maternal thing locked in the crypt of the psyche, the dead maternal body, Restuccia suggests that patriarchy leaves these daughters with a mother already dead such that they can neither separate from her nor identify with her. If the maternal body is an abject dead body, then patriarchy is to blame for insisting on matricide for the sake of culture.[19]

Given Kristeva's diagnosis of the male obsessional neurotic, it could be said that not only abused or melancholy women but also abusive men identify with a depressive mother. On Kristeva's analysis, the obsessional neurotic seeks revenge against his mother through other women; he is abusive. He takes revenge against his mother for burying him in her pain

(Kristeva 1995, 63). Thus identification with a depressive mother can lead to masochism in women and sadism in men. On the social level, it seems that identification with a depressive mother perpetuates the oppression and abuse of women; it creates abusive men and abused women. Maternal depression becomes a vicious circle that perpetuates the very causes of that depression, the denigration of women in general and mothers in particular. In an important sense, the causes of maternal depression are at stake in diagnosing women's oppression and vice versa. Again, the social causes of depression are overlooked in medical and psychological discourses on depression. In the next section I show how shame originating from the lack of social acceptance and support contributes to women's depression. And, in the last section of this chapter, I explore the dynamics of social melancholy and how they both differ from and are covered over by traditional accounts of melancholy and depression.

Shame and Depressive Identity

Many psychologists conclude that shame plays a major role in depression; not surprisingly, then, more women experience feelings of shame than men (see Lewis 1986; 1987b, 97, 105). In the psychological literature, shame and depression are linked, and they are much more likely to be experienced by women. Moreover, shame is related to one's sense of oneself as a subject and agent rather than to one's actions. We could say that shame is constitutive of identity in depressed women. An analysis of the differences between guilt and shame not only points up how shame is about identity while guilt is about action but also begins to explain traditional psychoanalytic theory's attention to guilt rather than to shame as another form of its masculinism. Shame (often compounded by guilt) results in a sense of double or debilitating alienation from one's own experience that is directly related to one's social context and position as marginalized or excluded within mainstream culture. In a sense, shame operates on an ontological level while guilt operates on an ontic level. Oppression uses both guilt and shame. But shame is more deeply seated in subjectivity than guilt.

The psychologist Helen Block Lewis (1987b, 105), both a follower and feminist critic of Freud, explicitly links women's depression and shame: "An empirical study of guilt and conscience in the major depressive disorders suggests that 'negative self-esteem' rather than guilt 'forms the cornerstone' in depressed patients of all types. Shame may be understood as the affective-cognitive state that accompanies 'low self-esteem' . . . depressed women undergraduates were more likely to blame their *characters* for bad events than they were to blame specific *behaviors.* (If anything, blame for behaviors was negatively correlated with depression.) If we equate blame of self for its character with shame and blame for behaviors with guilt, we may glimpse a convergence of evidence from behavioral and psychoanalytic sources suggesting the role of shame in depression." It is important to note that Lewis finds blame, even self-blame, negatively correlated with depression. To blame oneself is already to begin to articulate shame as guilt. And this articulation is a form of sublimation that can become a means of directing internalized negative affects outward once blame is placed with social institutions instead of on individuals. Shame operates at an even deeper, less articulate, unsublimated level than blame or guilt. Insofar as shame is farther from sublimation than guilt, it is not only more effective in the colonization of psychic space but also more often linked with depression as the split between words and affects. In "Shame and Gender," Sandra Bartky (1990, 85) maintains "that women typically are more shame-prone than men, that shame is not so much a particular feeling or emotion (though it involves specific feelings and emotions) as a pervasive affective attunement to the social environment, that women's shame is more than merely an affect of subordination but, within the larger universe of patriarchal relations, a profound mode of disclosure both of self and situation." Depressed women feel flawed or defective in their very being. Lewis explains that as long as mainstream views of women as less rational or otherwise lacking continue to be valued or internalized by women themselves, then shame and humiliation are turned inward rather than outward as anger or rage at oppressive stereotypes and are thereby transformed into depression (111). To various extents, as I have shown in the first half of this book, women and other marginalized people cannot help but internalize the values of mainstream culture, since it governs their lives. On the other hand, articulation, interpretation, and revaluation can transform shame to enable sublimation, which restores a sense of agency and self-esteem.

Lewis suggests that women's dependent positions in society contribute to their tendency toward shame. On the one hand, insofar as women were (or are) traditionally financially dependent on men, they were socialized to put the greatest stock in the love relations that secured their well being; on the other hand, they were excluded from positions of power that could give them full autonomy. Shame is opposed to autonomy. Lewis explains: "That women are more prone to shame than men is a long-standing and widespread observation. . . . Two factors join in fostering women's greater shame-proneness." First, loving identifications are central to the development of their personalities, and the loss of love threatens their sense of self and causes shame. "Second, the widespread exclusion of women from positions of power in work fosters a culturally sanctioned adjustment in women's position of economic dependency and devotion to family" (1981, 194). Lewis (1976, 312) concludes, "Women patients suffer a special penalty for their exclusion from and admiration of the aggressive arena. It is particularly the fate of women in our society to be reared into the expectation that they will live in an arena of gentleness to others and then to be shamed and shame themselves for these very qualities." Shame and the resulting depression are social pathologies that serve the colonization of psychic space and undermine women's sense of themselves as agents in the world.

Given that several psychologists postulate that shame is the flip side of interest, it is reasonable to assume that insofar as depression is characterized by loss of interest in the world and others, sustained experiences of shame will lead to depression (cf. Tomkins 1995, 401). This loss of interest has significant implications for subjectivity, if we take seriously the phenomenologists' insistence on the role of interest or what they variously call *intentionality* (à la Husserl) or *care* (à la Heidegger) in consciousness and subjectivity. As interest in the world withdraws, the structure of subjectivity itself is undermined. The directionality of consciousness as consciousness of something always directed at the world and others withdraws into catatonia. The care that Heidegger describes as conscious interest in the world inherent in *Dasein* can beome disinterested or decathected such that engagement with the world is cut off. The subject experiences itself as a damaged, defective, or flawed being who deserves to be ostracized. The agency of forgiveness, the accepting third, within the social is necessary to support the subject's assertion of individuality and singularity so that shame is transformed into the possibility of belonging to the community. Without that forgiveness, subjectivity is constituted by shame as inferior or bad in the sense of defective.

Those excluded or abjected by dominant values are made to feel ashamed, not about something that they have done but about who they are. Shame is directed at the very being of the marginalized subject. Several psychologists postulate that shame is a "keystone affect" in identity formation insofar as it appears very early in infancy before any notion of prohibition.[20] Shame appears before infants have any sense of the distinction between right and wrong, between being and doing. As a result, shame is associated with the infant's being. Shame is constitutive of identity not only because it attaches to one's being or self but also because it is the result of the interruption of pleasure or interest in relation to another or others. Shame is not originally the result of doing something that is prohibited, but rather the result of being unable to maintain social relations.

Shame is a response to a break in effective contact with another that aims toward reconnection and communication.[21] It is the underside of communication and communion with others.

Shame is associated with primary relations with others that are constitutive of one's own identity and sense of self. It is "a negative experience of self," an "implosion" or "destruction of self in acute self-denigration" that comes from "the vicarious experience of the other's negative evaluation" of oneself (Lewis 1987b, 95, 108). Support and acceptance within the social are necessary for a positive sense of self. If mainstream culture provides only abject images of self, then the result is social melancholy. Social melancholy is the result of losing a lovable self. While classical melancholy is the result of losing a loved other that produces feelings of guilt in the self for aggressive or hostile thoughts toward that other, social melancholy is the result of losing a lovable self that produces feelings of shame in the face of aggressive or hostile thoughts from others. Shame affects one's sense of self-identity as lovable. Recurring experiences of shame are constitutive of self-identity insofar as they undermine the individual's sense of himself or herself as lovable. Shame results from a break in communion with others triggered by their negative response to the shamed individual. Negative responses directed at an individual in response to what he or she is rather than or in addition to his or her actions accumulate to form a sense of the self as defective or bad and therefore unlovable.[22]

The relation between shame and subjectivity can be further discerned in a close examination of the difference between shame and guilt. Sandra Bartky (1990, 87) pinpoints the difference between shame and guilt: "Shame, then, involves apprehension of oneself as a lesser creature. Guilt, by contrast, refers not to the subject's nature but to her actions. . . . Shame is called forth by the apprehension of some serious flaw in the self, guilt by the consciousness that one has committed a transgression."[23] Bartky concludes that shame undermines one's trust in one's self and in that regard is deeper than feelings of guilt over a specific act. In a more recent analysis of shame, the literary critic Eve Kosofsky Sedgwick (2002, 4) corroborates the distinction between shame and guilt: "Shame attaches to and sharpens the sense of what one is, while guilt attaches to what one does." Shame is attached to being, while guilt is attached to doing; and mainstream presumptions about identity are attached to the distinction between being and doing.

While one is held morally responsible for what one does and can therefore be praised or blamed, found innocent or guilty, shame is related less to morality than to inferiority. If guilt is associated with evil in a moral sense, then shame is associated with bad in the sense of inferiority. Shame brings with it the sense of being defective or flawed. If "guilt is about moral transgression; shame is about inferiority" (Tomkins 1995, 85, 399–400; cf. Miller 1985, Bartky 1990).

If shame is constitutive of self-consciousness, then guilt is constitutive of conscience. In this sense, shame is prior to guilt and appears before the infant has a sense of right and wrong. Psychologists from Freud to Kohlberg have postulated that conscience is a later stage of moral development than shame. Freud ([1923] 1955, 52) suggests that guilt is an unconscious by-product of the resolution of the oedipal conflict. And both Freud and Kohlberg maintain that girls and women have a lesser developed sense of guilt and therefore a lesser developed moral sense. Lewis (1976, 183, cf. 301) argues that sexism in psychiatry, psychoanalysis, and psychology accounts for why theorists have concentrated on guilt rather than shame; she claims that Freud theorized guilt rather than shame because he "originally developed the superego concept with men in mind." Freud gives priority to guilt as oedipal because of his emphasis on autonomy and the centrality of the male ego in his theories; because he views attachment as feminine and shame as the result of girls' inferior genitals, he associates shame with the pre-oedipal and gives it little attention (cf. Bouson 2000, 9). Because shame is more basic than guilt and the Oedipus complex, however, it is more directly related to subject formation and identity construction. This explains why shame is constitutive of identity and subjectivity in a way that guilt is not. Although on the Freudian model, guilt remains unconscious and is a by-product of the Oedipal complex and central to melancholic ego formation, it remains associated with action rather than being. Even in its role in ego formation and the conflict between superego and ego, it is related to particular actions or desires. Shame, on the other hand, is not the result of any action or desire on the part of the subject (except perhaps the desire for communion with others after it has been broken off, an interaction that makes those excluded feel inferior and ashamed).

Shame becomes a vicious spiral that perpetuates itself through guilt and shame over being ashamed that haunts marginalized self-consciousness as it turns shame received from others inward against itself (cf. Bouson 2000, 10). Being ashamed of one's own shame is associated not only with being shamed by dominant values but also with being the depository for the shame and guilt of dominant culture. Once again, those excluded and oppressed are given the burden of a double alienation, a double shame, that shores up the privileged subject's confidence, autonomy, and agency by projecting unwanted affects, particularly shame, onto those othered. Resonant with my analysis in part I, privileged subjectivity maintains its privilege and dominance precisely through projecting its own shame over its brutality and the blood, sweat, and tears of others through which it has bought its own security onto those very others. Just as colonization operates through projecting unwanted affects onto so-called barbarians to justify the violence of manifest destiny, the colonization of the psychic space of women, people of color, gays and lesbians, and others excluded from dominant values and positions of privilege operates through projecting unwanted affects onto so-called overly emotional, sensitive, or irrational others to justify their inferiority and the violence of oppression aimed at them. Like the alienation of oppression, the shame of oppression is a doubling and defensive operation on the part of privileged subjects.

Lewis (1987b, 107) identifies this doubleness with a negative type of self-consciousness that results from shame, which "involves more self-consciousness and more self-imaging than guilt. The experience of shame is directly about the self, which is the focus of a negative evaluation. In guilt, it is the thing done or undone that is the direct focus of negative evaluation. We say 'I am ashamed of myself' and 'I am guilty of having done (or not done) something.' Because the self is the focus of awareness in shame, 'identity' imagery is usually evoked. At the same time that this identity imagery is registering as one's own experience, there is also vivid imagery of the self in the other's eyes. This creates a 'doubleness of experience' which is characteristic of shame."[24] Lewis's account of the double experience of shame resonates with both Du Bois's notion of double consciousness and Fanon's pain-filled discussion in *Black Skin, White Masks* of the shame that results from racism. Shame, like the Freudian notion of guilt, splits the subject into harsh, judging superego—the eyes-of-the-other—and shameful ego. Unlike the Freudian notion of guilt, however, the double experience of shame is not the result of a desired or imagined action on the part of the subject. Rather, shame is the result of internalizing the contempt of others, which becomes contempt toward the self. Racialized shame is the result of internalizing a cruel, racist superego. So, too, the shame of sexual difference is the result of internalizing the cruel, sexist superego of mainstream patriarchal culture, the culture that led Freud to suggest that women are ashamed of their inferior sex organs and suffer from penis envy.

In an insightful study of shame and trauma in the writing of Toni Morrison, J. Brooks Bouson (2000, 10) also concludes that shame is related to inferiority: "Shame sufferers feel in some profound way inferior to others—they perceive themselves as deeply flawed and defective or as bad individuals or as failures—and this internalized shame script grows out of early shaming interactions with parents or significant others." Those excluded and abjected within mainstream culture are not only shamed but also become the bearers of shame for the entire culture. As Bouson argues, "In a white male American culture that is 'shame phobic'—for it places value on 'achievement, competition, power, and dominance'—African Americans not only have been viewed as objects of contempt, they also have served as containers for white shame. Because white Americans have historically projected their own shame onto blacks, African Americans have been forced to carry a crippling heavy burden of shame; their own shame and the projected shame of white America" (15). I would extend Bouson's claims to women and other marginalized and abjected groups who are not only made ashamed of their very being but also forced to carry the shame of white men. For example, feminists have done important research on the emotional division of labor that assigns women the "lion's" share of affective burden so that men are free of it.[25] Shame is one of the heaviest parts of that affective burden.

Given this analysis of shame and the development of a psychoanalytic social theory of a loving paternal agent, or loving third, it could be said that shame is the affect that attaches to the withholding or denial of this supportive and accepting social force necessary for subject formation. The loving paternal agent or loving third term in the relation between mother and infant could be associated with a loving superego. Kristeva argues that contemporary culture lacks not the stern father of the law but rather a loving imaginary father as a counterbalance to the stern paternal superego. I would go one step further and argue that we need to replace the stern, punishing superego with a loving social agency, which not only makes idealization possible but also authorizes or legitimates each subjectivity in relation to idealization. In other words, idealization is available to all rather than being the privilege of the beneficiaries of oppression. Some theorists might argue that we need to do away with the superego or idealization altogether. But signification, communication, and sublimation—everything that makes us beings who mean—depend on idealization. It is not that we need to do away with the superego and its goals, expectations, and ambitions for us. Rather, we need a loving social agency through which we internalize not only the need for social order but also our legitimate access to it. Subjectivity requires some sense of individuality and agency, which not only result from but are themselves forms of transgression or revolt against the community. To assert oneself as an individual is to assert oneself as singular within the social. Acceptance back into the community requires a forgiving agent within the social that operates in relationships with others. If this forgiving and accepting agency is missing, the result is shame, as positive relations with others are interrupted. Shame is not connected to acts of transgression or prohibited acts so much as to the assertion of individuality and difference themselves. Shame is associated with one's sense of self in its most singular sense, with what makes one a unique individual. In this regard, shame not only isolates the individual from the social but also is the result of isolation from the social.[26] Prior to prohibition, shame is the feeling that one is bad, defective, flawed, and that these traits—or, better, these ways of being—are responsible for the loss of positive community with others.

Those excluded or abjected because of their race, sex, gender, sexuality, or class have to negotiate shame as a constitutive affect of their identities. This negotiation can lead to depression, or it can lead to transformation, humor, solidarity, or political action. Sedgwick sees shame as a particularly transformative affect not only because it is the first and permanent structuring of identity before prohibitions or good-evil binaries but also because it is related to performance. She maintains that shame "generates and legitimates the place of identity—that question of identity—at the origin of the impulse to the performative; but does so without giving that identity-space the standing of an essence. It constitutes it as to-be-constituted." Her analysis suggests that shame questions identity in such a way that calls attention to the relational and social nature of identity construction.

Sedgwick gives the example of the phrase "shame on you," which she points out not only has no subject, no I, but also projects shame onto another, thereby effacing its agency and deferring this second subject, the object of shame. Shame effaces the agency of both subject and object, but does so by displaying the constitutive relation between them. Sedgwick (2002, 21) argues, moreover, that "shame on you" is a performative utterance that confers shame by pronouncing shame; and shame is a self-effacing affect that is itself performative: "'Shame on you' is performatively efficacious because its grammar—admittedly somewhat enigmatic—is a transformational grammar: both at the level of pronoun positioning, as I've sketched, and at the level of the relational grammar of the affect shame itself. . . . shame effaces itself; shame points and projects; shame turns itself skin side outside; shame and pride, shame and dignity, shame and self-display, shame and exhibitionism are different interlinings of the same glove: shame, it might finally be said, transformation shame, is *performance*." Shame is performative in the sense of motivating performances as self-display and exhibitionism inherent in various types of political activism, and exaggerations of race, sex, or gender roles as parody, comedy, or even tragedy. Sedgwick concludes that because shame is constitutive of identity and not just part of someone's personality, and because it is performative, it can transform identity: "The forms taken by shame are not distinct 'toxic' parts of group or individual identity that can be excised. They are instead integral to and residual in the processes by which identity itself is formed. They are available for the work of metamorphosis, reframing, refiguration, transfiguration, affective and symbolic loading and deformation; but unavailable for effecting the work of purgation and deontological closure" (21). Insofar as shame signals the longing to belong, it can engender alternative forms of community. Unlike other affects, for example, disgust, contempt, or anger, even a chronic state of intense shame contains the hope and wish to reconnect with others (cf. Tomkins 1995, 400–402).

While we may not be able to purge shame from the psyches of those oppressed, we can imagine that some of the transformations and metamorphoses engendered by shame (where necessity is the mother of invention) will transform the social environment that gives rise to the shame of oppression. The transformations born out of the shame of oppression can lead to a sense of shared culture and solidarity through the negotiation of shame that creates community and belonging, even if on the margins of the mainstream. These performances of transformation may provide the space for an accepting and forgiving third within the social that allows individuals deemed different, queer, or otherwise inferior by mainstream culture to belong to a community.

Social Melancholy

The shame associated with oppression and manifest in depression affects the very subjectivity and identity of those othered. The shame of oppression turns back against the subject in a way that guilt does not. On Freud's analysis, guilt is a normal and even healthy part of the oedipal conflict; it actually shores up the ego. Shame, on the other hand, undermines the ego. Just as the shame of oppression has a radically different dynamic than the psychoanalytic notion of guilt, the depression or melancholy of oppression has a different dynamic than Freud's notion of melancholy. In the last chapter, I summarized some of these differences; here I explore in greater detail how social melancholy differs from the melancholy discussed by Freud and his followers. European notions of universal alienation as inherent in subjectivity cover over concrete and violent forms of alienation specific to oppression; psychoanalytic notions of melancholy and clinical notions of depression cover over the social factors that contribute, even cause, another form of melancholy or depression unique to oppression. Once again, the dynamics of social melancholy work almost in the reverse of traditional psychoanalytic notions of melancholy. To appreciate the differences, we need to first revisit Freud's theory of melancholy.

In "Mourning and Melancholia," Freud ([1917] 1989) describes melancholia as an identification with a lost love object. Freud distinguishes mourning from melancholia. The former is a healthy working through the loss of a loved one; the latter, a neurotic identification with the lost love in order to deny the loss. He says that while in mourning "it is the world which has become poor and empty; in melancholia it is the ego itself." Melancholia displays "an extraordinary diminution in self-regard, an impoverishment of ego on a grand scale" (Freud [1917] 1989, 584). This diminution of self-regard caused by the subject's identification with the lost love is also hatred toward the lost loved one for leaving. More than this, Freud attributes these self-reproaches to the melancholic's assumption of the blame for the loss of the loved one (587–88). As Freud describes it, the subject holds onto his or her love for the lost object through identifying with it. In this way, although he or she berates the lost object as himself or herself, he or she refuses to give up the love relation with the lost loved one. Freud maintains that "in this way an object-loss was transformed into an ego-loss and the conflict between the ego and the loved person into a cleavage between the critical activity of the ego and the ego as altered by identification. . . . The narcissistic identification with the object then becomes a substitute for the erotic cathexis, the result of which is that in spite of the conflict with the loved person the love-relation need not be given up" (586–87).

The melancholy of oppression, however, is not Freud's internalization of a lost love but the internalization of the loss of a loved or lovable self-image.[27] Confronted with abject images of themselves from mainstream culture, even as they are part of that culture, women and mothers suffer from the loss of a lovable image of themselves. Their melancholy is caused by the loss of the self as an active agent and positive force in the world. The oppressed melancholic's wounded ego is not the result of a loss of an other, but the result of a loss of a self. Just as Freud describes the loss of the other as formative of the melancholic's own ego, the loss of a positive self-image is formative in the melancholy of oppression. The melancholy of oppression fragments the ego and undermines the sense of agency and thereby renders the ego ineffective and passive. So, if there is no image of womanhood or motherhood that can discharge the affects of women and mothers, if the experiences of womanhood or motherhood are absent within the culture, then the missing woman or mother self becomes the melancholic object for women. Rather than guilty thoughts or actions, their beratement attacks their sense of self manifest as shame over their very being. They are made ashamed of being women. Shame and depression are the result of a loss of any socially sanctioned discharge of affects, especially negative affects.

Social melancholy as it is manifest as depression also differs from Freud's (and his followers') theory of melancholy insofar as melancholics hold onto love, refuse to lose it, by incorporating it into their own egos. For melancholics there is still the hope that love is possible and that although the source of that love remains inaccessible to their conscious lives, they have faith in a love that has its source in denial. Within the terms of Kristeva's theory, melancholics still have faith that words can discharge affects despite the fact that they are cut off from their true affects and their words betray them. Depression, on the other hand, is a complete loss of faith in the ability of words to discharge affects. Depressives are reduced to silence because they have given up on words to express the painful affects of their lost loves, the loss of themselves. With depression, the split between words and affects can become so extreme that it leads to catatonia and even suicide. My hypothesis is that the lack of accepting or loving social support is a major factor in women's depression. Without positive images of women that are not always tinged with abjection, in terms of the dynamics of the psyche, it is difficult to avoid depression, or what I am calling social melancholy.[28]

People constantly exposed to negative and denigrated images of themselves cannot help but feel insecure about whether they are lovable or can be loved.[29] To feel loved and lovable is possible only in a culture with positive self-images. In a culture where women and men of color have been pathologized, abjected, ridiculed, and hated, it is difficult for them to avoid some incorporation of self-hatred or a sense of inferiority or lack of legitimacy. The lack of social support can lead to feelings of emptiness, incompleteness, and worthlessness; at the extreme, the lack of social support can lead to the split between words and affects that Kristeva identifies with the depressive position. Within patriarchal cultures where maternal affects are not valued, it is no surprise that we lack the social space in which these affects can be sublimated or discharged. Women's experience generally, and women's depression more specifically, remains subterranean within dominant discourses. Therefore, the depressed woman has given up on finding the words to discharge or manifest her affects. The silence, especially women's silence, which so often accompanies depression, is a socially proscribed silence and its cause. Women's depression should be diagnosed as social melancholy rather than individual pathology, or merely biological chemical imbalance.

Throughout her work, the philosopher Judith Butler suggests that there is a link between oppression, melancholy, and a lack of social space within which to mourn lost homosexual loves, especially those lost to AIDS. In *Gender Trouble* (1991), she applies Freud's theory of melancholia to gender, arguing that melancholia is the result of an unmourned or ungrieved loss that is interiorized. Specifically, the homosexual love object is the melancholy object that cannot be mourned and is therefore interiorized. She continues this line of argument in *The Psychic Life of Power* (1997), where she maintains that heterosexual subjectivity is formed by virtue of the disavowal, even double disavowal, of homosexual love objects; woman takes up a feminine gender identity and man takes up a masculine gender as an incorporation of the homosexual love prohibited within heterosexist culture. Butler (1997, 138–39) suggests that this heterosexual melancholia permeates all sexuality, including homosexuality. She suggests that all subjectivity is formed through melancholic loss and the incorporation of that loss; we are all the consequences of loss and prohibition that constitute our identities as subjects (cf. 24–25).[30] And yet there is a tension in her work between moments in which she maintains that all subjectivity is the result of a wound or loss and others where this wound or loss seems specific to the exclusion and abjection of homosexual love. In these later moments, which I find more promising in her work, Butler describes a grief disavowed by culture, a grief foreclosed by homophobia and heterosexist norms: "Insofar as the grief remains unspeakable, the rage over the loss can redouble by virtue of remaining unavowed. And if that rage is publically proscribed, the melancholic effects of such a proscription can achieve suicidal proportions. The emergence of collective institutions for grieving are thus crucial to survival, to reassembling community, to rearticulating kinship, to reweaving sustaining relations" (148). The social space is not available to mourn particular losses, the "ravages of AIDS," for example, and therefore those deaths are not seen as worthy of grief and, by implication, those lives are not worthy (138). But, as my analysis has shown, diagnosing the melancholy of oppression requires going beyond Freud's theory of the interiorization of a lost love (and therefore beyond Butler's use of it). We need the social space to mourn the loss not only of loved others but also of loved and lovable images of ourselves, those who have been marginalized and excluded as abject or shameful. The melancholy of oppression results from the double loss of a sense of oneself as an agent and the loss of the sense of oneself as loved or lovable.

Social melancholy is the inability to mourn the loss of a lovable self because there is no affirmation or acceptance of this lovable self within mainstream culture. Social melancholy is not followed by guilt over hateful thoughts or actions toward the lost love but rather by shame over one's very being. When the only available images of oneself are always tainted with the abject or perverse, then shame is the result. Sexist, racist, and homophobic ideals and values in the United States produce social melancholy that is then misdiagnosed by psychoanalysis, psychology, and medical science as individual pathology: depression, schizophrenia, or perversion. The double loss of any positive sense of self inherent in social melancholy is the result of dominant values that represent the targets of discrimination as objects or inferiors lacking any complete, normal, or fully rational agency or as abject or denigrated. Insofar as love and agency are both activities of subjectivity, and insofar as both love and agency are necessary for a sense of self, let alone a sense of self-worth, stereotypes attack the very sense of self of those oppressed; they attack one's subjectivity and agency.

Lacking socially acceptable words or symbols to discharge affects that have been excluded within mainstream culture, marginalized people are not only shamed and then silenced but also vulnerable to depression, a consequence of the inability to manifest or discharge affects in language. This inability sets up the vicious circle of oppression whereby oppressive stereotypes can become self-fulfilling prophesies that debilitate their objects through shame, depression, disease, and lowered productivity. If depression is reaching epidemic proportions, especially among young women and mothers, rather than pathologize or biologize women, mothers, or other marginalized people, we need to examine the pathology of our culture and diagnose its *social* diseases.

CHAPTER 8

Sublimation and Idealization

At stake in the depression of oppression and the silencing of the affects of oppression is the ability to sublimate, that is, the ability to translate affects and bodily drives into words or other forms of signification. Oppression undermines the ability of those othered to sublimate; and sublimation is the origin and operator of all that we know as human. Sublimation is what makes us linguistic beings. The inability to sublimate leads to depression and silence. But again, to explain the relationship between sublimation, subjectivity, and oppression, we need a more social theory of sublimation than traditional psychoanalysis provides.

Freud's theory of sublimation is based on an individual's ability to redirect aggressive drives into socially acceptable forms of expression such as art and intellectual pursuits. We need to develop a social theory of sublimation that interrogates what counts as socially acceptable and for whom. If sublimation is the movement of drives into socially sanctioned forms of signification, then it has everything to do with social sanctions and prohibitions. If women and other marginalized or oppressed peoples are denied the social space in which to articulate their affects, especially the negative affects of oppression, then it could be the case that those othered are also denied the social support for sublimation. Yet for Freud and his followers, sublimation is the hallmark of subjectivity. It is necessary for the continuation of humanity. Human beings have the ability to sublimate aggressive animal drives into signification—rap music and symphonies, subway art and museum art, street poetry and academic literature and philosophy. But the ability to sublimate has everything to do with social context, support, and subject position.

While traditional psychoanalytic theory has been instructive in formulating a theory of subjectivity, it has neglected subject position and social context and thereby sacrificed not only its social, political, and historical relevance but also its truth. Subjects, subjectivity, and agency always exist only in a political and social context that affects them at the foundation of their constitution. One's social position and history profoundly influence one's very sense of oneself as an active agent in the world. Yet the contradictions and inconsistencies in historical and social circumstances guarantee that we are never completely determined by our subject position. It is possible to develop a sense of agency despite, or in resistance to, an oppressive social situation. Our experience of ourselves as subjects is maintained in what I have called the tension between our subject positions and our subjectivity.[1]

Although Julia Kristeva begins *Revolution in Poetic Language* by criticizing phenomenology and linguistics for studying a dead or sleeping body instead of a living, moving body in its social context, she too ignores differences in social positions and their relation to subjectivity and agency. And while recently she has returned to the theme of revolution and revolt—suggesting an analogy between psychoanalysis and politics—her provocative cultural analysis in her latest work still does not theorize the effects of different social positions on the psyches of those othered by oppression. Inspired by her suggestive analyses of sublimation and revolt, reformulate a social psychoanalytic theory that in its discussions of subjectivity accounts for subject position.

Sublimation and Psychic Space

Through Kristeva's notion of the imaginary father, or loving third, it is possible to interpret the lack of this loving paternal agent as the lack of social support that can lead to women's depression.[2] Reading the accepting third as a social support can help delineate how women and other oppressed people identify with the pathologies of mainstream culture. Although Kristeva's explanations of the imaginary father do not explicitly identify it with social support or the accepting third as existing within the social, this notion can be usefully interpreted as a primary form of social support necessary for psychic development, creativity, and love. My aim is to develop a psychoanalytic social theory that brings the social and attention to subject position back into discussions of the psyche and subjectivity. By doing so, we can begin to diagnose the affects of social oppression and domination on psychic development. We can formulate a notion of psychic life dependent on social support. In other words, we can formulate a psychoanalytic social theory that explains the intimate and necessary relationship between subjectivity (the structure of agency) and subject position (the historical and social context that supports or undermines agency) based on accepting support, responsivity, and forgiveness.[3]

Kristeva's provocative notion of the imaginary father can help supply the missing link between social and psychic space. The imaginary father can be read as a social support for identity that is operative not only in secondary narcissism but also in primary narcissism. The lack of this support can lead depressives to feel emptiness, incompleteness, and worthlessness; at the extreme, the lack of social support can lead to the debilitating alienation and colonization of psychic space that results in depression. Kristeva (1989, 378, 373–74) identifies the lack of the "loving father" with a deficiency or abolition of psychic space that leads to depression and suffering: "beyond the often fierce but artificial and incredible tyranny of the Law and the Superego, the crisis in the paternal function that led to the deficiency of psychic space is in fact an erosion of the loving father"; the "abolition of psychic space" leaves us homeless, "extraterrestrials suffering for want of love." Ultimately, this lack accounts for "new maladies of the soul" (Kristeva 1995). Without the imaginary father, there is no bridge between drives/affects and language/representation; and, because there is no bridge between drives and words, there can be no movement between the two. To avoid associating this support with paternity only, I call the imaginary father the accepting third, by which I mean the social meaning that adds a third dimension to the relationship between mother and child.

Psychic space depends on the movement between drives and language or signification; that is, psychic space *is* the movement between drives and signification.[4] If the psyche is reduced to one side or the other, either drive or word only, then psychic space collapses. It is the movement, even tension, between the two that sustains psychic space. Movement is possible only if space is traversable; space is traversable only if it is open. Kristeva describes the robust psyche as an *open system*, which biologists describe as interdependent through a flow of materials, energy, and information across system boundaries separating the system from its environment.[5] The colonization of psychic space operates by closing this system of exchange through an overpowering, cruel superego that forces psychic repression through social oppression. As Fanon so eloquently describes it, affects become atrophied and perverted such that the only exchange between the othered subject and the oppressive environment is toxic. Instead of opening up the psyche to what has been repressed, namely, positive self-images and negative affects toward the oppressor that have been turned inward, the colonization of psychic space closes down or debilitates the psychic space of those othered. As I have shown in chapter 3, this process works through a toxic exchange of affects that leaves both colonizer and colonized cut off from their affects and bodily drives. The colonized become infected with the drives and desires of their colonizers. As Fanon's analysis suggests, both colonizer and colonized suffer from neuroses: the colonized become obsessive and the colonizers become phobic.

So, too, do women in patriarchal cultures become infected with patriarchal drives and desires that turn them into objects and undermine their agency. Moreover, within patriarchal culture, women are denied the accepting third, which should be provided by social institutions and values that support the transfer and sublimation of women's drives and affects into language. Instead, patriarchal social institutions and values only allow for the articulation of sexist drives and desires, which to greater or lesser extents become internalized by women. By foreclosing the possibility of articulating the negative affects of oppression, let alone the original drives and affects of those othered—whatever they could possibly be within the context of dominant values that always already colonize psychic space—the colonization of psychic space attempts to kill psychic life and close psychic space at the same time that it presupposes it; it presupposes the internalization of values that keep those othered disciplining themselves, and this internalization in turn presupposes psychic life and open psychic space.[6]

The colonization of psychic space inherent in oppression operates in large part by denying access to the operations of meaning making, of confining those othered to a world of meaning not of their making and, moreover, confining them there as incapable of making meaning. Without available meanings to support their sense of self, or if the readily available meanings undermine their sense of self or relegate this particular self to abjection or exclusion, then any incorporation of that social meaning will cripple rather than nourish the psyche. Identification with, or incorporation of, restrictive meanings debilitate psychic space. And, without an open psychic space, the movement of drives and affects into language becomes impossible, and depression or repression is the result. The open structure of psychic space through which sublimation is possible depends on the connection between words and affects. It depends on a primary identification with the meaning of language, that is, the operation of making meaning one's own through assimilation that allows nourishment both for the body and for the soul or psyche. As I show in the next section, the identification with meaning is possible through an identification with the imaginary accepting third, which transfers social meaning into the subject, thereby authorizing that subject to act as an autonomous agent.

Without the support of that accepting third (or social meaning itself), the colonization of psychic space leads to depression because it prevents the sublimation of drives and affects into symbols and signification. In traditional psychoanalytic theory, the connection between representation and affect is called sublimation. According to Freud, the ability to sublimate drives, and their manifestation in affects, into representation and artistic practices, is the source of human civilization and creativity. Without the ability to sublimate bodily drives and affects into representation and artistic practices, we lose the ability to create meaning for our own lives. Without the ability to sublimate, we become depressed and life seems meaningless. Psychic space depends on sublimation.

In sum, psychic life and open robust psychic space depend on the discharge of drives and affects into signification, which requires social support. The colonization of psychic space operates through withholding the social support necessary for this discharge. The lack of social space not only prevents the articulation of the painful and negative affects of oppression but also undermines the possibility of sublimation for articulating affects and bodily drives. The lack of social support for the negative affects of oppression, the silencing of those affects within mainstream culture, creates a type of double, or even triple, bind for those othered by that culture. On the one hand, dominant values within mainstream culture do not provide positive self-images for those othered and excluded, oppressed or repressed, which leads to the colonization of psychic space by abject self-images. This abjection is compounded by the lack of social space, or even social taboos, for talking about the truly painful affects and shame caused by racism, sexism, and homophobia. The result is that those othered are shamed and forced to carry the burden of shame for privileged subjects, who project their own shame for benefiting from the oppression of others onto those very others. The privilege of those empowered within mainstream culture is maintained through a taboo on speaking of the negative affects of oppression. For example, in the United States it is impolite if not taboo to speak of one's own experiences of racist or sexist discrimination. The new use of the rhetoric of equality and color blindness denies the very existence of racism or sexism. On the other hand, the lack of social support and the colonization of psychic space undermine the othered subject's ability to sublimate and thereby make it difficult to translate bodily drives and affects into signification. Those othered within mainstream culture are in the double bind of being made ashamed of their negative affects at the same time that they are denied the positive social support that enables sublimation of those negative affects. This double alienation from one's own affects is debilitating unless alternative communities and forms of social support can grow out of the silence that we share.

The only way to explain the colonization of psychic space is with a new theory of *social* melancholy and *social* sublimation, something that traditional psychoanalysis does not provide. Only a social theory of psychoanalysis can address the subject position of those egos that psychoanalysis is trying to fortify and explain why so many of those egos required fortification, why they are not getting it from mainstream culture, and why they are in fact suffering as a result of their own abjection and exclusion from that culture. Any theory of subjectivity, whether it is philosophical or psychological, must include consideration of subject position, which is one's social position in relation to the dominant values of one's culture. Without considering subject position, theories of subjectivity are not only irrelevant to the lives of those othered but also and moreover complicit with oppressive values that would silence those othered to shore up the privilege of those empowered by dominant values. Still, given the analysis of depression and social melancholy in the last chapter, and given that rates of depression in women are reported as being twice or even three times as high as those in men, the question of women's ability to sublimate—and its relation to social context—is as relevant as ever.

Can Women Sublimate?

Are women less able to sublimate than men? Freud thought so. In *Civilization and Its Discontents*, he says that "women soon come into opposition to civilization and display their retarding and restraining influence. . . . The work of civilization has become increasingly the business of men, it confronts them with ever more difficult tasks and compels them to carry out instinctual sublimations of which women are little capable" (1961, 50). According to Freud, women are not capable of instinctual sublimations because their anatomy does not permit them to *act* on those very instincts that must be sublimated in order to become civilized—presumably incest with their mothers and, surprisingly . . . urinating on fire. Freud identifies control over fire as one of the primary achievements of primitive man that allowed him to become civilized. In a footnote in *Civilization and Its Discontents*, he hazards a conjecture on the origins of civilization as the origins of control over fire:

> The legends that we possess leave no doubt about the originally phallic view taken of tongues of flame as they shoot upwards. Putting out fire by micturating—. . . was therefore a kind of sexual act with a male, an enjoyment of sexual potency in a homosexual competition. The first person to renounce this desire and spare the fire was able to carry it off with him and subdue it to his own use. By damping down the fire of his own sexual excitation, he had tamed the natural force of fire. This great cultural conquest was thus the reward for his renunciation of instinct. Further, it is as though woman had been appointed guardian of the fire which was held captive on the domestic hearth, because her anatomy made it impossible for her to yield to the temptation of this desire. (37)

As I argue elsewhere, in this theory, civilization begins when man curbs his desire to display his virility by urinating on phallic flames. Women cannot sublimate the desire to pee on the fire because they cannot first act on the desire. We might wonder why Freud doesn't conclude that women necessarily sublimate this desire, since they can't act on it; that their anatomy demands sublimation whereas men's does not: that in women, nature has ensured sublimation of aggressive instincts and therefore the advancement of the species. Instead, Freud identifies civilization, law, and morality with man's virility and its sublimation, where this sublimation is also described as man's virile act of control over himself.[7]

In the fire scenario, man must control his erotic energy and redirect it through sublimating for the sake of civilization. On Freud's theory, sublimation is the sublimation of erotic energy. But, if erotic energy is blocked by oppression, then so is the possibility of sublimation necessary to psychic life. Cynthia Willett diagnoses the effect of oppression on psychic space and the ability to sublimate in terms of this erotic energy. In *The Soul of Justice: Social Bonds and Racial Hubris*, she argues that oppression undermines erotic relations necessary for social and psychic life. For example, she suggests that social eros is perverted in patriarchal cultures that devalue motherhood and reduce the mother-child bond to animality devoid of eros; and practices of slavery in the United States undermined social eros by preventing erotic bonds between slave men and women and their children. Willett (2001, 185) concludes that "the draining of erotic energy under conditions of oppression challenges our expressive capacities and blocks the energy for libidinal relationships and social change." Willett's analysis resonates with my exploration of the transmission of affect in chapter 3. Recall that Fanon's writings suggest that negative affects are projected onto the colonized or oppressed and that positive affects such as love and eros become the privilege of the dominant subjects. Oppression blocks the flow of erotic energy not only in relationships between people but also in the relationship between drives and words, between affects and their representations, and thereby undermines the very ability to sublimate that defines our subjectivity and humanity.

In *Totem and Taboo*, Freud gives another explanation for the origins of sublimation and thereby humanity and subjectivity. Freud's by now familiar story is that of what he calls a band of brothers who kill and eat what he calls their father, and afterward totemize the father out of guilt and develop prohibitions against murder and incest to prevent any one of them meeting the same fate. On this account, there was one superior male (the father) who horded the females and shunned the other males (the sons or brothers). Individually, none of the other males could take on and overpower the superior male; but one day they banded together to kill the superior male and assimilate his power. They do together what none of them could do individually. This requires some sort of communication and societal bond. At this point, however, they are not much different from a pack of wolves who act together to attack their prey. What distinguishes them from wolves, however, is that they *idealize* their "prey," the superior father or ancestor, to the point that "the dead father became stronger than the living one had been"; and they not only assimilate his power but also restrict that power through internalized prohibitions. These prohibitions are the result not only of their guilt over their deed but also over their sense of lack in comparison to this now all-powerful father figure and their fear that they themselves could meet the fate of the father if they do not curb their newly assimilated power (Freud [1913] 1989, 501). Freud's analysis resonates with Nietzsche's description in *On the Genealogy of Morals* of the origin of guilt as debt to ancestors who become idealized to the point of becoming gods in relation to whom we are all lacking. In Freud's totem scenario, as in the fire story, society begins through man's virility and his ability to control that virility, his assimilation of power and his ability to control that power. In a sense, man turns his power against himself to control it and become social.

This turning of power against itself is the origin of sublimation; what Freud describes in *Totem and Taboo* is the origins of humanity as the initiation of idealization and sublimation. These are the primary features that distinguish man from animals. Until the moment of the totemic meal, this horde is a group of animals. Only the prohibition after the fact, which is a result of the idealization of the strongest animal now become a totem or idol, and the subsequent sublimation of both aggressive and sexual drives into more socially acceptable forms, transform this group of animals into human beings. Before this moment, they are undomesticated animals, and the so-called father is no more than the strongest of them. Only after this moment of idealization does their killing become murder and their eating "the father" become cannibalism; only then do certain forms of sex become incest and bestiality.[8] This moment is the institution of prohibition that brings with it society and human temporality. This scene is the scene of the institution of memory and repetition required to idealize, represent, and ultimately become speaking animals who use symbols, who split reality and the ideal. At this moment, they themselves become split beings, animals who mean. No longer do they inhabit the timeless world of animality; now they have a memory of their deed that compels them to repeat it symbolically to remind themselves of their debt to their ancestor and their obligations to each other (cf. Freud [1913] 1989, 500–501).

Kristeva reads Freud's *Totem and Taboo* not only in terms of mimesis, assimilation of authority, and representation but also in terms of memory and time. She suggests that the institution of memory in the totemic rituals represses a timelessness, the timelessness that I have been associating with the animal. Her invocation of archaic timelessness gives us another motive for the repetition of rituals that assimiliate the authority and power of the primal father. Rather than just repeating the crime as a reminder of our own lack and debt, on the one hand, and the mobility of power and our part of it, on the other, we are repeating the timelessness of animal experience that frees us from prohibition, guilt, and responsibility. Rather than merely repeat guilt and prohibition, the ritualization and idealization open the space for a repetition of timelessness within the confines of human temporality. The story of totem is not just the story of taboo. Desire does not have to be conceived of as the flip side of prohibition but as a longing for archaic timelessness of our animal past. We long for this timelessness, for pure bodily experience, for the absolute unity of being and meaning, what Freud might call the death drive. Kristeva (2002c, 429) describes this timelessness as a lost time, an archaic timelessness, and following Proust, a pure embodied time, which prepares us for benevolence and forgiveness.

Sublimation is thus a process not only of idealization à la Freud's totem but also of assimilating the timelessness of the drives or unconscious (of the animal) into time (the temporality of the human). Art, writing, and intellectual activities take authors outside themselves into this timelessness within time. Sublimation puts writers in touch with the otherness that is outside time, or the eternal or divine within signification. This sublimation must be within time, which requires reflective distance. It is too late for us to go back to being animals. Now, we touch animality only by virtue of sublimating timelessness and unconscious drives into time, by bringing them into temporality. If we are not able to sublimate this pure embodied timelessness into time, the body turns this inability into somatic symptoms. On the one hand, we cannot "go back" to pure embodied experience; on the other, forms of extreme repression of that experience of that timelessness lead to somatic symptoms. These archaic timeless drives must have expression either through sublimation as forms of signification or as somatic symptoms and bodily pain. We can imagine that the infant's experience is like the animal's in its timelessness or time before time. Indeed, we can imagine that the infant inhabits a space before space, a unified space without separation, distance, or the split inherent in becoming a being who means. But once the infant begins to acquire forms of signification, which is immediately upon birth into our social world, it also begins to enter the realm of discrete time and space. Our longing for timelessness, then, can also be seen as a longing for our own prenatal state, the state of animality.

Throughout his writings, Freud suggests that women are too close to the state of animality to gain the distance from it necessary to lose it and then regain it through sublimation. As we know, Freud maintains that women are less able to sublimate, that they have an inferior sense of justice, and that because of their natural inclination to the domestic sphere and family life they are a threat to civilization. As we also know, this view was dominant up until at least the mid-twentieth century. Unfortunately, this view continues today, albeit in more subtle and invisible forms.

In *Powers of Horror* and *Black Sun*, even Kristeva maintains that women are less able to sublimate than men because they cannot distance themselves from the maternal body in order to regain it through words. Unlike Freud, Kristeva does not maintain that women have an inferior or underdeveloped sense of judgment. Rather, she diagnoses female sexuality as melancholy because women cannot get the proper distance from the maternal body and its semiotic connections. This is not the distance of philosophical speculation or the distance required for self-reflection, but rather a metaphorical distance that makes primary identification possible and acts as the very condition of possibility for any sense of self (Kristeva 1997, 163). This means that if women cannot gain this distance, their very identity and sense of self will be undermined—they may end up identifying with the abject maternal body from which they cannot separate and therefore cannot sublimate abjection in order to love their mothers or themselves, or any others. The distance of metaphor is the distance between bodies and words, particularly the maternal body and words, which is traversed as bodily drive force is transferred into words. The substitution of words for bodily needs associated with the maternal body is a metaphorical transference of the maternal semiotic into the symbolic that is possible only because of the space between them. This distance is the operation of idealization; it is psychic space itself, which allows us access to our bodies and to others (cf. Kristeva 1995, 6). Without that distance, women's psychic space and the ability to sublimate bodily drives and affects into signification is undermined. In her earlier work, Kristeva focuses on male authors who sublimate the maternal semiotic and abject into signification, even into great literature. But she also suggests in this work that women cannot transgress the social prohibition against the maternal body by sublimating it or bringing back this repressed maternal semiotic within language because they are too close to it. Rather, they must follow the accepted social codes perfectly to gain respect, even if this respect comes at the price of their own abjection and implicit exclusion from that code. Women are put in the paradoxical position of having to endorse a social code that devalues them and represses the maternal body as something natural rather than cultural.

In her later work, Kristeva (2002c, 178, 207–8, 229, 345–46) suggests that modern culture is suffering from the inability to sublimate or idealize. Modern culture confuses reality with the ideal order and cannot gain or maintain the distance necessary to sublimate and idealize (cf. 287). The new maladies of the soul are sicknesses of the imagination. We have lost the ability to imagine, including, and perhaps most important, to imagine the meaning of our own lives. We have become trapped within ourselves, Narcissus without the light necessary to see even his own reflection let alone its relations to others. The balance between narcissism and idealization has been thrown off by the culture of the spectacle, leaving us cut off from our affects and unable to love ourselves or others (cf. 172–74, 211). Given Kristeva's earlier hypothesis about women's difficulty sublimating because of an identification with the maternal body that is reduced to animality within patriarchal culture, this lack of imagination is compounded for women, who are trapped within the crypt of their psyches with an abject and lifeless maternal body.

What Kristeva's theory lacks, and what I hope to provide in this chapter, is a social theory of sublimation that explains why and how if it is more difficult for women to sublimate than men, this is because of the restrictions and retrograde values of patriarchal culture that keep women subordinated to men. And, in the next chapter, I develop a social psychoanalytic theory of idealization that attempts to navigate between idealization conceived of as a cruel, punishing superego or totalitarian law and the abandonment of idealization or laws altogether, which of course is impossible. We need a theory of sublimation, idealization, and linguistic code or laws conceived of as social support for individual singularity and differences rather than as assimilation of difference, a theory that does not assume that idealization requires an impossible ideal against which one is always lacking and therefore punished, a theory that does not propose that idealization requires the restriction or repression of desire and drives. We need to explore how sublimation, idealization, and systems of meaning can be enabling and restorative—how they support subjectivity for beings who mean.

Before returning to the technical dynamics of sublimation in relation to subjectivity and the social, it is important to insist that just as the notion that alienation is constitutive of subjectivity covers over specific forms of racist and sexist alienation, the notion that prohibition is constitutive of subjectivity covers over specific forms of racist and sexist prohibitions that in fact work against the constitution of subjectivity for those othered by dominant values. And despite the prohibitions against murder and incest that supposedly found civil society, women and girls are victims of rape, murder, and incest every day; moreover, only relatively recently have rape and incest been taken seriously as crimes, and many of these crimes still remain invisible and unreported. And only within the last decade has the United Nations started to consider rape as a war crime. Even more invisible are the ways in which women and other marginalized peoples are excluded from the production of social values and meaning. The daily oppression, harassment, and humiliation of women and others have become so normalized within our culture that it has become almost obscene or inappropriate to point them out.

Recall the examples of sexism from Marleen Gorris's film, where simple things like a boss touching his secretary's hand to make her stop stirring her coffee (even while stealing her ideas without giving her credit) or the isolated world of the housewife whose husband doesn't appreciate what she goes through every day to care for the children or the jeers that the waitress faces in the diner every shift make these women feel ashamed, humiliated, and devalued. Even the well-educated career woman with her well-educated career husband faces subtle forms of domination when she is excluded from conversations dominated by men or not taken seriously in her profession because she is "speaking as a woman and not as a psychiatrist." Even if we were to accept that subjectivity is constituted through prohibition, we must insist that the prohibitions—both explicit and implicit—that are leveled against those othered within mainstream culture undermine, rather than circumscribe, the boundaries of subjectivity. Exclusion and prohibitions levied against particular groups because of sex, race, or sexual preference do not work to shore up autonomy, subjectivity, agency, and a sense of belonging to a community or society. To the contrary, just as the debilitating double alienation of racism undermines the subject's sense of autonomy and agency, the prohibitions of oppression undermine the subject's sense of autonomy, agency, and belonging.

To better understand how these prohibitions undermine sublimation, I propose to investigate in greater detail how sublimation is related to subject position and social acceptance. Throughout the previous chapter and this one, I have diagnosed social melancholy or depression as the result of a disconnect or gap between drives and affects, and words. Affects are unable to make their way into signification because they are not supported by the social or readily available social meanings. Sublimation is the process of drives and their affective representations being transferred or redirected into signification. If social space shuns the negative affects of oppression, and moreover silences them, in addition to denying any positive self-images for those othered, then the ability to sublimate is undermined. And sublimation is necessary for psychic life. So, without supportive space within the social, oppression leads to the colonization of psychic space. To understand the importance of sublimation in the constitution of subjectivity, we need to better understand the dynamics of both sublimation and how infants enter language through a type of primary sublimation of drives and affects into signification.

In what could be called both primary and secondary narcissism, Kristeva associates the ability to sublimate with the loving imaginary third, what I have interpreted as social support, or the accepting third, that is meaning. Kristeva (1995, 121, 122) calls the loving third the "the keystone for the capacity to sublimation" and the guarantee for the "ability to idealize." "As the zero degree of symbol formation," this imaginary third leads to "the position of subjectivity, that is being for and by the Other" (122). In the infant (and subsequently, too), the imaginary third instigates and supports the transfer from the maternal body into the social, from needs to demands or language. The joys of the primary relation to the mother's body are transferred into language acquisition by virtue of this identification with the loving imaginary third, which could be associated with the semiotic within the symbolic and signification. The primary identification with the accepting third is not an identification with the symbolic element of the other's speech but rather with the semiotic element of language. The infant first identifies with the tones and rhythms of language, and its first discharge of drives and their affective representations are through sounds and babbling that imitate the sounds of words. This is the beginning of the operation of idealization that makes meaning and community possible.

In its pre-objectal/presubjective state, the infant originally identifies with the semiotic and nonreferential meaning of discourse, which is not a pure signifier but full of drive force and affects. It is precisely because this is not an identification with an object but rather with what Kristeva calls a metaphorical transference to the place of meaning itself that the drives underlying signification play a primary role in the infant's language acquisition and the ability to both idealize and sublimate social meanings. And it is only through this displacement of drive force that the transition from need to demand is filled with *jouissance.* Only through the displacement of semiotic drive force can the maternal body so crucial to the infant's survival make its way into language and not only be named but, more important, be loved insofar as affects are discharged through signification.[9] The infant can need the maternal body without entering the realm or meaning; but only through its entrance into the realm of meaning can it love its mother or have any self-conscious relation with her.

What Kristeva describes as the primary metaphorical transference is a transference to the place of the Other (or meaning), of others ultimately to the place of signs themselves. Through this primary identification with the imaginary or idealized third, we put ourselves in the place of meaning. We assimilate language and thereby find ourselves through it. We become meaningful by belonging to the world of meaning. If this third is a positive and supportive third, then we find positive self-meaning through that transference. But if there is no positive meaning for us within the social, no "loving third," then we are thrown into a narcissistic crisis having to identify with our own meaninglessness or abjection. This is why Kristeva proposes that the imaginary father is a counterbalance to the abject mother.

The imaginary father, or accepting third, is a conglomerate of maternal and paternal, needs and demands, drives and law. An identification with this mingling of maternal and paternal positions (needs and demands) loads language with preverbal and nonrepresentable drives and affects. It is not a matter of articulating affects, which is impossible, since, strictly speaking, they are nonrepresentable; rather, it is a matter of supporting them, giving them form, for-giving them, allowing them access to the symbolic. If, as Kristeva suggests, the symbolic is associated with the thetic phase of signification and its consequent position or judgment, then the imaginary father is the form provided for the semiotic by the symbolic prior to position or judgment. As such, the imaginary third is an accepting social agency prior to the judging or prohibiting social agency; the imaginary father is prior to, and a counterbalance to, the symbolic father of the law or superego. As I show in the last chapter, only this imaginary third prior to judgment makes forgiveness possible.

In psychoanalytic parlance, the absence of a positive sense of self and agency is the result of the absence of a loving ego ideal.[10] If the ego ideal, or superego, is only punishing, then we are left with paranoia or masochism (paranoia that we are constantly under the harsh surveillance of the law or masochism that we are constantly deserving punishment from the law). The narcissistic structure, which supports all subjective identity, also requires an accepting third term. This imaginary third is the flip side of the law, the love that supports a positive sense of self.[11] Without this accepting aspect of the social, the ego is left identified with an abject body excluded from the world of meaning or given meaning only as disgusting, animal, etc. Without accepting support from the social, we are homeless, without a sense of belonging.

The identification with the accepting third is a matter of allowing the primary relation to maternal omnipotence (ideal ego) compensation through the paternal law (ego ideal), the meaning of discourse itself. The accepting third facilitates the transition from the maternal body both as safe haven and as abject threat to the symbolic order governed by laws internalized in the superego.[12] By giving form to semiotic drive force, the accepting third or supportive social space allows the entry into the symbolic to be playful and sublimational instead of just threatening (cf. Kristeva 1989, 46). Between the maternal body and the father of the law is the accepting third that operates in between maternal and paternal functions. The authority of the mother's body is transferred to the superego, or paternal law, through the support of love, which is a union of maternal and paternal, of needs and demands, of drives and words. Love is one compensation for leaving the maternal body, and it is possible only through sublimation and idealization, which require a split between being and meaning or between reality and the ideal.

It is through the imaginary that we both acquire and maintain the ability to sublimate, to idealize, and ultimately to love. This is why the social agency that supports the infant's entrance into language is imaginary and not symbolic. The imaginary agency is necessary in order for the symbolic agency to attract the would-be speaking being. In other words, there must be some idealization of meaning, beginning with semiotic nonreferential meaning through metaphorical substitution, that precedes and sets up referential semantic meaning. This idealization may be nothing more than the infant's imitation of the sounds of language, that is, an identification with the semiotic element of language. But this imaginary support must also continue throughout the psychic life of all speaking beings. And this imaginary support is made available by social meaning and values that can be idealized. If those meanings and values contain positive images of the self and a subject with agency and autonomy, then the individual assimilates those images through an imaginary identification. But if those meanings and values contain only negative images of the self as shameful or abject and lacking agency and autonomy, then the individual idealizes only what it lacks and cannot be, the privileged subject with agency and autonomy, and identifies with its own shame and abjection.

The imaginary third is none other than the meaning of social signification. As we learn language—as we become beings who mean—we necessarily idealize forms of meaning in order to belong to a community of meaning: the concepts and symbols that make up signification are ideal forms of the things that they represent. When corrupted by colonization, oppression, or domination, this process of idealization can become the internalization of a cruel and punishing superego, even the superego of another culture in the case of colonization and occupation. But this process can also provide social support for the development of subjectivity with a sense of agency and belonging. This process of idealization does not punish but rather forgives (or fore-gives meaning). This is not the internalization of a harsh, judgmental superego but rather a metaphorical transfer to the place of meaning, an archaic identification with meaning that begins in bodily rhythms in tune with drive energy. But as I show in the chapters that follow, from the somatic source of meaning comes the possibility of form and for-givenness that does not punish through guilt and shame but rather forgives and thereby supports the singularity of each being who means.

Sublimation and idealization are necessary for robust psychic life because without them the subject becomes trapped within its own psyche and ultimately gives up on meaning, which leads to silence and depression. Without the possibility of sublimation and idealization, the borders between reality and fiction or imagination become blurred to the point where the subject lacks the distance necessary for an open psychic space through which drives and affects can make their way into signification.[13] Without the transfer of drives and affects into meaningful forms of signification, the individual stays at the level of the body, of reality, where drives and affects can be expressed only as somatic symptoms and pain. The distance or gap between imagination and reality is crucial for sublimation. Sublimation requires idealization, which gives birth to imagination. Through imagination and sublimation, we transfer inarticulate drives and affects into signification and thereby learn to live with and to love ourselves and others. Imagination and sublimation, which depend on supportive social meanings, sustain psychic space, while the lack of supportive social meanings undermines the ability to sublimate and impairs the imagination. In this sense, the colonization of psychic space is also an attack on the imagination and the ability to imagine oneself and one's social context otherwise. It is only by imagining the world otherwise that we are inspired to resist oppression and work for the decolonization of both our own and others' social and psychic space.

In sum, the connection between sublimation and the imaginary third supports my social theory of sublimation rather than traditional psychoanalytic theory's anatomical or psychological explanation for why and how it could be that women aren't allowed to sublimate as well as men can. Meaningful speech and a sense of meaning in one's own life depend on the connection between affects and words, drives and symbols. When affects and drives become disconnected from words and symbols, then there is a loss of the sense of meaningfulness. Only when bodily drives make their way into language supported by the accepting third will language have any real meaning for life. Social support allows one to make meaning one's own, not by possessing it but rather by belonging to language, to the world of social meaning. The metaphorical transfer operative in the function of this accepting third is a transfer to the place of meaning, which enables the subject to belong to meaning. But belonging is possible only if there is social support for what it means to be that individual, for the meaning of its very existence.

The loving third operates as a conduit between drives/affects and words/symbols and is crucial for one's sense of belonging in the world of meaning. Meaningful speech and a sense of meaning in one's life depend on the connection between affects and words, drives and symbols. Sublimation guarantees the ability to idealize and imagine. It redirects bodily drives into language and signification. This requires that the negativity of drive force be redoubled to create the negativity of signification, which in turn allows creative representation and the recovery of the (maternal) thing lost to the negation of signification. The accepting third is necessary for the transition from the dependence on the maternal body through the negativity of drive force and then the entrance into signification or language. In this sense, the primary sublimation that is foundational for language acquisition, more particularly for the connection between words and affects that makes language meaningful, depends on the accepting third. Retroactively, this primary sublimation is the foundation for all subsequent sublimation, that is, primary identification with the accepting third is retroactively implied in all secondary identification, and all secondary identification is based at least retroactively on primary identification.

Sublimation is facilitated by social supports that provide language and symbols with which individuals find and create the meaning of their own experience. We are all born into a world where meaning already exists. We do not choose the meaning of our language and cultural symbols. Rather, individuals must negotiate the language and cultural symbols that life presents in order to find themselves there. In other words, individuals find their own value and the value of their lives by virtue of negotiating the various meanings available in their culture. The ability to put drives and affects into language depends not only on the availability of words and symbols to discharge those affects but also, and more important, on the ability of society to authorize them. While in principle, according to psychoanalytic theory any word can discharge any affect or any affect can become attached to any word, the meanings available to us in our culture make some affects easier to manifest than others. Some affects are encouraged while others are refused. Some individual's or group's experiences are valued while other individual's or group's experiences are not. So the ability to sublimate—to manifest affects in words or representations—has everything to do with finding socially available meanings that can facilitate the transfer from mute experience to meaningful articulation.

What happens when the only readily available meanings for a particular experience are either nonexistent, prohibited, or abject and inhuman? How is sublimation possible for experiences or emotions that within mainstream culture can be articulated only through denigration or not at all, experiences so profoundly repressed that they are nearly foreclosed from the social? For example, how much of maternal experience and affect can be discharged within patriarchal cultural institutions, which are compounded by racism and classism? And how do women find the symbols to express not only "negative" affects but even their love and care that do not degrade or reduce them to merely natural animals destined by instinct to love their children? How many women can express the complexity of their feelings and experiences of their bodies, especially sex, menstruation, abortion, motherhood, childbirth, and menopause? And if they try, will they be ashamed and guilty? Where do women find positive social support and rich social symbols for the meanings of their experiences—especially their painful, angry, or frustrated experiences?

The connection between sublimation and available meaning and social support provides a social rather than anatomical or psychological explanation for why and how within patriarchal culture it is more difficult for women to sublimate. If positive social support is necessary for sublimation—for drives and affects to make their way into symbols and representations—and if within patriarchal societies women don't have accepting, positive supports within the social, then women would be less able to sublimate. In turn, if women are less able to sublimate—to articulate or discharge their drives and affects—then they will be more depressed. If women can't adequately sublimate their drives into words or creative activities because doing so requires social supports, then they will be less able to interpret their own experiences and find or create meaning, which requires sublimation. If women cannot discharge their affects and experiences in language or artistic activities as easily as men can, it is because women don't have the necessary positive social supports for their affects and experiences that remain unspoken, even taboo, within patriarchal cultures. Since these drives and affects must go somewhere, repression and ultimately depression are the only alternatives to sublimation.

Sublimation and Idealization as Imaginary Revolt

Kristeva's prescription for depression and melancholy is what she calls intimate, or psychic, revolt. Intimate revolt is a challenge to authority and tradition analogous to political revolt that takes place within an individual and is essential to psychic development.[14] It is a revolt in the psyche that enables us to live as individuals connected to others. Lack of the ability to revolt erodes any sense of belonging to the social. Feelings of not belonging relate to alienation that is experienced as a lack of authorization or legitimacy of one's affects and ultimately of one's agency and one's very being. The inability to revolt leads to depression and feelings of meaninglessness, hopelessness, powerlessness, and emptiness. Psychic revolt is essential to sublimation, through which one makes social codes and meaning one's own. In a sense, intimate or psychic revolt names the process of assimilating or sublimating social authority that makes individual autonomy possible. When this process is impaired or undermined, the individual's autonomy is likewise affected, and the result is a feeling of powerlessness and exclusion, which is the flip side of agency and autonomy. Without psychic revolt, which enables and authorizes sublimation and creativity, individuals suffer from various forms of borderline states in which negotiating the frontiers of relationships to self and others is precisely what is at stake. Intimate revolt is an ongoing process through which the borders of self and others are constantly renegotiated. Through intimate revolt, the individual assimilates the authority of the social and gains acceptance and a sense of belonging through responsiveness from others.

Entering the social order requires assimilating the authority of that order through a revolt by which the individual belongs to the world of meaning. Revolt, then, is not a transgression against law or order but a *displacement* of its authority within the psychic economy of the individual. The individual displaces the authority that it associated with the law and now sees that authority as its own. The displacement of the authority of the law authorizes the individual, and legitimates its agency and autonomy. As I analyze in greater detail in the last chapter, paradoxically, social authority becomes individual authority through the individual's revolt against that very authority; and only through revolt against the social order can the individual belong to that order as one who means. This revolutionary displacement gives the individual a sense of inclusion in meaning making and of belonging to the social that support creative activities and the sublimation of drives. Without the displacement of authority and the resulting feeling of belonging (belonging to the social and authority belonging to the individual), the individual does not feel included in the meanings of culture and therefore cannot find meaning in anything. This disowned individual cannot have meaningful experiences but only traumatic ones, because meaningful experience requires some assimilation into the social order. Trauma is what is unrepresentable as a result of the inability to assimilate the meaning of the traumatic experience into the social; trauma is what is meaningless or unknown within the social order (Kristeva 2000b, 29). Revolt, then, is necessary for meaningful experience. But this revolt presupposes not only the for-giveness of meaning but also more essentially the social forgiveness *for* meaning by virtue of which one belongs to a community as singular. I want to emphasize that this process of revolt is not a form of alienation that presupposes an individual inherently and eternally at odds with the social; rather, this revolt is a way to find or create for oneself a community of meaning to which one belongs as singular.

Psychic displacement of authority, or intimate revolt, is necessary for both autonomy and connection to others: "Through a narrative of free association and in the regenerative revolt against the old law (familial taboos, super-ego, ideals, oedipal or narcissistic limits etc.) comes the singular autonomy of each, as well as a renewed link with the other" (Kristeva 2002c, 440). Revolt as a return or questioning and displacement of the past, the old law, for the sake of renewal in the future engenders the social yet autonomous individual who belongs to a community by virtue of assimilation of its authority. On the level of psychic development, the infant becomes an individual through questioning and the ability to say no. Intimate revolt depends on this ability to continually question, which Kristeva calls a rebirth—perhaps because it recalls a childlike wonder and ravenous desire to ask questions. Questioning is a form of revolt necessary to psychic life, especially to sublimation and creativity through which the subject takes social codes or meanings and makes them its own. We become who we are through questioning; and we remain open to meaning and creativity only by continuing to question, continuing this infinite psychic revolt. Psychic space is sustained by infinite revolt, or questioning. These small revolts ensure both the individual's autonomy and its assimilation or belonging within the social symbolic order.

Questioning as revolt can be a counterbalance to depression and melancholia. Recall that the depressive gives up on words; questioning can counteract the depressive's feelings of powerlessness and meaninglessness by challenging words rather than giving up on them. If representation demands the negation of things in favor of words, then the depressive's refusal of words is the result of a melancholy relation to those lost things, most particularly the loss of the meaning of the body and positive body images. Questioning reopens the realm of words or signification through a challenge to signification itself that operates as an invitation to the depressive to refind lost bodies within words. Through the question, signification turns back on itself in the movement of a double negation that negates representations' negation of things.[15] Within the analytic context in particular, questioning, essential to analytic interpretation, becomes a negation of negation, repudiation of repudiation, a double negative (Kristeva 1995, 89). It could even be said that within the analytic context the negativity inherent in questioning becomes a triple negation of the depressed person's negation of the gap between words and things; that is, a negation of the negation of the fundamental negation at the core of signification, the signifier's negation of the thing. More than a loss, lack, or separation, however, the question—the form of intimate revolt—gives birth to creativity and psychic life itself. If negation is necessary for autonomy, and if it is the root of human experience, this is only because it gives rise to a negation of negation: the negation of representations' negation of things. This negation of negation is a reunion with the world of things, sensations, and affects—the world of the body—through language.

Questioning also prevents the conflation of word and thing, ideality and reality, that is symptomatic of the inability to idealize and therefore to sublimate. Recall that signification requires distance between reality and ideality; when this critical distance is denied or foreclosed, the result is somatic symptoms. When the subject is denied the distance necessary to idealize and sublimate, the distance between word and things, it becomes trapped within its body precisely as a thing, and it becomes unable to idealize the body in order to signify it. Trapped within the body without access to idealization, the only outlet for drives and affects is somatic symptoms, the body turned against itself.

Kristeva (2002c, 213) describes revolt as an interrogation rather than a rejection that "opens onto the symbolic as a double-negation, an indefinite questioning." Questioning arrives to usher the infant into discourse in a way that opens onto its infinite possibilities. There is always another question to ask, and at the beginnings of language acquisition the infant revels in asking yet another question—"Why? Why? Why?" Through this infinite questioning, negativity is transformed from a destructive or merely discriminatory force that separates self and other, inside and outside, and becomes the positive force of creativity and the nourishing of psychic space (226). The negativity of drive force becomes the positive force of signification through repetition and response from the other; it becomes the sublimation of drive force into language. In dialogue the infant enters the realm of signification when it can say no.[16] Its "no" is not only a sign of the infant's revolt and attempts at autonomy but also the hallmark of signification itself insofar as all signification is in a sense saying no to things in exchange for their idealized representations in words. Representation requires the denial of things in favor of their representations: the word is not the thing. This denial becomes a positive force because it institutes idealization. Things, bodies, reality are idealized through representation or signification. The infant enters the realm of symbols through this imaginary idealization.

Through idealization and imagination we regain the lost body, most significantly for the infant the lost maternal body. The "redoubled negativity" of signification "liberates" us from the repression in the face of the maternal body that was our first defense against desire or trauma (226). In a sense, then, the intimate revolt turns or returns libidinal drive force back on itself in the form of redoubled negativity that opens up the space for meaning, representation, and creativity—for psychic space itself. In other words, the negativity inherent in the infant's separation from the maternal body gives birth to the symbol of negation ("no") and all symbols, which in turn opens up that possibility of naming things and thereby recovering the lost things (most important, the lost maternal body) through words. The movement from the negativity of abjection to the negativity of signification requires this redoubled negativity or the negation of negation. More simply put, this process is the sublimation of drive force into language.

The repetition of negativity in bodily drive force discharged in relation to others who care and respond becomes a different order negation and moves the infant from the realm of needs and drives into the realm of demands or words. Drives make their way into language even as their negative force is transformed into signification as a compensation for the loss of the realm of needs. In a sense, signification is an overcompensation for leaving the realm of needs and things, insofar as signification transforms the negativity of drives into the negation inherent in language that becomes a positive force through idealization, representation, and sublimation. The idealization of things and bodies and the sublimation of drive force into language is a negation of the negativity of drives because through this process rejection gives way to assimilation and abjection gives way to identification. Through the realm of the imaginary, we come to the realm of the symbolic by virtue of the transformation of libidinal or drive negativity into the positive force of idealization. Through questioning as intimate revolt, negativity becomes a transformational force that opens up and maintains the world of idealization, sublimation, and creativity without which we face the colonization, even annihilation, of psychic space. And, this questioning is an infinite process.

Through revolt against the authority of the social and its linguistic codes, through questioning and the child's incessant why, the subject or fledgling subject assimilates the authority of the social and social meaning as its own. The subject is legitimated, and through this authorization constituted as a subject. Now the meaning of language and social codes—meaning that preexists the subject (which according to the theorists of alienation leads to alienation)—can become meaningful for each singular individual. The subject revolts against authority to authorize itself by assimilating that authority. In addition, the subject identifies with meaning through a metaphorical transfer that precedes even the subject-object split and thereby makes meaning its own. In this way, the subject enters the world of meaning as one who belongs and one who is capable of making meaning.

It is compelling to note that Frantz Fanon (1967, 231–32) also makes the connection between the body and questioning when at the end of *Black Skin, White Masks*, his "final prayer" is "O my body, make of me always a man who questions!" Fanon's suggestion that questioning has its source in the body resonates with Kristeva's analysis of questioning as a manifestation of bodily drive force and semiotic negativity. Fanon insists on the intimate connection between soma and psyche, and for this reason, he can say that the body questions. His analysis shows that colonization affects both the body and the psyche in ways that are inherently connected and that the colonization of psychic space operates through denying the colonized the social space for meaning making; the meaning of their bodies is given as unable to make meaning. For Kristeva, questioning is essential to psychic life because it transforms negativity from a differentiating or possibly even destructive force into the positive force of sublimation through revolt. Questioning or revolt against authority is crucial for psychic life. As psychoanalysis teaches us, this questioning has its source in the body and not some sovereign subject. The effect of sovereignty is created through revolt, and not vice versa. Both Fanon and Kristeva insist on accounting for the unconscious in its role in creating the sovereignty effect. Once we take into account the unconscious, we can never claim to be fully sovereign subjects. One thread in Fanon's writings suggests that the illusion of sovereignty is a symptom of the pathology of colonization. The new humanity that he envisions will be beyond property, ownership, and sovereignty.

Just as Fanon maintains that the debilitating alienation experienced by the colonized is different from, perhaps even the opposite of, the alienation that Hegel describes in his famous master-slave dialectic, Kristeva's intimate revolt is not the Hegelian revolt of slave against master or the fight (almost) to the death that ensues. Psychic revolt, while inherently related to others and the Other of social meaning, is not intersubjective. It is not the battle between two subjects or fledgling subjects for recognition. Rather, the transformation and revolution take place on the level of the unconscious. So, while for Hegel only reason can resolve the conflict that engenders self-conscious subjectivity, for Kristeva only the imagination operating at the level of the unconscious can engender self-conscious, but always only provisional, subjectivity.

The inability to revolt signals not only the inability to be creative or imaginative but also the inability to make or find meaning, and ultimately results in the collapse of psychic space. This revolt is associated with the ability to sublimate, the very mechanism that enables thought and language by translating and directing bodily drives. The ability to sublimate is the result of the accepting support of this imaginary third: "This primary thirdness allows a space between the mother and the child; perhaps it prevents osmosis as well as the merciless war where self-destruction alternates with destruction of the other" (Kristeva 2000b, 54). The accepting third allows us to break out of the Hegelian master-slave dialectic in which we must choose between annihilating either the other or the self and acts as a counterbalance, "thanks to which the subject is not mired in perversion but finds the resources (imaginary, strictly speaking) to continue the revolt integral to his autonomy and to his creative freedom" (54). This integral revolt is essential to creativity and psychic functioning and is supported by the loving third or accepting social meaning that is necessary for identification, idealization, and sublimation, all of which are necessary for love and meaning.

Through intimate revolt, the subject-in-process displaces the authority of the law, which it takes to be outside itself, onto its own individual authority, which it takes to be inside itself. In this way, the individual belongs to the social in a way that supports its own sense of agency as well as its relations to others. This revolt depends on an accepting imaginary third, who beyond the punishing father of the law accepts the individual/infant into the social through forgiveness. The individual's revolt against the father of the law requires the prior guarantee, so to speak, of the accepting third's forgiveness and support. Intimate revolt requires a sense that love is the other side of the law and that the individual can belong to the social. This sense of belonging is crucial for a sense of well-being insofar as it enables sublimation. Saying no to the (maternal) body requires the support of an accepting third who will forgive this negation and accept the individual back into the community.

In sum, without social support and positive self-images available in culture, girls, women, and those othered will suffer from the colonization of psychic space, which can result in the inability to sublimate, create, love, act, and, ultimately, to find or create meaning in their lives. Without that accepting social support, psychic space can become atrophied and impassable. Drives and affects, one's bodily experience itself, devalued in culture, become locked in some unnameable crypt, which makes of the psyche a prison that either flattens psychic space or confines or immobilizes affects and experience. In either case, drives and affects—the very passions that give meaning to life and love—become cut off from words and representations. One necessary antidote, if not the cure, for depressed women and other oppressed peoples, then, is having, finding, or creating the social space within which to articulate their drives and affects as positive, lovable, and loved and thereby supporting an open psychic space.

Making meaning for oneself is the seat of subjectivity and agency; and this is what oppression attempts to take away from those oppressed. Exclusion operates most effectively by preventing the assimiliation of authority that legitimates the individual and authorizes its agency. This authorization is a prerequisite for the capacity to sublimate through which an individual makes meaning its own (if always only provisionally) and thereby gains a sense of belonging to the community. Yet, despite oppression, empowered subjectivity and agency are possible for those othered within mainstream culture by virtue of their own resistance and revolt against oppression, which reauthorize agency and restore the capacity to sublimate and make meaning one's own. This resistance not only brings people together to create meaning for themselves but also begins to provide the social space necessary for open psychic space and empowered agency. As I show in the following chapters, creating the social space for resistance to racism and sexism provides the social support necessary to reverse and deter the internalization or epidermalization of oppressive values. As we create free and open social spaces, we begin to create free and open psychic spaces. Social revolt and psychic revolt go hand in hand; one is not possible without the other.

The identification with the accepting third becomes an identification with the agency of meaning itself. This identification is possible only if the fledgling subject finds itself within that meaning such that it can belong to the realm of meaning and signification. If there is no accepting third, if there is only the law or prohibition, then the affective transfer from drives to words is short-circuited, and the result is, at best, a depressive subjectivity whose agency is impaired. Likewise, if the social doesn't at some level sanction the psychic revolt necessary for creativity and sublimation by particular individuals, those subjects cannot inherit social authority and therefore are never quite legitimated as autonomous agents.

Just as it is clear that within Western culture inheritance of property is still patriarchal, the right to revolt and assimilate patriarchal power is socially sanctioned primarily for those who have traditionally had it, white men. But property is not the only thing that we inherit from our culture. We inherit the right and expectations to revolt against that inheritance and tradition. Paradoxically, it is this tradition revolting against itself that maintains that very tradition. In other words, because only those sanctioned as proper heirs to the tradition are given the place or space—physical and psychic—to revolt, only they properly assimilate the authority of that tradition. Others disenfranchised by those traditions are not authorized to revolt against them and therefore cannot assimilate their power and in turn are not legitimated as autonomous agents. As I show in the last chapter, the ability to revolt is linked to forgiveness, which is denied to those disenfranchised within mainstream culture.

Restoring the ability to sublimate requires enabling the ability to revolt against authority and thereby assimilate it. This authorizing move supports the transfer of embodied experience into language and signifying practices. It counteracts the silencing effects of oppression's deauthorization by restoring a sense of agency. It is the agency and authority of the social order that are transferred into an individual's signification by virtue of a process supported by the social order. This sanction is the accepting third that counterbalances the harsh paternal agent or, in the case of oppression, as a counter to the punishing, cruel superego of the privileged subjects. Although sublimation is drive force making its way into socially sanctioned signification, it still can be transformative and creative, especially when those who have not been heirs to social authority make ways to assimilate the law for their own purposes. We can imagine that revolt against an authority that excludes or abjects—a revolt against the oppressing superego of dominant culture—might open up the space for inclusion and belonging to those disenfranchised by that authority. This intimate revolt from the margins might open the space for authorizing and legitimating the individuality of those othered, those for whom individuality and the privileges of robust subjectivity and agency had been foreclosed by oppression. Alternative communities (such as hip-hop, Oprah's book club, feminist activism, lesbian folk music) may offer the support necessary for revolt that sustains and restores agency. Resistance itself is a form of sublimation that returns a sense of agency to othered subjects. But revolt against exclusionary authority and opening forgiveness to those excluded by this authority can be truly radical only if they take us outside the economy of property with its concomitant notion of ownership and sovereignty and into a different way to conceive of forgiveness, authority, and authorization altogether.

Part IV

Revolt, Singularity, and Forgiveness

To this point, I have analyzed how oppression and domination colonize psychic space through debilitating alienation and the transmission of affects, especially negative ones such as depression, shame, and anger. I have diagnosed the colonization of psychic space as the denial of the social space within which to sublimate drives and affects, especially the negative affects of oppression. Moreover, I have identified that lack of social space with the absence of social support in the form of positive meaning and self-images within dominant values and mainstream culture. This positive meaning is associated with a loving accepting third that supports the infant's move from the maternal body into signification and continues to support the ability to idealize, sublimate, imagine, and create throughout one's psychic life. In sum, I have diagnosed as social pathology what continues to be identified as individual pathology by the operations of colonization, oppression, domination, exclusion, and discrimination.

In addition to analyzing the dynamics of the colonization of psychic space, I have explored how the negative affects of oppression can be transformed into a way to regain a sense of agency and community. I have shown how the fluidity of subject position and power affect subjectivity and agency such that modes of domination can be turned against themselves and become modes of resistance. Fanon's analysis of the radio and the veil, and Alvarez's literary illustrations of how one nail of domination can take out another, has shown that just as the fluidity of power in relation to psychic space can lead to negative affects and their repression that colonize psychic space and undermine subjectivity and agency, this same fluidity can also lead to resistance and restoration of subjectivity. With Fanon, it is possible to imagine a humanism beyond the economy of property, one that does not turn bodies into property, subjectivity into ownership, or agency into sovereignty.

In the last chapter, I analyzed how imaginary or psychic revolt can restore the ability to sublimate and authorize the agency of those othered. The assimilation of social authority necessary to authorize subjectivity that has been denied to those marginalized might be gained through alternative communities and countercultural social supports. Moreover, the authorization of marginalized or othered subjects can be revolutionary, as those individuals and groups decolonize their psychic space and become meaning makers not only for themselves but also for others by providing an accepting social space. This alternative space can transform dominant values and mainstream culture both in terms of the interaction between centrist and marginal spaces and in terms of a regained sense of agency and empowerment for those who had been othered. Their self-confidence in itself becomes a form of resistance, which empowers them to assimilate cultural clichés in order to make them their own and, in the process, transform them.

In this part, I continue to consider the relationship between the social and the psyche, particularly insofar as the social is formative of singularity, individuality, and one's sense of belonging to the world of meaning. Here, I address the question of how one can be an individual and at the same time belong to a community: How do we belong to the social as singular? Again, I return to the relationship between idealization and sublimation in the evolution and maintenance of individuality as singular, only now using Julia Kristeva's theory of female genius to bring together my previous discussions of the need for positive self-images within the social and the need for idealization and sublimation to sustain psychic life. Finally, I explore the relationship between the social and the psyche in terms of individuality, singularity, and belonging to the community through forgiveness by developing a notion of forgiveness as a prerequisite for individual agency and the singularity that both makes individuality possible and at the same time always suspect. In the end, this model of forgiveness stands as an alternative to the model of alienation with which I began. Rejecting the hypothesis that alienation is inherent in subjectivity, I conclude by considering how it is forgiveness, not alienation, that instigates subjectivity.

Chapter 9

Revolt and Singularity

> For better or for worse, the next century will be a female one—and female genius . . . gives us hope that it might be for the better.
>
> —Julia Kristeva, *Hannah Arendt*

Throughout part II, I associated social melancholy with the loss or denial of lovable self-images or cultural meanings, which are replaced within oppressive cultures with abject and shameful self-images. The lack of positive images undermines idealization by undermining the move from the body or real to the ideal realm necessary for signification. Stuck in the body, without access to social space or signification within which to transfer or sublimate internalized abjection and shame, marginalized or oppressed people are left with somatic symptoms and emotional pain. Idealization is necessary for sublimation and robust psychic life: it is necessary for the transfer of drives and affects into signification; and therefore, it is necessary to turn bodily symptoms into words or works of art.

In chapter 8, I insisted that idealization is a necessary prerequisite for sublimation. This conception of the relationship between idealization and sublimation links them both to subject or ego formation, especially to one's sense of agency, autonomy, and belonging. Through idealization and then sublimation, the individual is authorized by the social and enters the realm of meaning as a meaning maker, as an agent. One enters the realm of meaning as an individual insofar as one sublimates one's bodily drives and affects into signification; but insofar as one does so through preexisting forms of signification and meaning, one also belongs to a community of meaning and to a community of meaning makers. Through idealizing social meaning and then identifying with it, one can make meaning one's own to discharge one's affects into signification and sublimate bodily drives. Psychic revolt or transgression not only gives the subject a sense of belonging to the social but also transforms the social through that revolt and belonging.

In important ways, this theory of sublimation, and of the relationship between idealization and sublimation, is radically different from Freud's. Freud limits his discussion of sublimation to sexual drives as they are redirected into art and intellectual activities; he rarely considers any other possible drives in relation to sublimation, and he rarely examines the relationship between drives and affects. If affects are psychic manifestations of drives, then a theory of sublimation must also account for the role of affects. Freud's theory does not. In addition, as many feminists have argued, the sexual drives that Freud considers are the products of the male libido, which for Freud is the only kind of libido. In his discussions of great artists and their processes of sublimation, he considers only men. This is not just because most of those considered great artists were men (because women were excluded from greatness in the realms of art and intellectual pursuits, restricted as they were to the domestic sphere), but also because his theory limits sublimation and its fruits to men's virility and control over it. Just as for Freud civil society begins with men sublimating their virility, culture and especially high culture—art, literature, philosophy—are the results of men's control over themselves, more specifically over their desire for sex. In an important sense, within the Freudian scenario, for great male sublimators, high culture becomes a substitute for sex with women. By opening sublimation onto the affective representations of drives and not just the male sexual drive, my aim is to develop a notion of sublimation that includes women as well as men. But to open the world of sublimation to women, it is necessary to open the world of idealization to women.

Moreover, for Freud sublimation is not constitutive of subjectivity. He separates idealization from sublimation by suggesting that while sublimation concerns only the object, idealization concerns both subject and object: "Sublimation is a process that concerns object-libido and consists in the instinct's directing itself towards an aim other than, and remote from, sexual satisfaction. . . . Idealisation is a process that concerns the object; by it that object, without any alternation in its nature, is aggrandised and exalted in the subject's mind. Idealisation is possible in the sphere of ego-libido as well as that of object-libido" ([1914] 1955, 94). Freud does not consider sublimation constitutive of the ego because it is simply a matter of redirecting drives toward another object and therefore is primarily about objects as the aims of drives. The theory that I have been developing, on the other hand, considers how sublimation is not only constitutive of identity and the subject but also the linchpin of subjectivity and agency. Recall the difference between the ideal ego (the narcissistic relation to the maternal body) and the ego ideal (the prohibitions and standards instilled by parents and culture to which the individual tries to conform).

Both the ideal ego and the ego ideal form the subject's ideal agencies. Without some form of idealization, signification is impossible. To use language, we must idealize meaning. This is not to say that we idealize it in the sense of imagining it as perfect or all-powerful, although the use of the notion of idealization in traditional psychoanalysis suggests this form of idealization. The punishing superego feeds off of this type of idealization—an impossible goal in the face of which the individual is always lacking. But idealization is also the process through which we can imagine something greater than ourselves, for example, a community of meaning. The operations of metaphor and metonymy inherent in signification require idealization, but not idealization as perfection. Meaning does not require a form of idealization linked to the notion of the good as the perfect ideal. Rather, here idealization is the process of imagination that gives form to images and concepts apart from things and allows us to sublimate bodily experiences into signification and thereby communicate.

As I have shown, the operation of what Kristeva calls the imaginary third is a form of idealization that supports the transition into signification and the sublimation of bodily drives and affects through loving rather than threatening. Rather than an identification with a punishing superego and its demands, this form of idealization is an identification with the meaning that supports the transformation of bodily needs into communication and communion. At stake in this analysis is the necessity to conceive of idealization and meaning—socialization—as providing a sense of agency and authorization through an identification with the support that it provides rather than merely through punishment or exclusion of difference. This is an identification not only with the connection and belonging but also with the revolt and singularity that the realm of idealization and meaning provide. We can't give up on idealization and signification just because they require form and perhaps even laws or regulation. Rather, we need to analyze the ways in which this form-giving agency is not only fluid and supportive but also enables revolt against punishing and cruel forms of idealization that become dogmatic and are used to justify exclusion, colonization, and oppression.

Idealization involves both the ability to form ideas or mental images and concepts as separate from perceptual experience and the ability to idealize someone or something as beyond the self. Both forms of idealization enable the separation between the world of bodies and things and the world of images and symbols. Both forms enable the transfer of bodily affects into signification and make movement between these worlds possible.

Just as it is necessary for us to idealize meaning and identify with it in order to become beings who mean, so too is it necessary to idealize others in order to inspire passion, interest, and caring in ourselves. We gain our own strength, courage, and greatness from those others whom we idealize, not because they are perfect but rather because they inspire us. This form of idealization is a form of investment without ownership that yields our own interest in the world and others. We can be passionate about something because others have been. We can hope for a better future because others have had hope. We can be inspired by the stories of greatness of others, especially in the face of colonization and oppression. This investment is also an acknowledgment of our dependence, an acknowledgment that our subjectivity is formed out of interest in the world and others that comes through the nourishing circle of interdependence and support. We are clothed by the investment in geniuses whom we idealize as beyond ourselves and yet as inspiration for our own greatness. Both aspects of idealization—the ability to form ideas or concepts and the ability to identify with someone or something beyond oneself—require imagination and nourish and sustain it. Imagination is definitive of subjectivity and a sense of agency; and through the agency of imagination, affects are transferred into symbols and sublimation becomes possible.

This analysis of idealization raises several questions: What images, ideas, or concepts do racist and sexist cultures provide women and racialized others to idealize? What people, geniuses, or heroines do they have to idealize? Traditionally, we have idealized male fantasies of beautiful women and heroic (white) men. We have admired the genius of great (white) men who changed the way that we look at the world, men like Newton, Darwin, Freud, and Einstein. But there are few, if any, women or racialized others whom we idolize as geniuses who have changed our experience of the world. As Christine Battersby so persuasively documents in *Gender and Genius* (1989), not only are all of our geniuses men but also throughout history (men's) theories of genius reserve genius for men; many theories of genius, like Freud's theory of creative sublimation, maintain that genius is the result of some kind of control over male virility. Many of these theories, like Freud's, also propose that women (and racialized others) are closer to nature, more intuitive and emotional, and therefore less civilized and incapable of the sublimation necessary for great genius (see Battersby 1989).

Feminists, including Battersby, working in various disciplines have insisted that women must reclaim women's genius and creativity from the dustbins of history. For example, some feminists like the psychoanalyst Luce Irigaray and the literary critic Hélène Cixous have attempted to rewrite myths to empower women; the philosopher Margaret Simons has persuasively demonstrated that many ideas attributed to Jean-Paul Sartre rightfully belong to Simone de Beauvoir and that she is a genius as both a philosopher and a novelist; and the literary theorist and historian T. Denean Sharpley-Whiting has shown the unacknowledged female influences on Fanon and on many of the ideas attributed to the male proponents of the negritude movement.

Ordinary Female Genius: Kristeva

Rejecting Freud's notion of sublimation—which is reserved for men controlling and redirecting their virility—and instead relying on a social theory of sublimation is a first step toward reconceiving of genius, particularly female genius. And, given my theory of social melancholy, it would seem that allowing the social space for female geniuses would also provide positive images of women to counterbalance negative images prevalent in mainstream patriarchal culture. In her recent trilogy *Female Genius*, Kristeva not only argues that Hannah Arendt, Melanie Klein, and Colette are geniuses, she also begins to sketch a theory of a particularly female genius.

Although Kristeva does not fully develop a theory of female genius when she valorizes three great women writers in three volumes, she does introduce and conclude the trilogy with some suggestions about female genius that have implications for genius and psychic life in general. She suggests that genius and geniuses are necessary for psychic life: we need geniuses to validate the exceptional within our own lives, which is as true for women as it is for men. Psychic life depends on a sense of validation and legitimization of the possibility of creativity and greatness for all of us. We need to idealize geniuses and identify with them. But to imagine idealization as identification, we also need to reconceive of genius as a type of social phenomena and the product of the lives of ordinary people who do extraordinary things.

Extraordinary within the Ordinary

Kristeva's description of genius as the extraordinary within the ordinary resonates with Michael Howe's analysis of genius in *Genius Explained*, where Howe also insists that genius cannot be explained as the product of some mysterious force or as the property of rare individuals born with genius, but rather as the result of a combination of social factors and environment, and individual biographies.[1] Like Kristeva, Howe sees the heuristic value in geniuses as figures who can be idealized to open up an identification with the extraordinary within the ordinary. Howe takes up specific cases of genius, particularly Mozart, Darwin, George Stephenson, Michael Faraday, and Einstein (and even a few women in passing), to show how their social context and particular biographies led to what we consider their genius. He concludes his study by insisting that genius is the result of ordinary people who do extraordinary things and that this should give us hope about our own possibilities:

> One of the reasons for people being reluctant to let go of the idea that geniuses are a race apart, distinct from everyone else by virtue of their inherent qualities as well as their marvelous accomplishments, is the fear that geniuses will be diminished if we remove the magic and mystery surrounding them. I do not share that view. On the contrary, it is not until we understand that they are made from the same flesh and bones as the rest of us that we start to appreciate just how wonderfully remarkable these men and women really are. They show us what humankind is capable of. And it is only when we acknowledge that geniuses are not totally unlike other people that our minds open up to all that we can learn from them. (1999, 205)

For Howe, it is the fact that geniuses are made of the "same flesh and bones" as the rest of us that not only makes them special but also inspires us to maximize our own capacities for greatness. Genius gives us a sense not of what we lack, but of what we can become. Like Howe, Kristeva describes genius as the extraordinary within the ordinary. She suggests that in a world that is increasingly run by computers and machines, the need for genius is more urgent because geniuses show us the extraordinary in humanity beyond automation or standardization: "In our day, it would appear, the word 'genius' stands for paradoxical occurrences, unique experiences, and remarkable excesses that manage to pierce through an increasingly automated world" (2002c, 400). The excesses in everyday life open up the meaning of human existence. Moments of creativity and imagination are such excesses—the interest on our investment in the world and others. These moments of excess are moments of sublimation, which are necessary to legitimate singularity, to belong to the social, and to make life meaningful. Certainly, the excess of genius is the result of sublimation, which I have described as the process of bodily affects as they are transferred into signification—poetry, prose, philosophy, music, physics, etc. This creative excess requires sublimation, and it is available to all of us.

Yet the possibility of sublimation and creativity is missing from the lives of girls and women and other marginalized people insofar as they are circumscribed by values, meanings, and images that foreclose their agency as meaning makers. The extraordinary within our midst, the excess within the everyday, begins to decolonize psychic space and frees the imagination from the restrictions of traditions even from within those very traditions. The social support necessary for agency and subjectivity is founded on the genius of everyday life because agency is the result of the ability to make meaning in one's life, which requires social support. Reconceiving of the value and contribution of women is just one part of the decolonization of psychic space through which we can restore the ability to sublimate cultural signifiers into women's lives so that women can belong to the social as singular individuals. Creating the social space for female genius not only provides positive images of women as geniuses within mainstream culture but also and thereby opens the psychic space necessary for women to sublimate in their everyday lives because the ability to sublimate requires the operations of idealization and positive support from the social.

Like Howe, Kristeva describes the genius as a subject who finds itself at a historical intersection and crystallizes its possibilities (400). She maintains that the genius belongs to all of us as a "therapeutic invention" by which we, too, create and live; geniuses allow us to imagine the extraordinary within our ordinary lives (400). This is because for Kristeva, like Howe, genius—female genius at least—is related to the biographies of individuals whose lives are inseparable from their inventions and innovations. We are fascinated by the ordinary lives of geniuses because the ordinariness of their lives also infuses our own with genius. We endow geniuses with a biography so as to gauge how the biography both can and cannot explain the excess and surplus of genius (401). The genius is an ordinary woman in an important sense indistinguishable from any other, except for her accomplishments insofar as they are recognized by others. More than this, genius is a relationship between the life of a singular individual and those who receive genius and consecrate it. We make geniuses for our own good because they allow us to cultivate the fantasy of creativity and originality essential to psychic life. Geniuses allow us to believe that we, too, can "be someone" (401).

Within normalized and normalizing traditions, and standardized and standardizing systems, there is space for the excess of sublimation that leads to extraordinary creativity, to genius. More than this, there is a need for genius, particularly female genius, not only to counterbalance abject and degrading images of women but also to acknowledge and idealize both extraordinary women and, more important, the extraordinary in the lives of ordinary women. Women and other marginalized people need the supportive social space to express the excesses of their particular genius. The figure of the genius is one antidote to degrading stereotypes of women that impair psychic space and the movement of bodily drives and affects into signification, which can result in depression. Genius provides the inspiration that ordinary women can take the clichés of culture and speak through them as individuals who belong to that culture as singular. If sublimation is a form of revolt, genius allows women to sublimate and thereby revolt against patriarchal culture in order to belong to that culture now transformed by their interventions. New geniuses inspire creativity, rekindle interest, and thereby open psychic life to sublimation and idealization as an antidote to the depression caused by oppression.

Implicit in Kristeva's analysis are two types of female genius: one that is documented by the creative and intellectual writings of great women and another that is too often not documented and underappreciated, the everyday genius of ordinary women, which speaks to the singularity of all individuals. Both forms of female genius have been and continue to be devalued within our culture, which continues to be controlled by patriarchal values. Against the colonization of psychic space that results from a lack of accepting social support, female geniuses, heroines of the spirit, can help women find value in their own everyday genius. On the one hand, the idealization of female geniuses (and positive figures of women's contributions to the social that are recognized and supported by mainstream culture) starts to provide the antidote to the social melancholy that results from the loss of a loved and lovable or socially acceptable self-image. On the other hand, the recognition of genius as the extraordinary within the lives of ordinary women opens up the social space for an imaginary identification with the possibility of creativity and the extraordinary within our own lives that promotes the sublimation of repressed affects into signification. Both forms of female genius, which are in a sense social genius and available to all of us, promote the idealization and sublimation necessary to overcome social melancholy.

On the one hand, genius in the more traditional sense of extraordinary accomplishments, like those of Arendt, Klein, and Colette, provide women geniuses to idealize and with whom to identify, which makes idealization possible. Female genius provides girls and women with positive figures and meanings with which to identify in order to experience themselves as agents within the social sphere. On the other hand, the notion that genius demonstrates the possibility of the extraordinary—creativity and sublimation—within the ordinary shows girls and women that they, too, are capable of sublimation that gives meaning to their lives and to their experiences as girls and women.

Sensory Experience

By recognizing the major contributions of several extraordinary women who have marked this century's history through their lives and works, Kristeva's trilogy is a call to the singularity of each woman. Only through the realization of their singularity can women and other oppressed and marginalized peoples begin the decolonization of psychic space. Creating meaning for oneself, for one's life, through sublimation is what makes each individual singular. In what she diagnoses as a standardized world that shuns creativity and thereby singularity, in passing Kristeva suggests that women's lives circumscribed as they have been by patriarchal cultures within the domestic sphere—confined to the world of the body and excluded from the life of the mind—might actually be our only hope against the threat of massification, automatization, and standardization of global capitalism. The everyday lives of women who have been socialized to be more sensitive to the sensory can protect the possibility of singularity in a world that is becoming more automated. Within patriarchal culture, women are socialized to be more sensitive to the sensory, especially to the details of everyday domestic life and bodies, bodies of children in particular.

Until recently, this sensory realm has been degraded and excluded from most of the history of intellectual production. Yet it is access to this sensory realm and the ability to translate it into signification that makes life meaningful and acts as a counterbalance to depression. Women's relation to the realm of the sensory and of the body again suggests, contra Freud, that they should be more capable of sublimation than men insofar as they are closer to their bodily drives (of course, Freud maintains that it is the ability and necessity to forcefully overcome and redirect these drives—the sexual drives—that leads to sublimation). As many feminists and others have argued, Western philosophy and culture in general have associated women with the body and domestic sphere and men with the mind or intellect and the public sphere. This split between body and mind leads to a culture in which bodily affects are cut off from signification. If our culture assigns affects to women and social signification to men, then how can we expect either men or women to sublimate bodily affects into signification? Given this split, it would seem that women are too close to bodily affects and too far from signification to be able to translate one into the other; and men are too far from bodily affects to even redirect them into signification. Our culture encourages the split between bodily drives and affects and signification by perpetuating gender stereotypes that put men and women on different sides of the divide between words and affects. This kind of split can only lead to feelings of emptiness and meaninglessness in both men and women. As I have argued elsewhere, traditional gender roles are themselves pathological (Oliver 1995).

But, as the roles of men and women mix and become closer, women's attentiveness to sensory experience and the sensory aspect of relationships can and will be translated into signification; and men's public or intellectual personae will become more in touch with bodily affects associated with the sensory realm of experience. Given this analysis of the need for sublimation and idealization that depend on the transfer of bodily experiences into signification, we can only hope that cultural prescriptions for gender roles that colonize psychic space give way to the singularity of sensory experience and its articulation beyond, or at least within, categorizations that perpetuate not only the split between affects and words but also marginalization and discrimination.

The flavors and textures of everyday life can give meaning and joy if they are valued and have meaning within culture. Food, clothes, home, garden, beautiful and functional domestic spaces can be valued and even display female genius, the extraordinary within the ordinary. Women's relationships to the materiality of life display everyday genius. The traditional realms of women's lives—domestic space with its food, clothes, and shelter—are the very realms within which the extraordinary manifests itself in the ordinary. Because of their traditional roles as wives and mothers, the genius of everyday life is women's genius; for Kristeva, this is particularly mothers' genius: "Mothers can be geniuses, not only geniuses of love, tact, self-denial, suffering, and even evil spells and witchcraft but also of a certain approach to living the life of the mind. That approach to being a mother and a woman, at times warmly accepted and at times outright refused or wrought with conflict, bestows upon mothers a genius all their own. . . . women are also able to work toward unique, innovative creations and to remake the human condition" (Kristeva 2002c, 403). Women and mothers do not realize their own genius because our culture has yet to learn to value it, let alone recognize it. In creating new human beings, many mothers are each singular innovators, reinventing the child anew every day. They invent ways to comfort, to teach, to train their children. And each child is unique and requires new games and new ways to comfort, teach, and train. Because each mother, and each mother-child relation, is unique, Kristeva suggests that mothers might represent "our only safeguard against the wholesale automation of human beings " (402). Insofar as child care cannot be automated or performed by machines, insofar as it requires women to give birth to children if not necessarily to raise them, it requires singular relationships that introduce children to language and sociality.

Yet this innovation is not valued as such by our culture, a culture that reduces mothers to fetal containers or legal guardians. Only by valuing the genius of women and mothers in the domestic sphere, especially in relation to children—or, as Kristeva insists, in relation to the continuation of the species—can women begin to value their own lives as closer to the sensory sphere of existence, the sphere in which children are raised and dwellings are made into homes. Acknowledging the everyday genius of women in relation to the sensory sphere can bring the importance of that sphere back into the social and thereby transform the social. It could possibly open a social space for the sublimation of the sensory into signification such that men and women could find meaning through forms of creativity that heretofore have not been valued as such. Valuing the everyday genius particular to women even as their experiences have been circumscribed by patriarchal values can lead to the decolonization of psychic space and transform our society and culture in ways that benefit all of us. Similarly, valuing the genius particular to other marginalized and racialized people even as their experiences are circumscribed by heterosexist and racist restrictions can also lead to similar benefits.

This decolonization is possible only if the values and meanings particular to these groups as they have been defined and confined by racist, sexist, and heterosexist cultural values become available to all of us; that is, that their genius is valued as a contribution to mainstream or dominant society and thereby becomes available for everyone. Of course, this is a paradox insofar as first we must acknowledge the specific genius of women and other marginalized people whose genius has been erased, ignored, or abjected; then we must value that genius as important to the history and sustenance of society such that rather than categorize genius as women's or blacks', etc., we can value this genius as it is found in the ordinary lives of all of us. This operation is radically different from simply assimilating or co-opting the genius of those othered, valuing it now only as part of dominant culture while continuing to devalue the contributions to culture of those othered. Only by revaluing and then overcoming the categorization inherent in sexism and racism can we begin to decolonize psychic space and begin to approach each individual as singular. In a sense, then, the very categories that must be valued to decolonize psychic space and overcome oppression must also give way to singularity beyond such categories. But, in the practice of our everyday lives, we are far from the possibility of conceiving, let alone acknowledging, singularity. So at this point it is crucial to analyze how racist and sexist culture create particular kinds of genius despite and because of marginalization and social restrictions. Female genius cannot be separated from the lives of women as women circumscribed by certain cultural restrictions and patriarchal values.

Everyday Revolutions: Alvarez

Acknowledging female genius, in the monumental and the everyday forms, gives hope that girls and women can make available cultural meanings their own through sublimation supported within the social sphere. In Julia Alvarez's fiction, girls and women turn the stereotypes of their culture, even patriarchal culture, into forms of creativity and resistance. Her fiction thrives on both types of female genius and displays the relations between genius that is consecrated and recognized by culture, and genius in the ordinary lives of women; in her work, these two types of female genius are always intertwined. Through the genius of the everyday, her heroines initiate revolutions that resonate throughout all levels of experience. Their revolutions are not monumental actions that overthrow governments but everyday struggles with authority that enable and empower resistance. Alvarez's heroines show how the very trappings of femininity, womanhood, and motherhood can be used against patriarchal values and institutions to open up a space for women's resistance to domination.

A turn to literature may enable a more vivid description of affects as they make their way into signification. Literature allows for a first-person account of emotions in dialogic relations in a way that theory usually does not. Analysis of how the singularity of female genius appears in everyday situations imagined and described in Alvarez's fiction may give us another kind of understanding, or perhaps I should say a feeling, of what Kristeva calls the semiotic element of signification. Fiction can *show* tensions between subjectivity and subject position, between singularity and social codes, that philosophy can only attempt to *describe.* The metaphorics of literature and the imagined dialogues and dialogic relationships between people engaged in power struggles or intimacy brings us closer to the semiotic and unconscious dimension of signification. Contemporary literature written by women is especially relevant in a discussion of women's attempts to sublimate affect, including the negative affects of oppression. Literature provides one means for women not only to sublimate but also to articulate experiences of discrimination, motherhood, sexuality that have been repressed within patriarchal culture. Alvarez is especially adept at both showing and representing women's everyday genius through forms of revolt against patriarchy that employ its very restrictions against themselves.

A Regular Revolution

Alvarez's first novel, *How the García Girls Lost Their Accents* (1991), documents everyday struggles of women and girls against restrictive traditions. The novel tells the stories of four sisters—Yolanda, Sandi, Carla, and Fifi—who are exiled from the Dominican Republic along with their parents because their father was involved in an attempt to overthrow the dictator Trujillo. In a chapter titled "A Regular Revolution," Alvarez suggests that revolution is a matter of "constant skirmishes" on a mundane level (111). She compares the four daughters' revolt against their parents' authority and against patriarchal authority to their father's participation in the revolt against the Trujillo dictatorship. Her fiction suggests that small revolutions (intimate revolts) happen every day. The girls plot their revolution using the accepted patriarchal codes for chaperones, and young ladies' proper behavior, against those very codes. Alvarez shows how patriarchal traditions are turned against themselves to undermine patriarchal authority. She imagines how everyday practices of domination also open up everyday modes of resistance, how power is not only the power to dominate but also the power to resist.

In "A Regular Revolution," Carla, Yolanda, and Sandi are trying to rescue Fifi from getting pregnant and stuck marrying their sexist island cousin Mundín. Here, Mundín is called a "tyrant," and the girls are staging a "revolution": "A coup on the same Avenida where a decade ago the dictator was cornered and wounded on his way to a tryst with his mistress" (127). The girls use traditional restrictions on girls and women to their advantage when they insist that their cousin and chaperone, Manuel, take them home early without the lovers Mundín and Fifi. They use Manuel's responsibility for them to combat the "male loyalty" that "keeps the macho system going" (127). Manuel's sister tells him that she has cramps from her period and needs to go home; he suggests that the rest of the girls wait in the hotel room until Mundín and Fifi are "done," but the girls remind him that "girls are not left unescorted in public." Manuel is forced to take them home without the lovers, which blows their cover, while the girls rallied with "¡Que viva la revolucíon!" The "first bomb" explodes on the women's side of the patio when the sisters are asked, "Where is Fifi?" They answer that she is with Mundín (unchaperoned), and then "there is an embarrassed silence in which the words *her reputation* are as palpable as if someone had hung a wedding dress in the air" (129). The girls use the excuse of menstruation and the patriarchal convention that girls are not to be left alone without their chaperone to expose the breach of another convention that girls are not to be left alone with their *novios*. Their motives, however, are not to protect their sister's reputation or virginity but to protect her from the oppressive patriarchal culture that would demand marriage, family, and subservience to her husband.

One Nail Takes Out Another

The central plot of Alvarez's novel *In the Time of the Butterflies* (1994) also revolves around revolution, specifically the four sisters Mirabal—Dede, Patricia, Minerva, and Maté—and their involvement in the underground revolution against Trujillo. Again, the women's resistance is not painted in the broad strokes of bloody battles and guerrilla uprisings but in the everyday makeup of femininity. Alvarez's story of the Mirabal sisters is as much about their own mundane revolutions against the restrictions of patriarchy as it is about a rebellion against the restrictions of dictatorship. In fact, the dictator's authority is depicted as founded on the macho image of a patriarch who has his way with women.

Like *How the García Girls Lost Their Accents*, *In the Time of the Butterflies* describes how patriarchal conventions are used to undermine patriarchal values and institutions and how the trappings of femininity are used to fuel revolution, this time political as well as personal: the church, crucifixes, and praying become forms of rebellion (237). The sisters use the script they learned from the nuns for writing out Bible passages to list the ammunition in their hiding places (168). The sisters' mental and physical discipline while in prison is compared to keeping the baby on a feeding schedule (235). Maté uses her long hair and hair ribbons to smuggle news stories to other prisoners and secret notes detailing the human rights abuses of the Trujillo regime to the Organization of American States's representatives when they visit the prison (246, 252). A young woman's diary becomes incriminating evidence against the dictatorship's abuses. Even the election of "Miss University" becomes the promise of democratic elections when Minerva tells Maté that "this country hasn't voted for anything in twenty-six years and it's only these silly little elections that keep the faint memory of democracy going" (136).

For the Mirabal sisters, love, family, and revolution are inseparable. Passion between lovers feeds passion for revolution, and the common struggle against the dictator fuels personal passion. For example, the struggle for freedom keeps Minerva and Manolo together through difficult personal times. Maté falls in love with Leandro when she meets him while he's delivering ammunition for the revolutionaries. She sees the revolution as her chance for personal independence from a family that treats her like the baby. More than that, she realizes that her looks and easy manner with men can serve the revolution. She writes in her diary, "now I can use my talents for the revolution" (143). Patricia becomes involved after her church group witnesses young guerrillas attacked by Trujillo's soldiers. She sees the face of her own son, Nelson, in the face of a dying young guerrilla and from that moment on is committed to saving her family by fighting Trujillo. All the while that these women are fighting against the national patriarch, Trujillo, they are also fighting against their own local patriarchs at home. They all have various skirmishes with their father and their husbands while asserting themselves against patriarchal conventions.

If, as Minerva says of the dance that cures her headache, "one nail takes out another," then she is the hammer (97). She knows how to strike one nail of patriarchy against another to get what she needs. When her father won't let her leave the farm to go to law school, and when El Jefe (Trujillo) wants to make her his mistress, she eventually convinces Trujillo to allow her to go to law school to be near him in the city (98). She pits the authority of Trujillo against her father's authority. When Trujillo suggests private meetings, she uses the patriarchal conventions of propriety and honor to argue that it would not be honorable for her to meet him alone (111). One nail of patriarchy takes out another.

Alvarez's novel describes how femininity and women's stereotypical roles as guardians of the family and of religion are put into the service of revolution, against the dictatorship and against patriarchy. Confessional diaries become means not only for personal therapy and self-surveillance but also for testimonies of injustice and suffering. The trappings of femininity like beautiful long hair are used to deliver secret messages to the outside world. Alvarez imagines resistance not only to the patriarchal power of the dictator but also to a more mundane patriarchal power that subordinates women in their everyday lives.

In the novel's postscript, Alvarez says that she presents neither the real Mirabal sisters of fact nor the Mirabal sisters of legend, but tries to demythologize their courage by describing ordinary people:

> What you find in these pages are not the Mirabal sisters of fact, or even the Mirabal sisters of legend. The actual sisters I never knew, nor did I have access to enough information or the talents and inclinations of a biographer to be able to adequately record them. As for the sisters of legend, wrapped in superlatives and ascended into myth, they were finally also inaccessible to me. I realized, too, that such deification was dangerous, the same god-making impulse that had created our tyrant. And ironically, by making them myth, we lost the Mirabals once more, dismissing the challenge of their courage as impossible for us, ordinary men and women. (324)

Alvarez presents the Mirabal sisters' genius as everyday genius. More than this, she presents their genius as female genius, the genius of penmanship, hair ribbons, feeding schedules, and girls' diaries. Alvarez's portrait of these heroines who gave their lives and their freedom for their beliefs paints a picture of ordinary women doing extraordinary things for themselves and their families. As her postscript suggests, like Kristeva and Howe, she believes that deifying or mystifying these women only takes away their genius by making it impossible for ordinary people. Moreover, she sees the deification of their genius as the same kind of operation that creates tyrants, superhuman men who maintain their control by evoking the fear of God.

By opening our imaginations to everyday genius, Alvarez and her own genius enrich our sense of possibility, agency, and empowerment. Alvarez's fiction is itself an example of the sublimation of affect into signification that not only sustains psychic life but also leads to creative genius. Her genius is her ability to use words to convey the complex emotions of women who are both oppressed and empowered by patriarchal restrictions that govern but never determine their everyday lives. Particularly in her historical novels, she moves beyond historical facts or accuracy to give us access to another level of truth, the truth of experience that can never be captured in facts or in history books. She believes that the life and truth of an epoch, especially the truth of affects and experience, cannot be told through history but can only be told through fiction: "For I wanted to immerse my readers in an epoch in the life of the Dominican Republic that I believe can only finally be understood by fiction, only finally be redeemed by the imagination. A novel is not, after all, a historical document, but a way to travel through the human heart" (324). Through her fiction, Alvarez not only shows us the affective dimension of experience, particularly women's experience, but also the semiotic dimension of language through which bodily experience can make its way into language, through which sublimation is possible. Perhaps the genius of her creative sublimation in her novels can also inspire us to create and articulate the affective level of our experiences; perhaps her courage in addressing the everyday conflicts, struggles, and resistance of women living with patriarchal values that abject and exclude them can encourage us to regain a sense of agency through mundane resistance.

The Real Revolution Can Be Won Only by the Imagination

In her latest novel, *In the Name of Salomé* (2000), Alvarez again imagines the world of everyday genius and how ordinary people are invested in, and rely on, the figure of genius in their midst. The novel alternates between the life of one of the Dominican Republic's most acclaimed nineteenth-century poets, Salomé Ureña, and the life of her daughter, Camille Henrîquez, a literature professor in New York. Salomé dies when Camille is only three years old, and throughout the novel Camille is searching for the remembrance of her mother. The novel makes it clear that Camille strongly identifies with her mother to the point of imaging that she is "somehow resurrecting her mother in her own flesh" (121), and yet she feels inadequate in the shadow of Salomé's greatness, and is the heir to maternal depression. Childless and unmarried, Camille wanders through the novel unable to sustain intimate attachments and mourning the loss of her mother. She feels guilty for her mother's death because, as the novel suggests, it is the pregnancy with Camille on top of tuberculosis that kills Salomé (325). Given Kristeva's theory of feminine depression, it could be said that Camille identifies with her dead mother, even the corpse of her mother; that is, she identifies with the abject mother. She is unable to separate herself from her mother and, as a little girl, imagines her mother lives inside her because she has her mother's name. She imagines that she is both Camille and Salomé: "Salomé Camilia, her mother's name and her name, always together! . . .' Here *we* are,' she [Camille] calls out" (331).

Unable to separate herself from her mother, Camille is guilt ridden and depressed. She cannot find the words with which to express the pain of her loss. Her identification with the lost mother results in the loss of herself. She desperately attempts to identify with her mother's creativity, with her poetry, and to become a poet herself, but she is inhibited by the maternal corpse/corpus that she has memorized and keeps locked up in the crypt of her psyche. While her brother Pedro can sublimate the loss of his mother into signification and like Salomé create through writing, Camille's creativity is stifled by cultural expectations for women, by the loss of her mother, and in particular by her brother's criticisms. While he has the social support necessary to find signifying practices through which to discharge maternal affect, she is expected to conform to the role circumscribed for her as a woman. Although Camille is a depressed character, her life is not without its own revolutions. She refuses to marry. She maintains a lifelong friendship with a lesbian lover, Marion. And she gives up her teaching position at Vassar to work for the revolution in Cuba. In her work toward literacy in Cuba, Camille realizes that "the real revolution could only be won by the imagination. When one of my newly literate students picked up a book and read with hungry pleasure, I knew we were one step closer to the patria we all wanted" (347).

For the women in Alvarez's novels, imaginary revolt operates as a counterweight to depression, in particular the depression that results from oppression. The opposition between depression and creativity is perhaps most apparent in Salomé. The everyday expectations of her as a wife and mother and her duties to her country as a woman take their toll. She gives up writing poetry for the sake of those duties, and the result is depression, disease, and ultimately death. With her poetry, she finds a way to sublimate her depression. As she repeats in the novel, "tears are the ink of the poet," and, rather than waste them by crying, she turns these painful affects into art. Through poetry she finds a means by which to discharge affects and sublimate bodily drives and sensations. Without that means, those affects, drives, and sensations become symptoms that manifest themselves in her body now unable to express itself. When she sacrifices her creative genius to take up roles traditionally assigned to women—wife and mother—she figuratively and literally suffocates.

As she does in *In the Time of the Butterflies*, Alvarez presents Salomé's genius as part of an ordinary life, more particularly a woman's life troubled by the restrictions of patriarchy. At several points in the novel, Salomé reflects on the irony of fighting for national liberation while she suffers the double standards and sexism of that nation: "Here she was—enslaved to her family's smallest demands and fighting for these larger freedoms" (151). She recognizes that "there was another revolution to be fought if our patria was to be truly free" (145), a domestic revolution to free women from patriarchal oppression, a revolution that Alvarez suggests can only be won by the imagination. Revolt against patriarchal institutions and values is one of imagination not only because it is necessary to change how we imagine ourselves as men and women but also because oppression takes its toll on the imagination and on the ability to imagine and create value and meaning in one's own life. Oppression colonizes psychic space and cuts off affects from words and thereby undermines the possibility of sublimation; this in turn leaves women feeling empty, depressed, and passive, without a sense of their own agency. In her novels, Alvarez not only describes this imaginary revolt in the lives and thoughts of her characters, but also through her own creativity as a novelist she opens up the possibility of imagining otherwise, of imagining strong women capable of agency and making meaning for their own lives, of imagining women engaged in intimate revolt.

In the Name of Salomé can be read as a lesson in the importance for psychic life of maintaining the space of creativity and sublimation. Without the intimate revolt provided by her poetry, Salomé suffers what her son calls "moral asphyxiation" (281). Although her husband, Pancho, falls in love with Salomé's poetry and image as the national poet, once they marry, Salomé's duties to him and his sense of her duties to the nation (which includes opening a school rather than writing poetry, particularly love poetry), and her duties to her children, overtake her passion for poetry. Her poetry is what keeps her alive, and when that is taken from her by the demands and expectations of patriarchal culture, she dies exhausted and depressed. Throughout the novel, poetry serves as an antidote to depression: "'Tears are the ink of the poet,' Papá had once said. But I was no longer writing, I could waste them now on my own sadness" (259). By sacrificing her voice for the sake of her family and her nation, in the end she sacrifices herself. Ultimately, the intimate revolt that sustains psychic life through creativity and imagination is an essential form of resistance against the colonization of psychic space that results in depression and psychic (if not physical) death. If depression is one symptom of the colonization of psychic space, a symptom with a female face, then resistance, particularly everyday revolt and female genius, is the prescription for psychic freedom.

Singularity and Individuality

What is at stake in both political struggles and revolts of imagination is renewing a sense of agency that allows each person to create meaning for themselves. We need robust psychic space to be creative, to revolt against an authority that demands that we conform. Belonging to culture, or creating meaning for oneself, is an ongoing process that is always relational, always tenuous, and always incomplete. In fact, there can be no singular individual or meaning for life and being without culture and language. The tension between the individual and the universal that is language and signification, and the revolt of the singular against the universal, makes belonging to the universal as singular possible, but always precarious. Kristeva (2002c, 408) describes the tension between singular and universal as "music composed of singularities, dissonant keys, and counter points that go beyond the fundamental tonalities." This conception of the relationship between the singular individual and the social is not the conception held by the philosophers of alienation discussed in chapter 1: the tension between singularity and society is not an opposition that leads to an abyss or fundamental alienation; rather, the movement between singularity and society is fluid and operates in an open system of exchange that makes possible belonging to the social as singular.

And, as Kristeva's musical metaphor suggests, these different and dissonant tones make up the composition that is our culture. Singularity is not individuality as it is normally conceived, as that which makes each person an autonomous subject. Rather, singularity radiates from the unconscious and creates what I call the *individual-effect*.[2] Singularity is the unique configuration of each individual's unconscious desires, wishes, pleasures, fears, repressions, anxieties. Strictly speaking, singularity is antithetical to signification and the social realm because as unconscious it remains inarticulate. It is the bodily drive force and its affective representations, which resist articulation, especially articulation conceived as representation. Singularity cannot be represented; it cannot be the referent of signification. Rather, like Kristeva's semiotic, it can only be transferred or translated into symbolic systems through the imaginary. The singularity of the unconscious is infinite, and its translation into finite forms of signification is never complete. This is why we keep speaking, singing, dancing, painting. This is why we keep trying to express ourselves, our singularity, using the only means available, the world of meaning into which we are born. This is how and why we communicate and commune. Singularity can only begin to be expressed or translated into the social through sublimation. But sublimation requires social support and social forgiveness.

Singularity cannot be reduced to individuality. *Singularity* connotes eccentricity, oddness, and strangeness along with uniqueness, whereas *individuality* is defined as indivisible, inseparable, self-same, and self-identical. If singularity is associated with the unique unconscious formation of each individual, it is indeed the eccentricity, oddness, and strangeness, even the uncanny, of unconscious desires and fears that are not in any way transparent to consciousness. The unconscious bodily drives or psychic energy is constantly dividing, moving, redirecting, and transforming itself; singularity, then, is the flip side—the unconscious—of the indivisible, self-same individual. Moreover, singularity interpreted as the strangeness of the unconscious as it haunts consciousness is the prerequisite for individuality. Our sense of ourselves as subjects and agents, that is, as individuals, comes through unconscious processes of sublimation and idealization.

While the individual is assumed to be autonomous and self-contained, singularity not only undermines our notion of the indivisible individual but also makes it possible. Individuality is an effect of singularity. The sense of ourselves as autonomous agents is formed through unconscious processes of transference between bodies and social codes that allow subjectivity to negotiate a relationship to meaning; this ongoing negotiation permits subjectivity to gain a sense of itself as a subject who means. Moreover, this negotiation, or revolt and assimilation, gives the subject a sense of itself as an agent and individual who belongs to the community. The unconscious processes of assimilating the authority of the social codes create the sense of individuality, which is always threatened by the singularity of the unconscious that produced it. In other words, individuality, autonomy, agency, and sovereignty are effects of unconscious processes that cannot be fixed or contained and yet create a sense of stability and unity in the subject, if always only temporarily.

Notions of the individual, individuality, and individualism that are familiar to us in American culture in particular cover over and erase the singularity that is their condition of possibility. The very definition of individualism suggests a defensive reaction to the fluidity and strangeness of the unconscious: the 1985 *Oxford English Dictionary* defines *individualism* as "the social theory which advocates the free and independent action of the individual. . . . The doctrine that the individual is a self-determined whole, and that any larger whole is merely an aggregate of individuals, which, if they act upon each other at all do so only externally." Psychoanalytic social theory, as I have considered it so far, could only interpret this view of individuals and their social relations as what Freud would call a reaction formation. A reaction formation is a defense against an unconscious threat or, in this case, the threat of the unconscious itself. This notion of individualism, presupposed by our legal and social institutions, is a defense against our profound and fundamental dependence on others, not only our physical dependence and our dependence on others for our sense of ourselves as subjects with agency but also our affective dependence on others; this notion of individuality covers over and denies the transmission of affect diagnosed by Fanon in the situation of colonization and oppression. Our effects on each other are not only "external" (physical, bodily, or social) but also profoundly "internal" (mental, affective, or psychic) insofar as they affect subjectivity itself. This notion of individualism covers over the fact that we are not primarily self-determined but determined by processes—both psychic and social—beyond our control, that our sovereignty and agency as individuals is always precarious because it is haunted by the unconscious processes that produce it. It erases the ways in which individuality is the effect of these unconscious processes. And without the acknowledgment of its founding possibility in unconscious processes, this notion of individualism becomes deadly and unforgiving.

Whereas individuality as it is conceived within Western democracies is built on the generalizable rights of individuals, singularity is not generalizable. The singularity that makes each individual unique is not and cannot be reduced to autonomy or indivisibility of the self, which is presupposed by our laws and social institutions.[3] Notions of individuality and individualism that equate individuals in the name of equality or equal rights cover over the singularity of each individual.[4] This is why the rhetoric of equality is so easily co-opted by repressive and conservative attempts to deny the singularity of experience, especially affective experiences of those othered and oppressed. Elsewhere I have argued that the rhetoric of equality and color blindness levels differences between the experiences of women and men of color in order to equate all individuals and foreclose what here I am calling the affects of oppression (see Oliver 2001).

Singularity is an antidote to the leveling and normalization inherent in discourses of equality. Kristeva (2002c, 400) suggests that the singularity of genius "keeps us from dying from equality in a world without a hereafter." This does not mean that we give up language or universal means of communication, nor does it mean that we deny equal rights to those to whom they have traditionally been denied. Rather, my analysis of singularity suggests that we need to question discourses of equality to guard against the ways in which they level differences, particularly the singularity of each individual. Genius is a reminder that we are not all the same. Even as it evokes the extraordinary within the ordinary, it does not level all experiences as the same.

Given this theory of sublimation and idealization, we must transfer singularity into social codes, realizing of course that this transfer is never complete. The psychoanalytic notions of sublimation and the unconscious allow us to renegotiate the relationship between the particular and the universal such that we are not left with a choice between leveling identity or alienating difference. Singularity and universality seem mutually exclusive only when we confuse singularity with individuality and forget that individuality, although crucial to our everyday lives, is no more than an effect of unconscious processes that involve sublimating the authority of culture to authorize the individual; singularity is another name for these unconscious processes. Kristeva forcefully describes this need for both universality and singularity in terms of the singular individual's relation to language:

> It is no longer a matter of conforming to the universal (in the best of cases, everyone aspiring to the same values, human rights, for example) or asserting one's difference (ethnic, religious, sexual) as untouchable and sacred; still less of fighting one of these tendencies with the other or simply and skillfully combining them. It is a matter of pushing the need for the universal and the need for similarity to the limit in each individual, making this simultaneous movement the source of both thought and language. "There is meaning": this will be universal. And "I" use the words of the tribe to inscribe my singularity *Je est un autre* ("I" is another): this will be my difference, and "I" will express my specificity by distorting the nevertheless necessary clichés of the codes of communication and by constantly deconstructing ideas/concepts/ideologies/philosophies that "I" have inherited. (432)

Singularity is the strangeness or uncanniness of the otherness within, that is, the unconscious. If I is/am another, it is because of the otherness of my unconscious, which is never truly mine even as it defines my singularity. The world of meaning into which one is born can express the specificity of the singular individual only through what I have described as social sublimation, the transfer of unconscious bodily drives and affects into signification such that they become meaningful for each as belonging, if always only provisionally. It is this social sublimation, not alienation, which turns the uncanny strangeness of the otherness within into signification. Singularity is the result of the sublimation of bodily drives and affects into signification through which the subject assimilates the authority of signification—social meaning or the universal—and thereby becomes a singular individual who belongs to the social. The assimilation of social codes and its requisite sublimation not only inaugurate subjectivity but also transform the social through the transgression or revolt necessary for assimilation and sublimation. It is not, however, the strangeness or otherness of the unconscious that is definitive of subjectivity but rather the translation of that otherness into signification. Subjects are beings who mean; and meaning requires the translation of bodily drives and affects into signification.

Kristeva's ordinary and monumental geniuses are so by virtue of renegotiating their singularity and the universal such that they can express themselves within the universal, even if that universal is one that excludes or abjects them. Their genius is finding ways to use and reinscribe available meanings not only to sublimate their affects but also to transform those available meanings and open up the social space for women's sublimation. The same would hold for other marginalized and abjected groups. As I show in the next chapter, this negotiation can take place only if the revolt, or "transgression," that is genius—that is, sublimation—presupposes forgiveness. Forgiveness opens up the possibility of negotiating between singularity and universality. Forgiveness is the counterweight to alienated individuals at odds with others.

CHAPTER 10

Forgiveness and Subjectivity

To forgive is as infinite as it is repetitive.
—Julia Kristeva, *Feminine Genius*

The philosophers of alienation propose that alienation is definitive of subjectivity because of the encounter with the hostile or inauthentic external Other, the other of Hegel's master-slave fight almost to the death or Sartre's accusing look. So far I have been developing an alternative to the notion that subjectivity is formed through such an encounter. I have argued that hostile and threatening encounters, especially in the forms of colonization and oppression, undermine subjectivity. Colonization and oppression operate by attacking subjectivity and agency, foreclosing the possibility of sublimation and idealization. It is not alienation and hostility that open up the possibility of sublimation and idealization necessary to enter the social and use language. Rather, it is forgiveness, a supportive, forgiving social agency—the agency of meaning or signification itself—that makes sublimation and idealization possible. It is not the judging Other of Freud's punishing superego, Sartre's look, or Lacan's gaze that inaugurates the entrance into and maintenance of the social; rather, it is the suspension of judgment or presupposition of forgiveness before judgment that instigates and sustains subjectivity.

Sublimation is possible only with social support that enables the assimilation of social codes into one's own vocabulary, so to speak. This assimilation requires a revolt against authority that allows the displacement of that authority. And this social authority authorizes the individual by virtue of its revolt. Without social support, however, this revolt and sublimation are forbidden. The revolt necessary for sublimation presupposes forgiveness and the suspension of judgment. Oppression and domination withhold social support for sublimation, on the one hand, and foreclose forgiveness for the revolt essential to singularity and thereby individuality, on the other. Through this double operation of withholding and foreclosing, oppression undermines subjectivity and agency. Instead of forgiveness, those othered face harsh judgment for their very existence, their very being. Becoming a being who means, becoming a singular individual, requires—presupposes—social forgiveness.

Hannah Arendt (1959, 213) predicts that "without being forgiven, released from the consequences of what we have done, our capacity to act would, [as it were,] be confined to one single deed from which we could never recover; we would remain the victims of its consequences forever, not unlike the sorcerer's apprentice who lacked the magic formula to break the spell." To conceive of forgiveness as a "magic formula to break the spell" requires thinking beyond our everyday conceptions of forgiveness and guilt. Philosophers of forgiveness, Hegel (on a perhaps eccentric reading), Arendt, and more recently Derrida and Kristeva, have in various ways made forgiveness a threshold of humanity: To be human is to forgive. If forgiveness is essential to human life, more specifically to human subjectivity and agency, then, conversely, the absence of forgiveness undermines humanity, subjectivity, and agency. Here, moving from Hegel's phenomenology of the role of forgiveness and confession in the dialectic of mutual recognition, through Kristeva's psychoanalytic notion of forgiveness as a support for sublimation and psychic life, to Derrida's hyperbolic ethics with its postulation of the impossibility of pure forgiveness, I develop a theory of forgiveness, not alienation, as the definitive feature of subjectivity and agency. In the end, I offer the forgiveness model of subjectivity as an alternative to the alienation model with which I began this book.

Rereading Hegel's account of forgiveness in *Phenomenology of Spirit* with and against Derrida and Kristeva gives us a sense of the role of forgiveness in constituting the subject as both individual and as belonging to the social. For all three theorists, forgiveness is a matter of negotiating between the singular (or, in Hegel's terms, particular) and the universal.

Going beyond Hegel's dialectical conception of individual and community, Derrida's analysis of forgiveness shows the importance of thinking forgiveness outside an economy of property and sovereignty. By supplementing both Hegelian and Derridean theory with a notion of the unconscious, however, only a psychoanalytic approach to the role of forgiveness in subjectivity allows us to imagine forgiveness without sovereignty and to imagine the possibility of negotiating between singularity and universality in a way that does not reduce one to the other. Using Kristeva's suggestions about the role of forgiveness in psychoanalysis, I postulate that the sublimation and revolt necessary to psychic life, or the singularity of subjectivity, presupposes forgiveness—not forgiveness from a sovereign agent who forgives but rather forgiveness as a social dynamic that enables and creates sovereignty, agency, and individuality. Still, some type of hyperbolic ethics is necessary to bring the psychoanalytic notion of forgiveness into social theory by insisting on ethical responsibility even for that over which we are not sovereign. And only a notion of the unconscious can make that responsibility radical enough such that we hold ourselves responsible not only for our actions and beliefs but also for our unconscious desires and fears. This responsibility entails an obligation to continually interpret our actions and their effects on others.

Particularity Requires Forgiveness: Hegel

Hegel's discussion of confession and forgiveness in *Phenomenology of Spirit* is a first step in understanding the relationship between subjectivity and forgiveness. For Hegel, forgiveness and confession are necessary for the constitution of the subject as an individual connected to the community. The dialectic of forgiveness and confession produces a subject who transgresses the community to become an individual and through that process realizes the necessity of belonging to the very community that it transgresses. For Hegel, consciousness becomes individuated—that is, we become subjects—through forgiveness and reconciliation, a reconciliation that Derrida rejects.

Hegel concludes the Spirit section of *Phenomenology of Spirit* with a discussion of forgiveness and confession that (again, temporarily) reconciles action and judgment, the particular and the universal, the unconscious and the conscious, which began in this section as the opposition between woman (Antigone) and man (Creon) that gave rise to the ethical order.[1] The reconciliation between action and judgment is initiated by the "confession" of the doer, or agent, who confesses to sharing with the judge the "evil" of their finitude, that is, of their subjective perspectives, and the limitation of their particularity. The agent realizes that the judge's attempt to pass judgment off as "the correct consciousness of the action" or the universal principle of action is just as much an action performed by a finite limited subject as the agent's own action (Hegel 1977, 405 §666). In a sense, the "evil" to which the agent confesses is merely that he and the judge both share mortality and finitude, that they are both fallible subjects, that ultimately they are both individuals. Hegel says that "no man is a hero to his valet; not, however, because the man is not a hero, but because the valet is a valet, whose dealings are with the man, not as a hero, but as one who eats, drinks, and wears clothes, in general, with his *individual* wants and fancies" (404 §665; my emphasis). The agent sees in the judge another individual who eats, drinks, wears clothes, and has particular wants and fancies. The judge or beautiful soul, on the other hand, will accept only duty for duty's sake, "pure" principle, and always finds in the agent's actions some aspect of the agent's particularity or desires that *contaminates* the action and renders it "evil" rather than pure: "No action can escape such judgment, for duty for duty's sake, this *pure* purpose, is an unreality; it becomes a reality in the deed of an individuality, and the action is thereby charged with the aspect of particularity. . . . Thus, for the judging consciousness, there is no action in which it could not oppose to the universal aspects of the action, the personal aspect of the *individuality*, and play the part of the moral valet towards the agent" (404 §665; my emphasis).

The agent's trespass is precisely his individuality with the particularity of action that it engenders.[2] In his confession the agent turns the tables and confesses that both he and the judge are individuals with particular desires; specifically, that they both have bodies with needs and wants that cannot be ignored or excluded from moral reasoning. Indeed, the agent's individuality in relation to the other and in relation to the universal is what makes responsibility and ultimately judgment itself thinkable. The judge cannot condemn the agent unless he can hold the agent responsible for the act. And the agent can be held responsible for the act only if he is an individual. The judge's judgment depends on that which he condemns as evil, individuality and its concomitant particularity. This is the contradiction that eventually leads the judge to forgive the agent's trespass, that is, the very seed of the agent's individual autonomy. Moral reasoning must be a negotiation between pure principles and the particulars of life.

Confession and forgiveness, then, turn on the mutual recognition of identity through limitation and difference.[3] The judge and agent recognize that what they share is precisely their individuality, that is, their difference.[4] Their individuality and concomitant particularity is what puts them at odds with one another, but it is also what brings them together and makes community possible. The universal, it turns out, is none other than this shared characteristic, individuality, which results from particularity, recognized in the Other. Reconciliation and mutual recognition result from an ongoing dialectic between belonging to the universal, or community, and asserting individuality by trespassing that universal. At this stage, the recognition that leads to reconciliation is a recognition of responsibility that comes with individuality and the indebtedness to the community that is painfully inherent in the trespass that inaugurates individuality.[5]

Hyperbolic Ethics of Forgiveness: Derrida

Derrida rejects Hegel's dialectic of mutual recognition and reconciliation because it assimilates difference and puts forgiveness into an economy of exchange. He takes issue with what he sees as Hegel's "logic of identification with the other that is assumed by the scene of forgiveness, on both sides, of the forgiver and forgiven, an identification that forgiveness assumes but which also compromises and neutralizes, cancels out in advance the truth of forgiveness as forgiveness from the other to the other as such" (2001b, 41). Yet, on my reading, Hegelian identification is precisely with the otherness of the other, with the other's difference. The identification comes with the realization of the particularity of individuals, a particularity so radical that it is only by virtue of the recognition of this universal property of individuality, of difference itself, that the judge and agent find any common ground. In one sense, Hegelian identification is already an identification with the impossibility of identification.

Against Hegelian reconciliation, in his latest published work on forgiveness, Derrida returns to Kantian regulative ideals and an insistence on the ideal of pure forgiveness. Derrida insists that *unlike* Kant, however, he does not think that duty for duty's sake is a pure motive. He objects to Kant's insistence that the moral law must be upheld out of duty, since that reduces it to paying a debt within the economy of exchange. But he embraces Kant's notion of a regulative ideal *outside duty*: "I should do what I have to do *beyond* duty. So I am ultra-Kantian. I am Kantian, but I am more than Kantian" (66; emphasis in the original). How is it then that Derrida's use of the Kantian notion of a regulative ideal does not bring to bear the now familiar criticisms of Kant's philosophy of the impossible?[6] An important difference between Derrida's postulation of a regulative ideal and Kant's is that for Kant the regulative ideal is related to a good and rational sovereign human will, while for Derrida the ideal of forgiveness must be without will and without sovereignty. It cannot be conceived by reason because it is not within rational calculation; indeed, it runs counter to reason. Yet it is not, like Kant's regulative moral ideal, in the end, accepted on faith. Derrida's regulative ideal is neither a matter of reason nor of faith, but beyond both. In a Kierkegaardian moment, he describes it as "a madness of the impossible" (2001a, 45; 1999, 7); if it is a matter of faith, it is the Kierkegaardian notion of faith as belief in the impossible. Whereas Kant's purpose in demanding purity is to establish the sovereignty of the will, Derrida's purpose in demanding purity is precisely to undercut the sovereignty of the will. For Derrida, presumptions about the sovereignty of the will continue to place forgiveness within an economy of exchange: For example, the idea that I can give forgiveness to another in exchange for reconciliation, the presupposition of truth and reconciliation committees that Derrida challenges. "Pure forgiveness," on the other hand, is beyond exchange.

In describing Hegelian forgiveness in terms of "the forgiver and forgiven"—terms that reappear in Derrida's own analysis—Derrida implicitly associates Hegelian forgiveness with will. However, for Hegel, it is the operation of the dialectic itself and not the individuals involved that forgives. Strictly speaking, the agency of forgiveness lies neither within the judge nor within the actor but rather within the dialectical movement between them. For Hegel, reconciliation is not so much a reconciliation of one party to the other, judge to agent, but rather, as always with Hegel, a reconciliation between universal and particular, between word and thing, between subject and object, between law and action, between language and affect, between meaning and being. For Hegel, the dialectical movement between universal and particular yields the individual, which is the reconciliation between what in Derridean terms can be called the unconditional and the conditional. As such, Hegel's notion of reconciliation is akin to Derrida's notion of decision, which is the result of the precarious and always tenuous reconciliation of the unconditional and the conditional.

Derrida maintains that the absolute unconditional pole of what he calls *pure* forgiveness is indissociable from the conditional pole of everyday forgiveness in all of its *contaminated* varieties:

> If our idea of forgiveness falls into ruin as soon as it is deprived of its pole of absolute reference, namely its unconditional purity [*sa pureté inconditionnelle*], it remains nonetheless inseparable from what is heterogeneous to it, namely the order of conditions, repentance, transformation, as many things as allow it to inscribe itself in history, law, politics, existence itself. These two poles, *the unconditional and the conditional*, are absolutely heterogeneous, and must remain irreducible to one another. They are nonetheless indissociable: if one wants, and it is necessary, forgiveness to become effective, concrete, historic; if one wants it to *arrive*, to happen by changing things, it is necessary that this purity

> engage itself in a series of conditions of all kinds (psycho-sociological, political, etc.). It is between these two poles, irreconcilable but indissociable, that decisions and responsibilities are to be taken. (2001a, 44–45; emphasis in the original)

The two poles, unconditional and conditional, cannot be reduced to one another, but neither can they be disassociated from each other. They determine decision and action, the two poles between which we live. What is decision then but a never-ending dialectical movement between the unconditional or universal and the conditional or particular that yields individual action? For Derrida, and on my reading for Hegel, these two poles are opposed to one another, and yet they are necessarily related; their reconciliation is not a reduction or conflation of one into the other but rather a tense and precarious intersection that threatens to derail itself at the next turn. As we know, however, Hegel is criticized for imagining an end to the process when the universal fully enters history, while Derrida insists that the universal, or unconditional—that is, pure—forgiveness cannot enter history but must endlessly serve as an ideal, impossible to realize.

The Hegelian and the Derridean notions of forgiveness need to be supplemented with a more robust account of the unconscious in order to move from the Hegelian notion of ethics in the service of law to a radically hyperbolic ethics. Only a notion of the unconscious can make us suspicious enough of the illusion that we have achieved our ideals or that the universal had been realized. The radical responsibility of a hyperbolic ethics that demands impossible ideals should also require that we account for the unconscious, especially if these impossible or *pure* concepts are always also and forever linked to the possible or to their so-called *contaminated* forms in everyday life. We are responsible not only for our actions and even beliefs but also for our fears and desires to which we have no direct access; we are responsible even for our ideals, including (or perhaps especially) the ideal of purity (as in pure forgiveness). And psychoanalysis provides a model with which to analyze and interrogate those ideals, fears, and desires.

Psychoanalytic Forgiveness: Kristeva

Turning to psychoanalytic theory, specifically Julia Kristeva's discussion of forgiveness, I develop a notion of forgiveness as the social support for subjectivity both in its singularity and in its relation to others. The agency of forgiveness enables us to become human beings and enter the world of meaning. On this model, we become agents, individuals, and "sovereigns-by-virtue-of-the-other," which are *effects* of forgiveness and not vice versa.

Restoring the victim's sovereignty effect is the consequence and not the prerequisite of forgiveness. The psychoanalytic model undoes our intuitive sense presumed by Derrida and perhaps by Hegel that forgiveness requires someone who forgives, a sovereign agent. Psychoanalytic forgiveness is a necessary condition for both agency and our sense of sovereignty and individuality.

To the Hegelian dialectic of confession and forgiveness, Kristeva adds the unconscious with its semiotic drive force. Still resonant with Hegel, mutual recognition becomes the recognition of otherness within the self, and reconciliation becomes the attempt to live with the otherness of the unconscious. Turning from Hegel to Kristeva leads from the intersubjective dialectic of mutual recognition to the agency of unconscious drive force working between two subjects-in-process. Language is still central, but while Hegel is concerned with bringing the concept in line with its articulation, with sense, Kristeva is concerned with bringing affects as representatives of unconscious drives into signification, that is, bringing the concept in line with non-sense. On the one hand, through these revisions of Hegel, Kristeva's psychoanalytic supplement can provide the basis for a theory of forgiveness that meets Derrida's demand for forgiveness without sovereignty. On the other hand, framed by Derrida's hyperbolic ethics, the psychoanalytic notion of forgiveness becomes ethical.

As in Hegel's *Phenomenology*, in psychoanalytic forgiveness what is confessed and forgiven is the agent's transgression of the social/universal inherent in asserting itself as a particular or singular subjectivity. Kristeva calls this necessary transgression an "intimate revolt," which is a form of continual questioning that enables, renews, and restructures both the singularity of the subjectivity and the social. Recall a passage quoted earlier where she says, "through a narrative of free association and in the regenerative revolt against the old law (familial taboos, [superego, ideals, oedipal or narcissistic limits] etc.) comes the singular autonomy of each, as well as a renewed link with the other" (2002b, 440). As I have shown earlier, questioning is a form of negativity or revolt that renews rather than destroys. We enter the social order as individuals through questioning; as children, we continually ask why. It is through the question that we fully enter the realm of meaning. Questioning transforms the negativity inherent in unconscious drives into the positive force of creativity. Maintaining a questioning attitude toward ourselves and our unconscious desires and fears is imperative for ethics, particularly for what Derrida calls hyperbolic ethics, with its radical responsibility.

Kristeva's revolt as questioning is akin to the Hegelian transgression inherent in becoming an individual with its concomitant particularity, a revolt or transgression that presupposes forgiveness. Forgiveness marks both the transgression against the social inherent in asserting oneself as a subject and the necessity of belonging to the social. For Hegel, transgression is linked to embodiment; for Kristeva, this embodiment is animated by unconscious drive force. The result of the addition of the unconscious to Hegel's dialectic of confession and forgiveness is an oscillation that brings the body back into the very logic and structure of the dialectic. Although for Hegel it seems that precisely what the agent confesses is that it has a body—eats, wears clothes, etc.—the role of that body in the dialectic of mutual recognition remains implicit. And for Derrida, it seems that within his analysis of forgiveness the body is the impossible real that pure forgiveness needs, but can never recover. For Kristeva, on the other hand, the body is the very location of what Hegel calls the dialectic of recognition, what in psychoanalytic terms becomes a dialectic of identification and differentiation. The semiotic element of language is associated with the rhythms and tones of the body that give signification its deeper meaning for our lives. Referential meaning, or sense, depends on this deeper meaning, or non-sense, to give life to language.[7] Just as Hegel's judge depends on bodily action, the symbolic as the position of judgment depends on bodily semiotic drive force.

Given its emphasis on unconscious drive force, however, psychoanalytic "confession" is not exactly an intersubjective enterprise. That is, the motor that drives forgiveness and recognition is neither intersubjective nor conscious. Rather, the action takes place on the level of unconscious semiotic energy, as it makes its way into language. Although language (or more broadly speaking, signification) is still the vehicle through which confession and forgiveness take place, the agent of forgiveness is unconscious. This secular form of forgiveness takes place between bodies for whom "communication" is a form of transference or a transfer of affects rather than a symbolic operation. Kristeva insists that the way in which interpretation, specifically analytic interpretation, gives meaning as a form of pardon (*par-don*, through-gift) "has nothing to do with 'explication' and 'communication' between two consciousnesses. On the contrary, this par-don draws its efficacy from reuniting with affect through metaphorical and metonymical rifts in discourse" (2002b, 26). Unlike Hegelian forgiveness, psychoanalytic forgiveness, because it takes place on the level of the semiotic, is not the result of intersubjectivity or mutual recognition. And although forgiveness supports subjectivity, insofar as it is not the act of a subject or even intersubjectivity, it is not the result of a sovereign will. Psychoanalytic forgiveness is forgiveness without sovereignty, forgiveness beyond recognition.

Forgiveness enables revolt by supporting the transfer of affects and drives—the unconscious—into signification. This transfer takes place in between two bodies engaging in communication, in the broadest sense of the term. So, although forgiveness is not the product of intersubjectivity or of one consciousness forgiving the other, it is dialogic in the sense that it happens between two communicating bodies, two bodies mediated by meaning, or what in psychoanalytic discourse we have come to call the third. The agency of forgiveness is the operation of this third that should not be attributed to either one party or the other. Rather, the agency of forgiveness is the effect of meaning as it is lived between people. The dialectical movement between semiotic force and symbolic structure is a dialectical movement between the body and language or law that both produces and presupposes forgiveness. To return to Arendt's metaphor, we are all like the sorcerer's apprentice who lacks the magic spell because the forgiveness constitutive of subjectivity is without sovereign; there is no sorcerer who can bestow or grant forgiveness. Rather, meaning, or what takes place between us, is the magic formula, so to speak, that makes forgiveness possible.

As the agency of the meaningful relation between two bodies, transference itself gives pardon; it is not given by one subject or the other. As the unconscious makes its way into signification through the semiotic dimension, the possibility of forgiveness emerges from meaningful response. The meaninglessness of life, more specifically the meaninglessness of trauma, is thereby forgiven by becoming meaningful. In this sense, the transference that facilitates forgiveness is the transference of unconscious drive force into language and conversely the transference of meaning into/onto the body with its experience.[8] Kristeva describes forgiveness as the "coming of the unconscious to consciousness in transference" (19).

But this transference is bodily and not intellectual. The type of meaning given in for-giveness is beyond or before intellection, understanding, or judgment. The suspension of judgment required for forgiveness, that is, the suspension of the superego, opens onto semiotic drive energy. This suspension of the harsh, judging superego enables the unconscious to make its way into language so that sublimation is possible. Sublimation is the movement of semiotic drive force into signification, affect into law, by virtue of the imagination, which is necessary for revolt, the life force of the psyche. Kristeva describes the intimate connection between sublimation and imagination in terms of the ability to speak our aggressive desires through social codes rather than acting on them; speaking these violent desires, however, presupposes forgiveness. Just as Hegel's dialectic of confession and forgiveness takes us beyond the struggle to the death in the lord and bondsman stage of self-consciousness, forgiveness in psychoanalysis forges a "third way between dejection and murder" (Kristeva 1989, 199). Forgiveness makes it possible to become a subject without murdering the other or dejecting or abjecting oneself. Through forgiveness, we sublimate our murderous and suicidal tendencies. At the extreme, rather than kill we confess our desire to kill; and this confession requires, that is, presupposes, forgiveness.

Sublimation requires not only social acceptance and support but also social forgiveness. Subjectivity necessitates the sublimation of particular bodily needs and affects into social codes. This sublimation is at once a trespass against those codes and an assimilation of them. Subjectivity requires trespassing social codes to assert one's singularity, which is itself the particular unconscious formation that makes each subject a unique being who means. Forgiveness allows the subject to trespass the social order and yet be accepted back into that order as one who belongs.

Sublimation allows the signification of the trauma of separation from the social required for subjectivity, required to become a being who means. And through this articulation of the affect of transgression, the individual speaks to and through the social as one who belongs. In other words, subjectivity, driven by affective unconscious impulses, necessarily transgresses the social and linguistic codes and then sublimates that transgression by resignifying it within those very social and linguistic codes now modified to incorporate the subject's singularity. This is the process of becoming a subjectivity who belongs to the social. Subjectivity depends on others to support its ability to transgress those very others to become an individual by virtue of singular unconscious processes of negation and displacement, sublimation and idealization. These processes presuppose forgiveness, or the subject could never carry out the primal transgression against those on whom it depends for its life in every sense.[9] Or, as Hannah Arendt suggests, this one act would be the last because without forgiveness the agent would never recover from the wound of separation. By releasing the trauma of separation from the social order back into the social order through the agency of our meaningful relations with others and with meaning itself, we can be sure that we belong to that order. As Kristeva (1989, 216) says, "It is possible to forgive ourselves by releasing, thanks to someone who hears us, our lack or our wound to an ideal order to which we are sure we belong—and we are now protected against depression."

What makes us human is not the split between being and meaning that alienates us from ourselves, but rather the forgiveness that makes it possible to transcend alienation, if always only temporarily, through creative sublimation in language or signification. We become heroes *precisely because* we eat, drink, and wear clothes with our own particular wants and fancies. We translate our own particularity/singularity, our finitude and limitation, our own unconscious desires and fears, into the universal, into language, and thereby unite being and meaning; we become beings who mean. Forgiveness becomes the acknowledgment that being is thinking (cf. Hinchman 1984, 183).

With psychoanalytic forgiveness, this reconciliation between being and thinking is an acknowledgment of otherness within the self, the unconscious within the subject, or drives and affects within language. This reconciliation is one that unsettles rather than unifies. It is based on unceasing questioning, questioning as trespass, which presupposes forgiveness. But this forgiveness does not erase or absolve otherness or transgression but rather brings us face-to-face with it by acknowledging that although we would rather exclude otherness, we owe our very existence to it. We owe our existence to the Other that is language or meaning through which we become beings who mean, and we owe our existence to the others who shepherd us into the realm of meaning. Psychoanalytic reconciliation is not the reconciliation of truth and reconciliation committees that might have us forget the past for the sake of unity. Rather, community—inherently tenuous, precarious, and suspect—is possible only by vigilantly and continually acknowledging otherness and negativity within.

It is this type of vigilance that motivates Derrida's insistence on pure forgiveness without which we risk falling into an "ecology of memory" that either forgets or, what amounts to the same thing, remembers only what is convenient (2001b, 41; 2001a, 32). And although Derrida argues that forgiveness is antithetical not only to reconciliation and to law and justice but also to psychoanalysis, he imagines what he calls therapy only as a form of forgetting the other (2001b, 41, 57; 2001a, 32, 41, 50). He maintains that when forgiveness becomes a means of working through, mourning, or sublimation, then it is no longer pure forgiveness but rather a form of forgetting that transforms the crime and criminal into something else.[10]

As I have described it, however, psychoanalytic forgiveness is a process of questioning to open onto otherness, a process that perhaps even Derrida would recognize as a type of reconciliation-otherwise. He says, "If by reconciliation . . . I refer to something which has no identification, no recovery, no therapy, as simply a certain relation to the other as such, then I say yes, that is what I have in mind by forgiveness. But that is not what one usually has in mind when one speaks of reconciliation, not only in Hegel but in others who speak of reconciliation, for whom reconciliation implies community, education, complicity, and so on" (2001b, 57). Reconciliation-otherwise would be an encounter with the other rather than an assimiliation. This forgiveness as encounter with otherness requires infinite questioning.

Concluding by bringing Derrida and Kristeva together on forgiveness may seem like a strange move, given that Kristeva insists that forgiveness cannot operate in the social realm but only between individuals, and Derrida is concerned with how the discourse of forgiveness has made its way into politics. Kristeva sees no role for forgiveness in politics, while Derrida analyzes the role of forgiveness in truth and reconciliation committees and other testimonies to "unforgivable" crimes such as the Holocaust and Apartheid. Yet they share the concern with how forgiveness can possibly be translated from what could be called the ethical realm—the realm of personal relationships—to the political realm. Although Derrida considers this translation in ways that Kristeva won't, he concludes that forgiveness is always corrupted by these translations into the realm of politics. For Derrida, forgiveness is always contaminated as it is "practiced" in any realm because it can never live up to the ideal of pure forgiveness—it is always contaminated by the economy of exchange.

The psychoanalytic social theory of forgiveness that I have been developing here proposes that the inauguration and sustenance of subjectivity depends on finding a forgiving, nonjudgmental social space or meaning. The ability to transgress or revolt presupposes this forgiveness. Restoring the ability to sublimate, idealize, and revolt to oppressed people to whom social forgiveness has been foreclosed requires the construction or reconstruction of a nonjudgmental social space or meaning. Forgiveness, then, is not about forgiving the perpetrator of some crime but about forgiving the transgression that is singularity and individuality. When talking about oppressed people or the victims of unforgivable crimes, forgiveness is not a matter of forgiving the perpetrators but rather of reestablishing the capacity for forgiveness within the victims. Forgiveness is not about the colonizers, the oppressors, the dominant groups, or heirs to power; rather, it is about restoring that definitive feature of subjectivity—forgiveness—to the victims.

Derrida's analysis is primarily concerned with the question of how we can forgive the unforgivable and what it would mean to forgive the perpetrators of such crimes. I would say that psychoanalytic social forgiveness, on the other hand, is not about forgiving the perpetrator—except insofar as we come to analysis feeling guilty—but about restoring the capacity for forgiveness in the victim. There is one concluding passage in "On Forgiveness," however, in which Derrida imagines how absolute victimization undermines the capacity for forgiveness and that what is at stake therefore is restoring the victim's sense of subjectivity and agency:

> It is also necessary to think about an absolute victimization which deprives the victim of life, or the right to speak, or that freedom, that force and that power which authorizes, which permits the accession to the position of "I forgive." There, the unforgivable would consist of depriving the victim of this right to speech, of speech itself, of the possibility of all manifestation, of all testimony. The victim would be then a victim, in addition, of seeing himself stripped of the minimal, elementary possibility of virtually considering forgiving the unforgivable. This absolute crime does not only occur in the form of murder. (2001a, 59)

Derrida's conception of deauthorization can be extended to describe the essence of victimization as it works in oppression. While not all victims are oppressed, I would argue that what Derrida calls absolute victimization as crime against humanity is victimization as part of a system of oppression directed toward a particular group of people. Only when victimization attempts to annihilate the subjectivity of a people or race is there absolute victimization in the sense of annihilating the position of the "I" forgive. Oppression, colonization, genocide, domination in various ways deauthorize the subjectivity of the victim by attacking the structure of subjectivity that makes it possible both to take the position of *I* (with what I have been calling its sovereignty effect) and to act as an agent. To begin to imagine forgiving the unforgivable requires the restoration of the oppressed person's agency and ability to take the position of "I forgive." As an attack against the very subjectivity of the subject, oppression is an attack against the very humanity of "man." Reestablishing the possibility of forgiveness is the only way to restore subjectivity and humanity to both the victim of oppression and the perpetrator.

The question, then, is not Derrida's question, whether we can forgive crimes against humanity, or unforgivable crimes, but rather how we can reopen the space of forgiveness for the victims of oppression, domination, torture, and genocide, and thereby reopen the space of forgiveness for humanity. Only then can we talk about forgiving the perpetrators of crimes against humanity. The connection between subjectivity and forgiveness runs deeper than Derrida's analysis suggests. It is not just that absolute victimization takes away the position of the *I* such that any statement of the kind "I forgive" is impossible; but, more significant, as my analysis of psychoanalytic forgiveness suggests, forgiveness is inherent in the constitution and maintenance of subjectivity and agency. This analysis has been an attempt to rethink the relation between subjectivity and forgiveness, and thereby open up a way to conceive of humanity without sovereignty, humanity without humanism.

This interpretation of forgiveness, however, also requires moving away from Kristeva's discussion of the role of forgiveness within the analytic session. This is why in my analysis of Kristeva's notion of forgiveness, I continually push it out of the analytic session and toward a social theory of the constitution of subjectivity. As I have shown, we can extrapolate Kristeva's theory of the operation of forgiveness in the analytic session to the social constitution of subjectivity itself. Just as the analysand requires that the analyst suspend judgment and provide a safe social space within which the analysand can articulate and discharge its affects, any subjectivity requires a safe social space and the suspension of judgment that is forgiveness. If the agency of forgiveness within the analytic session can be interpreted as transference itself, then the agency of social forgiveness can be interpreted as meaning itself. Moving away from Kristeva, I develop a psychoanalytic social theory of forgiveness that can help explain the dynamics of oppression as the foreclosure of this safe, forgiving social space within which those othered can sublimate their affects, especially the negative affects of oppression.

The psychoanalytic theory of forgiveness adds the unconscious to Derrida's discussion of social or political forgiveness. Without postulating the unconscious, we can never move away from the economy of sovereignty and property that contain forgiveness within an economy of exchange. But, without extrapolating from the interpersonal relationship within the analytic session to the social realm, we are left with a theory of forgiveness that can never be part of a social theory—ethical or political. Here, Derrida's notion of hyperbolic ethics can transform psychoanalytic social forgiveness into an ethics of forgiveness. Following Emmanuel Levinas, Derrida proposes a hyperbolic ethics to insist on its urgency and the necessity for constant vigilance. Its imperatives and responsibilities are hyperbolic because they demand the impossible, that we are hyperaware of how our actions and decisions fall short of our ideals. Like the infinite curve of a hyperbola, we can only continue to approach the asymptote that is our ideal. Moreover, we must be hyperaware of how our ideals themselves exclude others, even others whom we may not recognize.

The ethical imperatives of the ethics of forgiveness do not come from reason or external law but rather from the constitution of subjectivity itself and our obligation to that by virtue of which we are subjects, agents, and individuals who belong to the community. Ethical obligation is inherent in subjectivity insofar as the subject is by virtue of others to whom it is indebted for its agency, individuality, and sovereignty. These very traits—agency, individuality, and sovereignty—can lead to a defensive forgetting of that ethical obligation when they are cut off from their source in unconscious bodily drive force and affect. When the subject protects its individuality at the expense of its singularity and that of others, when it pits its individuality against that of others, when it asserts that its right to exist depends on denying that right to others, then it has forgotten its obligation to its founding possibility and its indebtedness to those others. Echoing Simone de Beauvoir, not one is free until all are free.[11]

Conclusion

Ethics of Psychoanalysis; or, Forgiveness as an Alternative to Alienation

It is telling that Frantz Fanon (1968a, 41) describes a "craving for forgiveness" among colonized peoples, a craving satisfied only by a "state of grace" when they rediscover the value in themselves and their culture. Exclusion from the realm of meaning as those incapable of making meaning, as those who do not belong, produces shame and alienation even more painful and treacherous than that imagined by the philosophers of alienation as inherent in becoming a being who means. Those excluded are made ashamed for what is deemed their abject difference; and their "evil" cannot be forgiven because it supposedly contaminates the purity of humanity. Their exclusion denies the forgiveness that should enable the individual to rejoin the social as one who belongs even after the trespass through which it asserts its singular individuality. But, in a racist or sexist society, if part of one's singular individuality is to be a man of color or a woman, this becomes a "trespass" that is not forgiven. And the absence of forgiveness becomes a kind of self-fulfilling prophecy whereby those othered and dispossessed by the social order are affected at the level of subjectivity such that sublimation becomes doubly difficult and meaning—not just referential meaning but, more important, the meaning of life—is abjected. Escaping this void requires trespass that transforms the very law that it breaks, revolt that opens the law onto otherness and transforms it from cruel superego into forgiveness, which in turn enables the transformation of shame into agency.

Forgiveness supports questioning the authority of our communities even as it enables their existence. The absence of forgiveness, on the other hand, undermines the possibility of both a sense of individuality and a sense of community. Exclusion and oppression turn on foreclosing the agency of forgiveness and making the judging superego absolute to the point of cruelty. Those excluded individuals or groups are subject to harsh judgment without the possibility of forgiveness. They are excised by law that claims an absolute authority without appeal, an authority that these individuals and groups are not allowed to assimilate or sublimate through revolt. Without the presupposition of forgiveness, revolt against this authority becomes a mammoth undertaking difficult to imagine.

Rather than forgive and support the transgression or revolt essential to subjectivity and psychic life, those excluded through oppression are punished for their attempts to individuate by assimilating the authority of the social. Whereas the heirs to law and authority are allowed to revolt and assimilate the power of the law because their forgiveness is presupposed, those othered by the law are excluded by the foreclosure of revolt and forgiveness. Subjectivity requires revolt and transgression to become a singular individual, but it also presupposes forgiveness to belong to the social. Rather than lead to sublimation, creativity, and belonging, the revolt of those excluded from the dominant values and social insitutions—if they pull it off—is seen as uppityness, perversion, or terrorism.

For example, throughout the first half of the twentieth century, blacks who occupied or tried to occupy positions traditionally held by whites were considered "uppity" at best (and aberrations of nature at worst) by racist ideologies. Feminist studies in linguistics have demonstrated that the same language used by men and women is interpreted differently: men who assert themselves and their authority are seen as strong and articulate, while women who do the same are seen as out of line or worse as screaming "bitches" (see Cameron 1985, 1992; Lakoff 1975). Even today, homosexuality and bisexuality are still considered perversions by various social institutions, including law, and much of mainstream culture. Only since 2003 has the Supreme Court finally recognized that gay people have the right to privacy, and their right to marry is still considered a heresy against the supposed sancitity of marriage by most lawmakers. And the rhetoric of terrorism can be used to describe anyone engaging in resistance to dominant ideology; for example, "ecoterrorism," "virtual terrorism," "economic terrorism." Moreover, the covert killing practices of the

West are rationalized as necessary to protect freedom, while the same kinds of practices by our "enemies" are considered terrorism and barbarism. The United States can colonize Iraq, kill thousands of people, destroy their cities, in the name of freedom, or, worse, in the name of justice as vengeance against the perpetrators of September 11. When the United States destroys buildings and kills people it is called "freedom fighting," but when our "enemies" do the same it is called "evil."

Fanon's (1965, 24) insight regarding this differential in the context of the Algerian occupation couldn't be more relevant today: "The European nation that practices torture is a blighted nation, unfaithful to its history. The underdeveloped nation that practices torture thereby confirms its nature, plays the role of an underdeveloped people. If it does not wish to be morally condemned by the 'Western nations,' an underdeveloped nation is obligated to practice fair play, even while its adversary ventures, with a clear conscience, into the unlimited exploration of new means of terror." The same is true for those oppressed within Western cultures and those exploited and oppressed by Western cultures: they must "practice fair play," wherein "fair play" is determined by the dominant group, government, or culture; if they don't, then they confirm their "nature" as cheaters and criminals or, worse, terrorists and monsters. Their revolt is not forgiven. Rather, the social support necessary for revolt is withheld, which necessarily leads to the affects of oppression, depression, shame, or anger—sometimes an anger that expresses itself as violence to be heard, if not also recognized as a form of resistance to domination. This withholding, or foreclosure, is an essential part of domination and oppression, which operate through the colonization of psychic space precisely by denying the possibility of sublimation, revolt, and forgiveness. Even as forgiveness supports the trespass that is singularity, it also enables sublimation of violent impulses and thereby prevents more deadly trespass.

In sum, forgiveness and acceptance, not alienation, define the human condition and subjectivity. We do not become beings who mean by virtue of alienation from being but rather by virtue of continually overcoming that alienation through signification. Through the sublimation of bodily drives and affects into signification, we regain, if only provisionally, our being as animals, that which we supposedly lose and mourn to become human. Signification and meaning become a way of working through that mourning. It is not, however, the mourning but the process of working through the mourning that makes us human. Alienation and melancholy are not definitive of subjectivity; rather, they undermine the very conditions of possibility of subjectivity and agency. The conditions of possibility of subjectivity and agency are social acceptance and forgiveness, not alienation from the social. Becoming a singular individual is not determined by alienation from the social. Rather, the trespass or revolt against the social necessary to assert one's singular individuality ends in alienation only when that individual's singularity has been erased in favor of some group characteristic that is used to justify the individual's exclusion from the social realm. When the trespass or revolt necessary to assert singularity and authorize individuality is forgiven, then the result is not alienation but a sense of belonging and an affirmation of agency, which are as essential to psychic life as they are part of the precarious and continuous process of becoming subjectivity.

Within the framework of psychoanalytic social forgiveness, however, the subject and the humanity at stake are not the same subject and humanity marinated in the economy of property presupposed by some of the philosophers of alienation. Rather, the subject is beyond the economy of property that makes subjects opposed to their objects, which can be owned and exploited; and humanity is beyond the economy of property that makes human beings sovereign over all other beings, which can be owned and exploited. The psychoanalytic notions of the unconscious—melancholy, sublimation, and idealization—can be transformed into social concepts that uncouple the subject and the human from sovereignty and thereby begin to move us outside the economy of property and ownership that ultimately justifies colonization, exploitation, slavery, and domination. By engaging the unconscious as that element of our psychic life that is outside time, linear logic, rationalization, and consciousness, we begin to conceive of forgiveness outside the economy of ownership and propriety. Only then can morality and moralizing give way to ethics.

Morality works through an economy of propriety and ideals of the good that are necessarily exclusionary insofar as they work by virtue of oppositions that divide people and actions into proper/improper, pure/contaminated, good/evil. Colonization and oppression operate through the imposition of these values on others until those others become "infected" with the dominant values, values that mark them as contaminated and evil. The colonization of psychic space is the result of this infection, an infection that leads to alienation, shame, and melancholy. Colonization and oppression justify themselves using morality, morality that covers over the fundamentally ethical structure of subjectivity. The privileged subject disavows the fact that it depends on others for its privileged sense of itself as a subject; it disavows the fact that its own subjectivity is necessarily a response to others and to the Other that is meaning into which it is born. Rather than acknowledge its primary and fundamental indebtedness to others and meaning, the subject enslaves and oppresses those others and uses the realm of meaning through rationalizations to justify itself.

Ethics as conceived here, unlike morality, is not a set of codes that divide people into good and evil, dominant and subordinate. Ethics is the acknowledgment that we are by virtue of response from others and by virtue of response from meaning through which we become beings who mean. Subjectivity, then, is inherently ethical. We are subjects or subjectivity only through our relations with others, and ultimately with otherness. But we can articulate an ethics and a politics of otherness or difference only by accounting for the unconscious. To make responsibility radical enough, that is, ethical enough, we need a notion of the unconscious, which makes us responsible even for motives, desires, and fears unknown to us. The fundamental imperative of hyperbolic ethics is that we should never be content with ourselves. It is an imperative to be self-critical, especially with our responses to others, most especially because there are those others whom we may not even recognize. We can never stop interrogating and interpreting our notions of justice, democracy, and freedom, which means that we can never stop asking ourselves why we do what we do, why we value what we value, why we desire what we desire, and why we fear what we fear. Yet, without engaging the unconscious, our self-interrogation and self-interpretations will never be vigilant enough. Only by postulating the existence of the unconscious as that which resists consciousness and rational thought will we be humble enough to continue to question our own motives, fears, and desires.

Only the notion of the unconscious gives us an ethics of responsibility without sovereignty. We are responsible for what we cannot and do not control, for our unconscious fears and desires and their affective representations. In addition, we are responsible for the effects of those fears, desires, and affects on others. As Levinas says, we are responsible for the other's response. This infinite responsibility entails the imperative to question ourselves and constantly engage in self-critical hermeneutics. It is this critical interpretation that also gives meaning to our lives and allows for the sublimation of bodily drives and affects.

Responsible ethics and politics requires that we account for the unconscious. Without doing so, we risk self-righteously adhering to deadly principles in the name of freedom and justice, which can then become the justification for war, imprisonment, and imperialism—all in the name of freedom and justice. Without interrogating our motives—conscious and unconscious—we risk making justice, democracy, and freedom into empty but dangerous clichés that we use to justify killing. We risk taking the defensive posture of individualism that protects itself by attacking others, becoming absolutely unforgiving. We risk denying the fundamental ethical relationality that is subjectivity. We risk a defensive, unforgiving posture that denies, even fears, singularity, the singularity that is the unconscious, a posture that maintains control by denying the existence of the unconscious or unconscious motives, desires, and fears. Yet only by acknowledging our unconscious fears, phobias, and desires can we hope to be self-reflective enough to contemplate an ethical response to others. And that reflection and acknowledgment presupposes forgiveness, that we will be forgiven for articulating, interrogating, and interpreting our own death drive and its concomitant phobias and desires. Perhaps by continually acknowledging the death drive within ourselves and being forgiven, we can begin to prevent killing and find an alternative to either murder or suicide. Only then can we begin to imagine forgiveness transforming alienation into a way of belonging to the social as singular.

Notes

Introduction

Freud and Freudian psychoanalysis has influenced so much work in so many disciplines that it would be impossible to fully situate my project within these ongoing debates and discourses. So, for the sake of this introduction, I can only sketch the scene on which I hope to intervene and give the reader a sense of what my project contributes to psychoanalytic theory, social theory, and the emerging field of psychoanalytic social theory.

1. Most of the essays in Christopher Lane's 1998 collection *The Psychoanalysis of Race* are good examples of insightful applications of psychoanalytic concepts that for the most part either leave those concepts intact or criticize them without developing new concepts.

2. For example, Anne Anlin Cheng in *The Melancholy of Race* (2001) uses Freud's theory of melancholy to diagnose Asian Americans' relations to American culture by interpreting and applying the concept of melancholy to various literary and artistic productions. David Eng and Shinhee Han combine Freud's theory of melancholia with Melanie Klein's theory of good and bad objects to diagnose the depressive position of Asian Americans within American culture. Eng and Han (2000, 667) argue that "processes of immigration, assimilation, and racialization are neither pathological nor permanent, but involve the fluid negotiation between mourning and melancholia." So, while they critically employ and combine psychoanalytic concepts in creative ways, for the most part they accept those concepts wholesale. Judith Butler (1991, 1993, 1997) also uses the concept of melancholy in a similar way when she argues that the separation between mourning and melancholy is not as clear-cut as Freud makes it out in order to diagnose the melancholy of homosexual desire. She also uses Julia Kristeva's notion of abjection in her discussion of lesbian desire in *Gender Trouble* (1991). And although Butler employs these concepts with imagination and to ends significantly different than either Freud's or Kristeva's, she does not so much revise the concepts as use them. Like Butler, and also Elizabeth Grosz, Teresa de Lauretis critically deploys Freud's notions of disavowal and castration to theorize lesbian desire. All three theorists present

novel theories of lesbian desire, but for the most part they do so by taking on Freud's (and Lacan's) concepts and showing how these concepts do or do not apply to what they are developing as lesbian desire or, in Butler's case, as the lesbian phallus (Butler 1993; Grosz 1995; de Lauretis 1994). In one sense, their theories are original in that they take Freudian and Lacanian concepts to their logical limits, but that leaves those psychoanalytic concepts intact.

Many cultural critics and feminists have used Lacanian psychoanalytic theory to analyze the gaze and desire. For example, Kalpana Seshadri-Crooks (2000) brilliantly argues that whiteness operates like the Lacanian phallus as an ideal against which we all fall short. Although she substitutes the concept of whiteness for the Lacanian phallus, she is still working squarely within the Lacanian framework and applying Lacanian concepts to literature and film. Rey Chow (e.g., 1998) provocatively uses Lacanian concepts to analyze various kinds of cultural productions; but once again she applies the concepts rather than transforms them. Of course, Laura Mulvey (1975) is famous for her use of Lacan's concept of the gaze when she argues that the cinematic gaze is male. Mulvey also uses Freud's notion of the Oedipal complex in her latest work (1996), but she takes on these concepts rather than transform them. Homi K. Bhabha (1994) uses Lacanian concepts to analyze race and desire, but again he does not transform those concepts by so doing. Of course, there are many more cultural theorists who employ concepts from psychoanalytic theory to diagnose and analyze cultural productions and institutions. Still, most of these theorists use psychoanalytic concepts critically, rather than turn psychoanalytic theory into social theory. One of the most successful attempts to use Lacanian psychoanalytic theory to develop a social theory is Teresa Brennan's *History after Lacan* (1993), wherein she provocatively diagnoses modern culture in terms of the time of the psyche. And Drucilla Cornell's (1995, 1998) introduction of what she calls "the imaginary domain" into legal and social theory is one of the singular most important recent contributions to developing a psychoanalytic social theory.

3. The Frankfurt school philosophers are well known for their attempts to meld Freud's theory of the individual with Marx's theory of political economy. But most of these theorists, and their contemporary followers (e.g., Jürgen Habermas and Alex Honneth), begin with psychoanalytic notions based on individuals and either extrapolate to the social or argue that the social and the psychic realms are analogous, even related, but essentially in conflict. While the Frankfurt school attempted to extrapolate some psychoanalytic concepts to the social (particularly, Herbert Marcuse, who used Freud's notions of repression and sublimation to critically diagnose capitalism), contemporary critical theorists following Habermas are more likely to see psychoanalysis and social theory as analogous but distinct; for example, Honneth (1991, 239) sums up the relation within Habermasian theory as one of analogy: "Just as psychoanalysis analyzes the individual process of will-formation from the perspective of an emancipatory cognitive interest in order to free a subject from the force of unrecognized constraints upon action, so a critical social theory correspondingly analyzes the process of species will-formation in order to free it from the force of uncomprehended dependencies."

Rather than turn to Marx for social theory, many post-structuralist theorists turn to Foucault. Perhaps Butler and de Lauretis come closest to transforming psychoanalytic theory in their attempts to merge Freudian psychoanalytic theory and Foucauldian social theory. Making Freud and Foucault work together does not, however, result in a psychoanalytic social theory in which the very concepts of psychoanalysis are transformed into social concepts. Like the attempts to mix Marx and Freud, the attempts to mix Foucault and Freud do not alter the basic ingredients. For examples of theorists who use Freud together with Foucault, see Butler (1997), de Lauretis (1998), Shepherdson (1995), Restuccia (2000), Lane (2000), and Trigo (2002).

4. Even as theorists like Butler and de Lauretis stretch the meanings of psychoanalytic terms to construct productive theories of lesbian desire or homosexual melancholy, those terms still operate within a discourse that takes over traditional psychoanalytic notions of the individual at odds with the social; like traditional psychoanalysis, the focus is often on the psyche rather than on the social. Even when Butler and de Lauretis focus on the social conditions that produce the psyche, they often fall back into some version of a family romance, even if it is a negative version, à la de Lauretis.

5. For example, this is true of Nancy Chodorow's early work in *The Reproduction of Mothering: Psychoanalysis and the Sociology of Gender* (1978), where ultimately she proposes that patriarchal gender roles are perpetuated by the fact that mothers and most caregivers are women. This is also true of Carol Gilligan's groundbreaking early work (1982) that began what is called care ethics now so prominent in analytic feminists' debates. Gilligan's thesis that men and women are socialized differently and therefore develop different moral attitudes, like Chodorow's theory, is heavily reliant on the fact that most caregivers are women.

6. See Oliver 2001 for criticisms of Derrida, Kristeva, Honneth, and Butler along these lines.

7. In the Frankfurt school, Marcuse is best known for his sustained engagement with psychoanalysis. He transforms the notion of desire, or eros, by arguing that it is constituted by capital and a second-order repression that he calls "surplus repression" (1955). Surplus repression is added onto Freudian repression and is determined by capitalism and a repressive political economy. He also proposes that to liberate eros from capital it is necessary to make it possible for workers to sublimate through the high arts and culture. He emphasizes the necessity of sublimation for psychic life, with which I heartily agree, but he conceives of sublimation in a traditional Freudian framework that limits it to individuals and high culture, and in important ways excludes women. And as provocative and critical as his use of psychoanalysis is, he still begins with the Freudian individual ego and extrapolates the concept of repression from the individual level to the social level.

More recently, feminists have used what has become known as object relations theory, a revision of Freudian theory that concentrates on the objects of drives rather than the subject. Jessica Benjamin and Nancy Chodorow are probably the best-known proponents of feminist object relations psychology. I differ from Benjamin

(1988, 1995) in resisting a Hegelian master-slave model of primary relationships and the notion that autonomy and individuality are won through struggle with others. I differ from Chodorow (1978) in focusing on the relationship between the psyche and the social as interactive rather than determinative. Sometimes Chodorow's work makes it difficult to imagine how changing gender roles is possible without convincing men to switch gender roles, especially in relation to mothering, which would be a radical social change. Cynthia Willett, among others, has also pointed out that object relations theorists continue rather than break down the dichotomy between affect and reason, between autonomy and connection, and ultimately, it seems, between the psyche and the social. I hope to undermine these dichotomies rather than reinforce them.

8. See, for example, Cynthia Willett's critical analysis (2001, 2002) of the shortcomings of Marcuse's attempts to make psychoanalysis into a social theory; Robyn Ferrell (2002) argues that Jessica Benjamin's theories in both *The Bonds of Love: Psychoanalysis, Feminism, and the Problem of Domination* (1988) and *Like Subjects, Love Objects: Essays on Recognition and Sexual Difference* (1995) do not go between psychoanalysis and feminism as she claims, but rather reduce the psyche to the social such that "the analysis she provides of the desire is exclusively in terms of power relations between subjects (pleasure is not the point), simplifying any intrapsychical dynamic to an implicitly Hegelian model of self-consciousness." For criticisms of Honneth's use of object relations psychoanalytic theory to develop his theory of subjects struggling for recognition, see Oliver 2001. In addition, many Hegelian critical theorists, including Benjamin and Honneth, premise their notions of subjectivity on recognition, a conception of subjectivity that I challenge as part of the very pathology of domination (Oliver, 2001).

9. For example, in *The Bonds of Love*, Jessica Benjamin suggests that the infant develops its individuality and autonomy in a Hegelian master-slave-type dialectic with its mother. Axel Honneth (1996), following Benjamin, also imagines relations with others as a constant struggle for recognition. And Judith Butler (1997) describes all subject formation as subjugation.

10. Of course, contemporary French philosophy (e.g., Foucault, Levinas, Deleuze, Derrida, Irigaray) has been an attempt to decenter the subject and move away from a subject-centered philosophy toward a relational, or other-centered, philosophy.

11. For an excellent analysis of how and why primary relationships are not intersubjective, see Cynthia Willett's *Maternal Ethics and Other Slave Moralities* (1995).

12. In *Witnessing: Beyond Recognition*, I develop a notion of subjectivity as fundamentally responsive as an alternative to recognition models of subjectivity.

13. This is the central argument of my book *Witnessing*.

14. Ed Casey brought this to my attention, for which I am grateful.

15. Sublimation is central to Marcuse's analysis (1955) of the affects of capitalism on desire. But in the end, he follows Marx when he argues that the workers exploited by capitalism do not sublimate drives into higher pleasures, namely, high

culture and art, because they do not have the time, and their desires have been repressed by capitalism. His notion of sublimation is very traditional because it is based on transforming individual drives into high art; unlike what I do here, he neither develops a social theory of sublimation nor expands the notion of sublimation to include all forms of signification.

16. For summaries of the main arguments in *The Colonization of Psychic Space: A Psychoanalytic Social Theory of Oppression*, see the introductions to each of the four parts, along with chapter 6, "The Affects of Oppression," and the conclusion, "The Ethics of Psychoanalysis; or, Forgiveness as an Alternative to Alienation."

I. Alienation and Its Double

1. For my criticism of Jacques Derrida and Judith Butler insofar as they advocate this position, see Oliver 1997 and 2001.

2. See Oliver 1997 and 2001.

1. Alienation as Perverse Privilege of the Modern Subject

1. Lewis Gordon (2000, 35–36) nicely interprets and summarizes Fanon's argument that Hegel's master-slave dialectic does not describe the situation of black slavery. See also Robert Bernasconi's "African Philosophy's Challenge to Continental Philosophy" (1997) and Lou Turner's "On the Difference between the Hegelian and Fanonian Dialectic of Lordship and Bondage" (1996).

2. See Oliver 2001, chap. 1.

3. Unlike Hegel's scenario, this resistance may indeed require killing white others, we might say, to create whiteness as Other. As Fanon (1968b, 295) says in *The Wretched of the Earth*, "From the moment that you and your like are liquidated like so many dogs, you have no other resource but to use all and every means to regain your importance as a man. You must therefore weigh as heavily as you can upon the body of your torturer in order that his soul, lost in some byway, may finally find once more its universal dimension." Violent resistance restores the sense of agency or action lost through oppression.

4. Many English translations of Marx are not sensitive to this distinction.

5. It is possible that Marx shortchanges some of the more social animals.

6. After a detailed analysis of why Marx's notion of alienation does not explain black alienation, McGary, oddly enough, concludes that he doesn't believe that black alienation affects many people. He claims that black communities provide support against alienation for most black people.

7. For a useful account of the development of Sartre's notion of alienation throughout his work, see Thomas Busch's "Sartre and the Sense of Alienation" (1977).

8. Thanks to Cynthia Willett for this formulation of my argument in her constructive review of an earlier version of the manuscript.

9. See Oliver 2001, chap. 1.

10. As I argued in *Witnessing: Beyond Recognition*: "This reversal of the mirror stage is akin to Freud's, and later Lacan's, stage of secondary narcissism. But, rather

than work to form the ego through an identification with another person as in Freudian or Lacanian secondary narcissism, racism makes an identification with the white oppressor both necessary and impossible for people of color. More than this, Fanon suggests that rather than solidify the ego, racist identifications undermine the ego. So, unlike the identifications with the other formative to the ego in secondary narcissism, the identification with the oppressive other in the reversed mirror stage works to compromise the ego and its agency" (34).

11. Fanon's claim that there might be a "normal" childhood within the colonial situation before the child encounters white society is problematic. If he is suggesting that childhood or family life is at some point a safe haven from the effects of colonialism, then I would disagree. On the other hand, if he is suggesting that within the colonized imaginary there is a space before or beyond racism and colonization, then I find this suggestion provocative. At this point, I merely cite Fanon's problematic claim, even though it demands further analysis.

12. Throughout *Black Skin, White Masks,* Fanon associates an either-or logic with colonialism. He refuses to accept the colonial either-or, that he is white or black, that he is meaning or being (see esp. 1967, 203).

2. Alienation's Double as Burden of the Othered Subject

1. In particular, see his criticisms of Alfred Adler in chapter 7 of *Black Skin, White Masks* (213–15).

2. Fanon describes the complex relationship between economic and technological control and the production of values and meaning in his essay "This Is the Voice of Algeria," which is on the role of radio in both the colonization and liberation of Algeria (1965, 69–98).

3. For an interesting discussion of the visibility of race/skin within Fanon's *Black Skin, White Masks,* see Doane 1991, 216–27.

4. In *The Soul of Justice,* Cynthia Willett (2001, 20) argues that white slaveholders exhibit a double consciousness that allows them to justify and continue their assault on their slaves: "It seems that the white slaveholder may exhibit a double consciousness when it comes to his relation with the slave. For this slaveholder, the slave is part brute but also part human. From this divided consciousness the white master derives the secret pleasures and powers of his crime." The representation as brute eases guilt over slavery and justifies it, but the representation as part human gives "the surplus pleasure and social power of whiteness." Willett's suggestion that the social power of whiteness depends on this assault on the human part speaks to the logic of oppression beyond slavery that works through humiliation.

5. For an in-depth analysis of the rhetoric of color-blindness, see Oliver 2001.

6. For a critique of Fanon's gender politics, see T. Denean-Sharpley Whiting's *Fanon and Feminisms: Theory, Thought, Praxis* (1997).

7. See, for example, Davis (1981), Combahee River Collective (1982), Lorde (1984), King (1988), Crenshaw (1991), Collins (1990, 1998), Willett (2001).

8. See especially King 1988.

3. Colonial Abjection and Transmission of Affect

1. Teresa Brennan develops this current in Freud's thinking when she proposes that affects can move from one body to another such that dominance can lead to, or establish, one person or group of people as what she calls the "dumpers" and another as the "dumpees." For the development of her theory of the transmission of affect, see *The Transmission of Affect* (2004). For another application of the theory of the transmission of affect, see Oliver 2001.

2. In *Black Skin, White Masks*, full of the pain of his own experiences, Fanon describes the affects on the bodily schema of the man of color from the Antilles who sees himself as white until he is interpolated as black by Europeans. Consider two passages in particular: First, when Fanon (1967, 148) says that "the Antillean does not think of himself as a black man; he thinks of himself as an Antillean. The Negro lives in Africa. Subjectively, intellectually, the Antillean conducts himself as a white man. But he is a Negro. That he will learn once he goes to Europe; and when he hears Negroes mentioned he will recognize that the word includes himself as well as the Senegalese." Second, where he says that "we have seen in fact that the Antillean who goes to France pictures this journey as the final stage of his personality. Quite literally I can say without any risk of error that the Antillean who goes to France in order to convince himself that he is white will find his real face there" (153n16).

3. Fanon takes his notion of bodily or corporeal schema from Jean Lhermitte's *L'image de notre corps* (1939). Lhermitte's book also influenced Maurice Merleau-Ponty's use of the notion of what he calls a postural or corporeal schema in his 1960 lecture "The Child's Relations with Others." There, Merleau-Ponty attributes the first use of this notion to the British neurologist Henry Head. Head first used the idea of body image in an article with Gordon Holmes, "Sensory Disturbances from Cerebral Lesions," that appeared in the journal *Brain* in 1911. He says, "Anything which participates in the conscious movement of our bodies is added to the model of ourselves and becomes part of these schemata; a woman's power of localization may extend to the feather in her hat" (188). He followed up this research in volume 2 of his 1920 *Studies in Neurology*. Merleau-Ponty (1960, 117) maintains that "the consciousness I have of my body is not the consciousness of an isolated mass; it is a postural schema. It is the perception of my body's position in relation to the vertical, the horizontal, and certain other axes of important coordinates of its environment." Merleau-Ponty also concludes that "this entire placement of the corporeal schema is at the same time a placing of the perception of others" (123). Even more than Merleau-Ponty, Fanon makes the corporeal schema social. Others have made a distinction between body image and bodily schema. See esp. Gallagher and Cole's "Body Image and Body Schema" in Welton 1999 and Weiss 1999.

4. For a detailed analysis of the pathology of the demand for recognition, see Oliver 2001.

5. See also chapter 1 of Oliver 2001 for more development of the argument that the colonial dependence on internalization of values is contradictory.

6. Kalpana Seshadri-Crooks (2000, 41) argues that the taboo against miscegenation both relies on and threatens the prohibition against incest: "The taboo

against miscegenation, which underpins other interdictory practices such as segregation, and various forms of discriminations, behaves like the prohibition against incest by organizing kinship relations, punishing transgressions, and offering the subject a place in the racial order. However, a closer examination of the racial interdiction will reveal that it does not so much bear a resemblance to the prohibition of incest, as it relies on it." "The prohibition of miscegenation must be understood not as a law that resembles the incest taboo, but rather as one that threatens it. . . . All raced subjects have cause to fear miscegenation as it could render the moral law inoperative. . . . *The prohibition of miscegenation should above all be understood as the tenacious refusal to grant legitimacy in order to preserve the possibility of incest*" (42–43; emphasis in the original).

7. I would go a step further and argue that the colonizers must take responsibility for colonial violence, including resistance by the colonized. The colonizers are ethically responsible for the responses that their actions engender, including violent resistance. More specifically, the colonizers are responsible for their affects and for the transmission of affects to the colonized. This does not mean that those colonized are not also responsible for their violent or deadly actions. See my book *Witnessing: Beyond Recognition.* See also Renate Zahar's interesting analysis (1974) of Fanon's discussion of violence, crime, and psychosomatic disorders as indexes of alienation.

4. Humanism beyond the Economy of Property

1. In *Witnessing: Beyond Recognition,* I suggest that theorists such as Jean-Paul Sartre, Julia Kristeva, and Judith Butler, among others, in various ways propose that subjectivity depends on excluding or abjecting the other.

2. Although ultimately she insists on sovereignty, Arendt (1959, 164) begins to develop a theory of action without authorship: "Although everybody started his life by inserting himself into the human world through action and speech, nobody is the author or producer of his own life story. In other words, the stories, the results of action and speech, reveal an agent, but this agent is not an author or producer. Somebody began it and is its subject in the twofold sense of the word, namely, its actor and sufferer, but nobody is its author."

3. "Only the modern age's conviction that man can know only what he makes, that his allegedly higher capacities depend upon making and that he therefore is primarily *homo faber* and not *animal rationale,* brought forth the much older implications of violence inherent in all interpretations of the realm of human affairs as a sphere of making" (Arendt 1959, 204).

4. Cf. Arendt 1959, 206: "Risks and dangers [are abated] by introducing into the web of human relationships the much more reliable and solid categories inherent in activities with which we confront nature and build the world of human artifice."

5. Patricia Williams (1991, 230) gives an example from her own experience of an exchange as investment in others outside an economy of property when she describes her interaction with a group of people who gave her a sense of belonging without debt or guilt: "My value to the group was not calculated by the physical

items I brought to it. These people included me because they wanted me to be part of their circle; they valued my participation apart from the material things I could offer. So I gave of myself to them, and they gave me fruit cakes and dandelion wine and smoked salmon and, in their giving, their goods became provisions. Cradled in this community whose currency was a relational ethic, my stock in myself soared. My value depended on the glorious intangibility, the eloquent invisibility, of my just being part of the collective—and in direct response I grew spacious and happy and gentle."

6. See Senem Saner's analysis (2004) of Fanon on the West's claims to own the concepts of freedom, democracy, and justice.

7. For example, Kalpana Seshadri-Crooks (2000) interprets Fanon as a kind of essentialist about race, while Mary Ann Doane (1991) interprets Fanon as a kind of nominalist about race.

5. Fluidity of Power

1. Theorists who attempt to combine Foucauldian discursive analysis and Freudian psychoanalysis include Judith Butler, Teresa de Lauretis, Frances Retuccia, and Benigno Trigo.

2. For a helpful analysis of Fanon's discussion of the role of radio in resistance, see Nigel Gibson's "Jammin' the Airwaves and Tuning into the Revolution: The Dialectics of the Radio in *L'An V de la révolution algérienne*" (1996).

3. For a discussion of the relation between psychoanalytic truth and historical truth, especially as they come to play in resistance, see Oliver 2001.

4. For insightful analysis of Fanon's discussion of the role of the veil in the Algerian revolution, see Eddy Souffrant's "To Conquer the Veil: Woman as Critique of Liberalism" (1996); and David Theo Goldberg's "In/Visibility and Super/Vision: Fanon on Race, Veils, and Discourses of Resistance" (1996).

5. For analyses of Fanon's remarks about women and the relation between his writings and feminism, see, for example, Sharpley-Whiting 1997, Chow 1998, and Doane 1991.

6. The Affects of Oppression

1. An exceptionally poignant example is the 1949 Hollywood film *Home of the Brave*, which delivers this message when African American soldier Peter Moss is told by his doctor that racism is all in his head. Moss suffered hysterical paralysis and war trauma after watching his buddy—who had just used a racial slur against him—get shot. His doctor tries to convince Moss that his suffering is not the result of the racial slur but the guilt that anyone feels when he sees a buddy get shot. In the end, the doctor "cures" Moss by yelling racial slurs at him until he is angry enough to walk again. Throughout the film, the doctor tells Moss—brainwashes him even—that racism is all in his head and that he is treated just like anyone else. At the end of the film, Moss is repeating the words of the doctor like a mantra with which he continues to hypnotize himself.

Ironically, when the doctor provokes Moss's anger using racial slurs, he uses the affects of oppression to deny the reality of both those affects and the experiences of humiliation that give birth to them. For a discussion of this film in terms of its apolitical message, see Oliver and Trigo 2003. *Home of the Brave* was directed by Mark Robson and stars James Edwards as Peter Moss (the only black character in the film); Lloyd Bridges as his friend, Finch, who is shot; and Jeff Corey as the white doctor who convinces him that racism is all in his head.

2. For example, see Teresa Brennan's groundbreaking research in *The Interpretation of the Flesh* (1992); see also Sandra Bartky's *Femininity and Domination* (1990) and Jennifer Hansen's "Remembering the Self" (1999).

3. It seems that viewers of the film suffer from the same blindness. The film critic Hal Erickson says that "the moral seems to be that murder is justified so long as it stems from dissatisfaction with the entire male population" (see review of *A Question of Silence* at www.allmovie.com). He describes the psychiatrist's refusal to find the women insane and thereby spare them from prison as her casting her lot with the killers. Erickson is surprised, even appalled, that the Dutch Film Finance Corporation, headed by men, would make such a film. Erickson does not see that by refusing to find the women insane, the psychiatrist guarantees that they will spend their lives in prison. Her comprehension of the everyday humiliations they suffer as women is interpreted as her justifying their actions rather than explaining them. Erickson, like the judges in the film, assumes that to judge these women sane is to justify or exonerate their crime. The film does not exonerate them; it is clear that they are guilty. Rather, the film explains how the everyday oppression that they all experience as women could lead to the rage that results in murder, an act that we don't expect from women, even when enraged.

4. For a discussion of how the film format intensifies the theme of women's isolation, see Gentile 1990.

7. The Depressed Sex

1. As T. Denean Sharpley-Whiting so eloquently elaborates in the first two chapters of *Black Venus: Sexualized Savages, Primal Fears, and Primitive Narratives in French*, during this same century, Sarah Bartmann, a female "Hottentot" from Africa, was exhibited all over Europe to spectators who paid to see her protruding buttocks. She was subjected to the most intense and objectifying medical gaze as she was examined and reexamined by a team of zoologists, anatomists, and physiologists. Sharpley-Whiting analyzes how these scientists characterized the so-called Hottentot Venus as bestial, primitive, and highly sexual. After her death, she was dissected, and the study of her genitals dominated the reports that followed. Sharpley-Whiting (1999, 16–43) argues that these discourses around Bartmann in the early nineteenth century shaped the nineteenth- and twentieth-century stereotypes of the oversexed primitive African woman.

2. There are several critical analyses of hysteria, among them Jann Matlock, *Scenes of Seduction: Prostitution, Hysteria, and Reading Difference in the Nineteenth-Century France* (1993); Sander Gilman et al., *Hysteria beyond Freud* (1993); Elaine Showalter, *Hystories* (1998); Julia Borossa, *Hysteria* (2001); and Juliet Mitchell, *Mad Men and Medusas: Reclaiming Hysteria* (2001).

3. Cf. the National Mental Health Association's description (1998) of depression: "Persistent sad, anxious or empty mood, loss of interest or pleasure in activities, including sex, restlessness, irritability, or excessive crying, feelings of guilt, worthlessness, helplessness, hopelessness, pessimism, sleeping too much or too little . . . appetite and/or weight loss or overeating and weight gain, decreased energy, fatigue, feeling slowed down, thoughts of death or suicide . . . difficulty concentrating, remembering or making decisions."

4. In her 1999 study of gender of melancholia, "Remembering the Self: Gender, Melancholia, and Philosophical Method," Jennifer Hansen presents a tour de force critique of the medical establishment's overmedication of women. She maintains that "physicians routinely administer Prozac to such depressed women, whether or not these women participate in therapy or not. This practice concretely illustrates how patriarchy deals with women's depression. The practice of masking women's depression follows both from long-standing cultural assumptions that women are inferior creatures in comparison to men and that women's rage needs to be contained so that women will not break out of the disciplinary matrix of 'femininity in which patriarchy subordinates them'" (1999, 22).

5. For examples of feminist critical analysis of medical and biological discourses, see Hansen, "Remembering the Self"; Alice Adams, *Reproducing the Womb* (1994); Gena Corea, *The Mother Machine: Reproductive Technologies from Artificial Insemination to Artificial Wombs* (1985); Helen Bequaert Holmes and Laura Purdy, eds., *Feminist Perspectives in Medical Ethics* (1992); Ruth Hubbard, *The Politics of Women's Biology* (1990); Evelyn Fox Keller, *Reflections on Gender and Science* (1985); Keller, *Secrets of Life, Secrets of Death* (1992); Kelly Oliver, *Family Values: Subjects between Nature and Culture* (1997); and Nancy Tuana, *The Less Noble Sex: Scientific, Religious, and Philosophical Conceptions of Woman's Nature* (1993).

6. See, for example, Benigno Trigo, *Subjects of Crisis: Race and Gender as Disease in Latin America* (2000); Sander Gilman, *Difference and Pathology* (1985); Gilman, *Disease and Representation: Images of Illness from Madness to AIDS* (1998); Susan Sontag, *Illness as Metaphor* (1979); Melbourne Tapper, *In the Blood: Sickle Cell Anemia and the Politics of Race* (1998); and, of course, the work of Michel Foucault.

7. This argument is persuasively made by Trigo in *Subject of Crisis* (2000); see especially p. 10 and the conclusion.

8. Various studies conclude that depression and other mental risks have physical effects not only by decreasing the body's tolerance for pain and increasing the likelihood of other illnesses and diseases but also by decreasing the ability to concentrate and to perform productively. One study found that chronic fatigue syndrome and fibromyalgia syndrome (increased pain) affect predominantly women, many of whom also suffer from depression (Skapinakis et al. 2000). The most dramatic result was reported in a spring 2000 study in the *American Journal of Psychiatry*, which concludes: "Early-onset major depression disorder adversely affected the educational attainment of women but not of men. . . . A randomly selected 21-year-old woman with early-onset major depressive disorder in 1995

could expect future annual earnings that were 12%–18% lower than those of a randomly selected 21-year-old woman whose onset of major depressive disorder occurred after age 21 or not at all. Early-onset major depressive disorder causes substantial human capital loss, particularly for women" (Berndt et al. 2000). For an insightful discussion of the medical establishment's teatment of depression in women, especially the use of Prozac, see Hansen 1999.

9. Although its language of "basic personality" may be outdated and it doesn't attend to gender differences, and we have made some progress since 1951, still, Abram Kardiner and Lionel Ovesey's *Mark of Oppression: Explorations in the Personality of the American Negro* provides powerful psychological evidence of the effects of racism on the development of the psyche, self-esteem, and agency.

10. Holzer et al. 1998.

11. My emphasis; National Mental Health Association 1998a.

12. The National Mental Health Association (1998a) reports that "historically, among health professionals, there has been a consistent under-diagnosis of depression in the African American community and an over-diagnosis of schizophrenia."

13. Didier Anzieu (1989, 86) points out a connection in Freud's theories between the ear and the superego.

14. Lewis Gordon (2000, 12) makes this point in *Existentia Africana* when he says that Fanon's resignation letter of 1956 indicates that "black defiance to black dehumanization historically has been constituted as madness and deviance." There Fanon (1968a, 53) says that "madness is one of the means that man has of losing his freedom."

15. For discussions of images of the mother in popular culture and film, see Kaplan 1992, Doane 1987, Fischer 1996, and Oliver 2002; for a discussion of images of the mother in medical and legal discourses, see Oliver 1997. See also *Noir Anxiety*, where Trigo and I suggest that in the Negro Problem films of the 1940s even racial impurity or a haunting blackness is traced back to the mother (Oliver and Trigo 2002).

16. David Allison and Mark Roberts (1998) expose the so-called Munchausen By Proxy Syndrome as a fraud. Women lost their children when courts ruled that they caused their children's diseases by worrying about them too much and projecting their own morbid fantasies on their children.

17. See, for example, Barkly et al. 1992, Kuhne et al. 1997, Faraone and Beiderman 1997. Cf. Perry 1999, Pelcovitz et al. 1998, Lee and Gotlib 1989.

18. For an insightful analysis of melancholy identification with the maternal body in Vilar's novel and other novels by Latin American and Latina writers, see Benigno Trigo's *Remembering Maternal Bodies: Melancholy in Latina and Latin American Women's Writing*, forthcoming from Palgrave.

19. I disagree with Kristeva's insistence that we must abject the maternal body. See my analysis of patriarchy's insistence on matricide in *Family Values* (1997).

20. Eve Kosofsky Sedgwick cites the work of the psychologists Silvan Tomkins, Michael Franz Basch, Francis Broucek, and Donald Nathanson, among others. See Sedgwick 2002. Sedgwick quotes Francis Broucek: "Shame is to self psychology

what anxiety is to ego psychology—the keystone affect" (Sedgwick 2002, 4; Broucek 1982, 369).

21. Michael Franz Basch (1976, 765–66) maintains, "The shame-humiliation reaction in infancy of hanging the head and averting the eyes does not mean the child is conscious of rejection, but indicates that effective contact with another person has been broken. . . . Therefore, shame-humiliation throughout life can be thought of as an inability to effectively arouse the other person's positive reactions to one's communications. The exquisite painfulness of that reaction in later life harks back to the earliest period when such a condition is not simply uncomfortable but threatens life itself."

22. Donald Nathanson (1987, 27) links shame directly to the constitution of a sense of self, particularly a sense of self as lovable: "The difference between the infant before the moment of shame (the infant in the moment of alert activity, of interest, excitement, or enjoyment) and the infant suddenly unable to function, this difference itself may be registered by the infant as a significant experience calling attention to and helping to define the self. In other words, I am suggesting that the physiological experience of the proto-affect shame is a major force in shaping the infantile self, and remains so throughout life. If this is true, then I suggest further that the adult experience of shame is linked to genitality, to self-expression, to physical appearance, to our entire construct of what it means to be lovable, initially and primarily simply because the episodes of shame experienced during the formative years (as these other psychic structures are established in the context of success and failure, of positive affect and of shame as the occasional accompaniment to failure) are crucial to the development of a sense of self."

23. The philosopher John Deigh (1983, 241), with whom Bartky engages, says, "Shame is felt over shortcomings, guilt over wrongdoings."

24. Lewis's description is reminiscent of Sartre's discussion of shame in *Being and Nothingness*, where Sartre insists that shame is always before the Other. For Sartre (1956), too, the experience of shame in the eyes of the Other is constitutive of self-consciousness by splitting the self in a kind of doubleness of experience. Sartre, like many theorists of shame, however, does not acknowledge the shame particular to oppression.

25. See, for example, Brennan's *Interpretation of the Flesh* (1992); see also Sandra Bartky's *Femininity and Domination* (1990) and Hansen's "Remembering the Self" (1999).

26. Cf. Sedgwick 2002, 4.

27. For a discussion of the melancholy of oppression in relation to race and the work of Fanon, see Oliver 2001, 36–37. For an in-depth analysis of Freud's theory of melancholy, see Hansen's "Remembering the Self."

28. In *Family Values*, I argue that stereotypes of paternity and maternity make feeling loved or lovable impossible (Oliver 1997).

My theory of social melancholy, the melancholy of oppression, is inspired by Teresa de Lauretis's analysis of lesbian desire. In *The Practice of Love*, she maintains that lesbian desire is constituted against a fantasy of castration, interpreted as a narcissistic wound to the subject's body-image. The subject is threatened with a loss of body-ego; what would amount to a loss of being itself. Here, de Lauretis follows Lacan in interpreting castration as a threat against what he calls the phallus, or, simply put, power. On Lacan's account of sexual difference, masculinity is *having* the phallus or power, and femininity is *being* the phallus or (sexually) powerful (in relation to masculinity). For de Lauretis (1994, 261–62), in terms of lesbian desire, castration is translated into the threat of the loss of a powerful image of oneself as a female body, or an image of oneself powerful.

De Lauretis proposes that lesbian desire sets up a fetish in the place of a lost or missing positive female body-image. In other words, for de Lauretis, when culture cannot provide a positive female body-image for the girl as she develops into a woman, she finds fetish substitutes to compensate for the missing desirable female body. Although de Lauretis refuses to extrapolate her theory to apply it to feminine sexualities in general, it is enlightening to do so. For example, when a girl is made to feel bad about her own body, when she is told that she is not feminine, that her body is not desirable or lovable, when the dominant culture tells girls both that they are not feminine enough and that to be feminine is bad, then they have difficulty finding a positive female body-image with which to fortify their own egos and self-esteem as women. The consequence is that women either have sadomasochistic relations to their own bodies and the bodies of other women, or they have to find alternative ways to value their bodies as women or create substitutes for the missing positive female body-image.

Against Freudian theory, in which the fetish is a substitute for the missing maternal phallus, de Lauretis argues that lesbian disavowal and fetishism have less to do with the lost maternal body or maternal phallus than the lost female body. The lesbian, unlike the heterosexual man, is not trying to find a substitute mother or a substitute for the maternal phallus, as Freud suggests (cf. Freud [1927] 1972 215; de Lauretis 1994, 265). Rather, she is trying to find a desirable and lovable female body-image. Against Freudians, de Lauretis describes masculinity in lesbians not as penis envy but rather as an embrace of one of the only symbols of desire for women available in our culture. That is, for de Lauretis, butch-femme lesbians fetishize available representations of desirable femininity (femmes) and desire for femininity embodied through masculinity (butch).

I would reject the notion that lesbian desire for a positive or desirable, lovable self-image is at odds with the desire for the maternal body. Rather, the maternal body is abjected within patriarchal culture, and this cannot help but affect girls, who are expected by that culture to identify with their mothers. This expectation can lead them to reject that identification with the abject and therefore perhaps with the feminine (since within the patriarchal imaginary the maternal and feminine are conflated), or it can lead them to identify with the abject maternal body and leave them in the melancholy position of mourning the loss of a loved and lovable feminine self. Against de Lauretis, I have argued here and elsewhere that rather than reject the relationship between women's desire or lesbian desire and maternity, we need to reconceive of maternity and diagnose the symptoms of the abjection of the maternal body on girls and women within patriarchal culture. Still, de Lauretis's analysis is extremely useful in imagining new meanings for femininity and masculinity, as well as lesbian desire.

Far from merely repeating heterosexual stereotypes of masculinity and femininity, de Lauretis argues that recirculated within lesbian desire, masculinity and femininity have new meanings that both acknowledge and deny the loss of a positive female body-image within patriarchal culture. She suggests that the use of masculine fetishes among butch lesbians is not a sign of penis envy but an acknowledgment that within our culture one way that desire for women is signified is through the trappings of masculinity (263). Insofar as masculinity operates outside the heterosexual matrix and within a woman-centered desire, for de Lauretis, it both avows and disavows masculinism. On the other hand, she argues that "the exaggerated display of femininity in the masquerade of the femme performs the sexual power and seductiveness of the female body when offered to the butch for mutual narcissistic empowerment. The femininity aggressively reclaimed from patriarchy by radical separatism, with its exclusive reference and address to women, asserts the erotic power of the unconstricted, 'natural,' female body in relations between women" (264). De Lauretis's lesbian fetishism is a denial of the stereotypical symbolism of sexual difference in patriarchy in an attempt to find or create real sexual difference by recovering a missing desirable, lovable, valuable, female body-image through fantasy. Lesbian fetishism disavows the loss of a desirable and valuable female body within patriarchy by resignifying the very symbols that effectively prevent a positive female body-image. The fantasy or imaginary dimension of fetishism opens up the possibility of desiring otherwise, what de Lauretis, following Freud, calls perverse desire.

Judith Butler also uses and revises Freud's notion of fetishism and disavowal against itself in her analysis of lesbian desire. In her essay "The Lesbian Phallus and the Morphological Imaginary," Butler challenges the Lacanian notion of the phallus by displacing it into the context of lesbian desire. She argues that given the Freudian-Lacanian theory of fetishism, other body parts should be substitutable and symbolizable by the phallus. Once Butler has established the psychoanalytic possibility of the lesbian phallus, she shows how this notion undermines the Freudian distinction between castration threats and penis envy and the analogous Lacanian distinction between being and having the phallus. In other words, the lesbian phallus calls into question the Freudian-Lacanian explanations for sexual difference. The upshot of Butler's analysis (1993, 84–85) is that to be consistent, once psychoanalytic theory posits the possibility of fetishism and phallus substitutes, then it has to allow for the mixing of masculine and feminine positions in all sexualities. This means that Freud is inconsistent in claiming that males suffer from castration anxiety and females suffer from penis envy, if fetishism is possible for both sexes. Fetishism opens up sexuality to the world of bodies constructed, lived, and experienced, through imaginary relations that are not necessarily determined by anatomy. Butler's analysis also challenges the Lacanian distinction between the feminine position of being the phallus and the masculine position of having the phallus. Again, if the phallus is a symbol that can represent various body parts and body-like things, as it does for the fetishist, then the way that the phallus determines sexual difference is opened out of the binary opposition between being and having. If Lacan is serious that the phallus is not the penis, then both men and women can both be and have the phallus. Having phallic power is not dependent on having a penis (88–89). Imagining the lesbian phallus deprivileges the masculine phallus by removing it from heterosexual normative relations and recirculating it in relations between women. This recirculation challenges not only the connection between the phallus and the penis but also the association between masculinity, maleness, and having phallic power. If lesbians and women can have phallic power, then sex can no longer operate according to the binary logic masculine-active versus feminine-passive. More than this, Butler's theory implies that sexuality can no longer operate according to the binary logic of mutually exclusive categories of heterosexuality and homosexuality. The conventions of normative heterosexual exchange become transformed in the homosexual context. And the alternatives opened in this exchange can be transformative when imported into heterosexual exchange to expand the horizons of normative sexuality. Butler, like de Lauretis, uses and bends the tools of psychoanalysis to imagine alternative sexualities beyond the binary of heterosexuality. By recirculating the masculinist terms of traditional psychoanalytic theory—disavowal, fetishism, phallus—in an economy of lesbian desire and relations between women, these theorists not only transform psychoanalytic discourse but also open up the possibility of theorizing lesbian desire and positive active desire between women.

29. For an extended analysis of how stereotypes undermine our ability to feel loved or lovable, see Oliver 1997. The National Mental Health Association (1998b) estimates that "the highest overall age of onset is between 25–44, with an increasing rate among those born after 1945, perhaps related to psychosocial factors such as single parenting, changing roles, and stress." For a discussion of empirical studies on depression, particularly in relation to drugs, see Hansen 1999. Whereas Hansen rejects psychoanalytic theory as sexist and turns to the philosophies of Simone de Beauvoir and Luce Irigaray in order to diagnose women's depression, I develop a psychoanalytic social theory of depression by reconceiving of both melancholy and sublimation as they are traditionally put forward in psychoanalytic theory. I try to develop a social psychoanalytic theory of melancholy, sublimation, and idealization.

30. For a sustained criticism of Butler's theory of subjectivity as subjection, see Oliver 2001.

8. Sublimation and Idealization

1. By *subjectivity* I mean one's sense of oneself as an "I," as an agent. By *subject position* I mean one's position in society and history as developed through various social relationships. For a discussion of the relation between subjectivity and subject position, see the introduction. See also Oliver 2001.

2. Kristeva introduces the notion of the imaginary father in *Tales of Love*

(1987) and develops it throughout her later work, especially *The Sense and Non-sense of Revolt* (2000b).

3. For a sustained discussion of the distinction between subject position and subjectivity, see Oliver 2001 and 2003b.

4. Psychic space is not just an inner drama or psychological interior. The belief in an interior depth or some natural element inside our heads distracts us from interpreting the meaning of our desires and actions, especially the surface value of our actions and especially of our words. Interpreting the surface meaning of words was the linchpin of Freudian psychoanalysis. The unconscious works through linguistic associations that must be interpreted as surface associations rather than as elements contained within some natural entity called the psyche or soul. This is what Kristeva (1995, 28) calls "the trap of psychology." That is, the "trap" of psychology is the notion of the psyche as an interior that does not operate as an open system but as a closed system, as a unified and autonomous soul or mind. Conceiving of the psyche as an open system brings social history into psychoanalysis. The psyche is a space of interaction and mobility between one's body and one's culture and language. Constant and free-flowing negotiations, transference, and translations between the bodily drives and cultural language are necessary to sustain robust psychic space. Without this interaction between body and culture, two related, unhappy consequences may result: the collapse of psychic space (through the reduction of the psyche to drive or to culture) and the imprisonment within a psychic realm that has become closed and turns in on itself. Interpretation—imagining, finding, or creating meaning—requires an open space full of free-flowing drive energy interacting with language. It cannot be conceived of as an entity or closed space, or it becomes a trap: "Psychic realm may be the place where somatic symptoms and delirious fantasies can be worked through and thus eliminated: as long as we avoid becoming trapped inside it, the psychic realm protects us. Yet we must transform it through *linguistic activity* into a form of sublimation or into an intellectual, interpretative, or transformational activity. At the same time, we must conceive of the 'psychic realm' as a *speech act,* that is, neither an acting-out nor a psychological rumination within an imaginary crypt, but the link between this inevitable and necessary rumination and its potential for verbal expression" (Kristeva 1995, 29).

5. In biology, interchange between system and its environment is necessary for the survival of open systems. Boundaries are amorphous, permeable, and ever changing: "Just as biologists speak of the 'open structure' of living organisms that renew their identity by interacting with another identity, it could be said that the adolescent structure opens itself to that which has been repressed" (Kristeva 1995, 136). Kristeva identifies the "adolescent" structure of the psyche with the creativity and imagination of writing that sustain and replenish psychic space.

6. For more on this contradiction, see Oliver 2001, chap. 1.

7. The psychologists Andrew Meltzoff and Keith Moore's studies (1977, 1983) on newborn infants' imitations of facial and manual gestures provide evidence to suggest that newborns are responsive to their social environment from birth. Shaun

Gallagher and Meltzoff (1996, 212, 227) conclude that these "recent studies of newborn imitation suggest that an experiential connection between self and others exists right from birth" that "is already an experience of pre-verbal communication in the language of gesture and action." See Oliver 1997, 2001, and Willett 1995.

8. These insights are inspired by Kalpana Seshadri-Crooks's powerful essay on Lacan and animality, "Being Human: Bestiality, Anthropophagy, and Law" (2003).

9. This primary identification with the semiotic element of language—not just the semiotic rhythms of the maternal body but those rhythms as they show up in the speech of the Other—allows a transition from the infant's identification with the maternal body and its assimilation of signification to the acquisition of language. This is why Kristeva (1989, 26) calls this primary identification a *reduplication of a pattern*, a semiotic pattern given form by its symbolic counterpart in the speech of the Other: "When the object that I incorporate is the speech of the other—precisely a nonobject, a pattern, a model—I bind myself to him in a primary fusion, communion, unification. An Identification. . . . if there is repression it is quite primal, and that it lets one hold on to the joys of chewing, swallowing, nourishing oneself . . . with words. In being able to receive the other's words, to assimilate, repeat, and reproduce them, I become like him: One. A subject of enunciation. Through psychic osmosis/identification. Through love."

10. The ego ideal refers to the ideal to which the subject tries to conform, while the ideal ego refers to the infant's narcissistic fantasy of omnipotence.

11. There are two facets of the paternal agency—love and law—that support the transition into signification: "It is on the basis of that harmonious blending of the two facets of fatherhood that the abstract and arbitrary signs of communication may be fortunate enough to be tied to the affective meaning of prehistorical identifications, and the dead language of the potentially depressive person can arrive at a live meaning in the bond with others" (Kristeva 1989, 23–24). We must have both the loving imaginary father and the stern father of the law, or the superego. But the superego, law, or signification itself will only operate as a satisfactory, even joyful, compensation for the maternal body if it is supported by the loving imaginary father or accepting third, that is, by the possibility of identifying with nonrepresentational and affective elements in language. Without the loving aspect of the paternal function (or the function of the accepting third party in relation to the infant and maternal body), the superego condemns affect, especially affect associated with the maternal body, to remain without an object. As a result, we have meaning without signification. To give this meaning to signification and signification to this affective meaning, we need the support of the accepting third. We need both facets of fatherhood (or third party), love and superego, to belong to the social.

12. "Nondesiring but loving father (not symbolic but imaginary) reconciles the ideal Ego [narcissistic omnipotence] with the Ego Ideal [superego] and elaborates the psychic space where possibly and subsequently an analysis can take place" (Kristeva 1989, 30). The infant's "identification" with the phallic mother [Ideal-Ego] is an identification with abjection. This identification is prior to the subject-object split, and that is precisely why it is an identification with abjection. The

abject is what calls into question boundaries; it is what is on the border, undefinable, uncategorizable. This not-yet-subject in relation to the maternal not-yet-object has fallen from the state of narcissistic omnipotence—when it takes its mother/self to be the all-powerful center of the universe—into abjection. The imaginary father addresses and supports the narcissistic crisis that results from the infant realizing that its mother/self is not the center of the universe. When it realizes that its mother desires a third party, then it finds itself at a turning point, a crisis point, where it can take one of many different paths into the symbolic order with more or less success.

13. Cf. Kristeva's analysis of the uncanny in *Strangers to Ourselves* (esp. 2002c, 286–87). See also Coward's interview with Kristeva where she discusses the necessity of idealization (346–49).

14. In *The Sense and Non-sense of Revolt* (2000b) and *The Intimate Revolt: The Powers and Limits of Psychoanalysis* (2002b), Kristeva revisits the theme of revolution so prominent in *Revolution in Poetic Language* (1984). In the earlier work, Kristeva identifies the possibility of revolution in language—a revolution she deems *analogous* to social revolution—with (maternal) semiotic forces in avant-garde literature. In *Powers of Horror* (1982), this semiotic drive force is not only associated with the maternal but more particularly with the abject or *revolting* (yet fascinating) aspects of the maternal. Here, the revolting becomes revolutionary through the return of the repressed (maternal) within (paternal) symbolic systems. While in her earlier work Kristeva was concerned with a revolution within language analogous to political revolution, in her later work she emphasizes the affects of the sociopolitical context on the possibility of individual revolts necessary to psychic life and still dependent on language and its semiotic drive force.

In *The Sense and Non-sense of Revolt*, Kristeva asks if revolt is possible today. She claims that within postindustrial and postcommunist democracies we are confronted with a new political and social economy governed by the spectacle within which it becomes increasingly difficult to think of the possibility of revolt. The two main reasons are that within media culture the status of power and the status of the individual have changed. In contemporary culture a power vacuum results in the inability to locate the agent or agency of power and authority or to assign responsibility. We live in a no-fault society in which crime has become a media-friendly spectacle, and government and social institutions normalize rather than prohibit (Kristeva 2000b, 5). The fact that these institutions are corruptible and full of scandals, however, undermines even their authority to normalize. The combination of the lack of locatable authority and the fact that government and social institutions are corruptible results in the breakdown of authority. Kristeva attributes the inability to revolt to this lack of authority. The problem, then, is that there is no authority against which to revolt. In a no-fault society, who or what can we revolt against?

In addition to the power vacuum, Kristeva identifies the impossibility of revolt with the changing status of the individual. The human being as a person with rights is becoming nothing more than an ensemble of organs that can be bought and sold or otherwise exchanged, what Kristeva calls the *patrimonial individual* (6). And how can an ensemble of organs revolt? Not only is there no one or nothing to revolt against, but also there is no one to revolt. Since we cannot locate power, because it has become both normalizing and corruptible, and because there is no clear-cut authority to obey, we try to abolish our own feelings of exclusion at all costs by renewing exclusion at the lower echelons of society. We cannot imagine the revolt necessary to make authority our own because we can't locate it, and so we feel excluded from the social. Therefore, within this paranoid culture where power is both everywhere and nowhere oppressing us, in order to feel included again, we exclude others.

15. In *New Maladies of the Soul*, Kristeva (1995, 89) describes this questioning as a form of symbolic castration, a particular form that calls into question castration as loss. Although castration relies on negation and rejection, she insists that in questioning, it cannot be reduced to them (87). She suggests that symbolic castration "owes its benevolent and brutal impact less to its status as a negation than as a question" and that "a question is not a negation" (88, 87). Rather, questioning is a form of castration that precisely overcomes negation.

16. "Libidinal negativity engenders the symbol of negation: or rather the symbol period, for all symbolism—notably that which presents itself as 'positive' in the judgment of affirmation—is the result of a nihilation of the Thing (of desire, of the object of desire) in favor of its representation" (Kristeva 2002c, 226).

9. Revolt and Singularity

1. Thanks to Lewis Gordon for turning me on to both Battersby and Howe.

2. This section on the relationship between singularity and the unconscious is indebted to conversations at the Dartmouth Institute for French Cultural Studies with Lisa Walsh and Shannon Lundeen, to whom I am grateful.

3. My discussion of the distinction between the singular and individual is indebted to conversations at the Dartmouth Institute for French Cultural Studies with Sam Weber, to whom I am grateful.

4. Kristeva (2000a, 10) says that "*singularity* [that] remains, today more than ever, beyond equality and, with it, the goal of the advanced democracies, that is, those based on consent in the negotiated handling of conflicts" (my emphasis).

10. Forgiveness and Subjectivity

I would like to thank Benigno Trigo, Mary Rawlinson, John McCumber, Walter Brogan, and Daniel Dahlstrom for conversations that helped me write this chapter.

1. If we analyze why Antigone is so important to Hegel, it becomes clear that her transgression is as much about her being a woman as it is about the action of throwing a handful of dirt on her brother's corpse. The evil, in Hegelian terms, of her particularity is that she is a woman. Creon is as much threatened by Antigone's womanhood as he is by her defiance of the civil law. Not only the civil law, but also Creon's manliness is at stake. Creon is explicit that the struggle is really about the superiority of man and inferiority of woman: "We must defend the men who live

by law, never let some woman triumph over us. Better to fall from power, if fall we must, at the hands of a man—never be rated inferior to a woman, never" (Sophocles 1982, 94). Antigone's trespass is her sex, which is why it is not forgiven. Given my analysis in chapter 7, it could be said that she is less guilty of an act of treason against the state than she is shamed into inferiority because she is a woman (cf. Oliver 1997).

2. It is important to note that for Hegel the universal is opposed to the particular, and the result of their dialectic interaction is the individual. The universal is the generic—law, language, thought—that is embodied in the individual. Here, then, it is the particularity of the individual's actions and desires that is at odds with the universal, and through the dialectic of confession and forgiveness, the individual becomes individuated as a subject by virtue of the realization of the universality of particularity.

3. Jean Hyppolite (1974, 523) emphasizes that for Hegel the reconciliation of forgiveness comes through *difference* and the mutual recognition of *two*: "The 'yes' of pardon which surges forth is the word of reconciliation, the recognition of the I in the other I—a remission of sins which causes *absolute spirit* to appear via this reciprocal exchange. Absolute spirit is neither abstract infinite spirit which is opposed to finite spirit, nor finite spirit which persists in its finitude and always remains on this side of its other; it is the unity and the opposition of these two I's. Thus the equation I = I assumes all its concrete signification if we insist on its *duality as much as on its unity*" (emphasis in the original).

4. Benjamin Sax (1983, 459) analyzes the importance of individuality in the language of confession and concludes that for Hegel, "equality is not based on uniformity or the reduction to an indifferent universal, but on the mutual recognition of individuality." Sax points out that the confession is of an individual's "unique selfhood" (457).

5. Cf. Jay Bernstein's discussion of "guilt" in Hegel's "Spirit of Christianity." Bernstein argues that since the German *Schuld* denotes responsibility and indebtedness, it does not imply moral guilt. We are all guilty in that we are responsible as individuals and indebted to the community. Bernstein (1994, 68) also argues that "tragic suffering is the recognition that transgressive action and the subject of that action are dependent upon the community from which the self separates itself."

6. See, for example, Robin May Schott's *Cognition and Eros: A Critique of the Kantian Paradigm* (1993); and her edited volume *Feminist Interpretations of Immanuel Kant* (1997).

7. For a discussion of the relation between these two types of meaning—referential and semiotic—see my introduction to the first and second editions of *The Portable Kristeva* (1997, 2002).

8. Kristeva (2002c, 29) describes the dynamic of transference in forgiveness as it operates in the analytic session: "Re-mission [forgiveness] and re-birth are thus acquired through the putting into words of the unconscious; they are acquired by giving conscious and unconscious meaning to what did not have any—for it is precisely this absence of meaning that was experienced as ill-being. Pardon is not

given to me by another. I pardon myself with the help of another (the analyst), by relying on his interpretation and on his silence (on his love) in order to make sense of the senselessness troubling me."

9. Kristeva's (1982) theory of abjection gives one explanation of how the infant maintains both connection and separation from the maternal body on which it depends.

10. In response to Derrida's criticisms of psychoanalysis, Kristeva (2002a, 282) says that forgiveness is not erasure but the recognition of suffering that takes place only in the private sphere and never in the public realm of governments. Derrida and Kristeva would agree that forgiveness is impossible within the realm of law and justice. But, while Kristeva maintains that forgiveness falls outside the realm of law and operates within the realm of the psyche, Derrida maintains that pure forgiveness should operate as a regulative ideal within the realm of law. For Derrida (2001, 66), then, forgiveness is not impossible in the social realm because it is private or between two but rather because it is a Kantian ideal that we can only attempt to reach by admitting that we fall short. Disregarding what Derrida calls hyperbolic ethics and the vigilance that it is meant to provoke, Kristeva (2002a, 283) calls his ideal forgiveness "utopian."

11. In *The Ethics of Ambiguity* (1948), Simone de Beauvoir comes to this conclusion through an existentialist ethics that maintains that we create ourselves free as part of the project of being human. But, as she insists, no one of us can create human beings as free, since no one of us defines human being. Not until all human beings are free, will we have created human beings as free. Obviously, I reach this conclusion through very different means.

Works Cited

Adams, Alice. 1994. *Reproducing the Womb*. Ithaca, NY: Cornell University Press.

Allison, David, and Mark Roberts. 1998. *Disordered Mother or Disordered Diagnosis? Munchausen By Proxy Syndrome*. New York: Analytic.

Alvarez, Julia. 1991. *How the García Girls Lost Their Accents*. New York: Plume.

———. 1994. *In the Time of the Butterflies*. New York: Plume.

———. 2000. *In the Name of Salomé*. Chapel Hill, NC: Algonquin.

Anzieu, Didier. 1989. *The Skin Ego*. Trans. Chris Turner. New Haven, CT: Yale University Press.

Arendt, Hannah. 1959. *The Human Condition*. Chicago: University of Chicago Press.

Barkly, R. A., et al. 1992. "Adolescents with Attention Deficit Hyperactivity Disorder." *Journal of Abnormal Child Psychology* 20 (3): 263–88.

Bartky, Sandra Lee. 1990. *Femininity and Domination*. New York: Routledge.

Basch, Michael Franz. 1976. "The Concept of Affect: A Re-examination." *Journal of the American Psychoanalytic Association* 24:759–77.

Battersby, Christine. 1989. *Gender and Genius: Towards a Feminist Aesthetics*. Bloomington: Indiana University Press.

Beauvoir, Simone de. 1948. *The Ethics of Ambiguity*. Trans. Bernard Frechtman. New York: Philosophical Library.

Benjamin, Jessica. 1988. *The Bonds of Love: Psychoanalysis, Feminism, and the Problem of Domination*. New York: Pantheon.

———. 1995. *Like Subjects Love Objects: Essays on Recognition and Sexual Difference*. New Haven, CT: Yale University Press.

Bernasconi, Robert. 1996. "Casting the Slough: Fanon's New Humanism for a New Humanity." In *Fanon: A Critical Reader*, ed. Lewis Gordon et. al., 113–21. Malden, MA: Blackwell.

———. 1997. "African Philosophy's Challenge to Continental Philosophy." In *Postcolonial African Philosophy*, ed. Emmanuel Chukwudi Eze. Cambridge, MA: Blackwell.

———, ed., with Tommy L. Lott. 2000. *The Idea of Race*. Indianapolis, IN: Hackett.

Berndt, Ernst, et al. 2000. "Lost Human Capital from Early-Onset Chronic Depression." *American Journal of Psychiatry* (June): 940–47.
Bernstein, Jay. 1994. "Conscience and Transgression: The Persistence of Misrecognition." *Bulletin of the Hegel Society of Great Britain* 29: 55–70.
Bhabha, Homi. K. 1994. "Interrogating Identity: Frantz Fanon and the Postcolonial Prerogative." In *The Location of Culture*, 40–65. London: Routledge.
Borossa, Julia. 2001. *Hysteria.* New York: Totem.
Bouson, J. Brooks. 2000. *Quiet as Its Kept: Shame, Trauma, and Race in the Novels of Toni Morrison.* Albany: State University of New York Press.
Brennan, Teresa. 1992. *The Interpretation of the Flesh: Freud and Femininity.* London: Routledge.
———. 1993. *History after Lacan.* New York: Routledge.
———. 1997. "Social Pressure." In *American Imago* 54 (3): 257–88.
———. 2004. *The Transmission of Affect.* Ithaca, NY: Cornell University Press.
Broucek, Frances. 1982. "Shame and Its Relationship to Early Narcissistic Developments." *International Journal of Psychoanalysis* 63:369–78.
Bulhan, Hussein Abdilahi. 1985. *Frantz Fanon and the Psychology of Oppression.* Boston: Boston University Press.
Busch, Thomas W. 1977. "Sartre and the Sense of Alienation." *Southern Journal of Philosophy* 15:151–56.
Butler, Judith. 1991. *Gender Trouble: Feminism and the Subversion of Identity.* New York: Routledge.
———. 1993. "The Lesbian Phallus and the Morphological Imaginary." In *Bodies That Matter: On the Discursive Limits of "Sex,"* 57–91. New York: Routlege.
———. 1997. *The Psychic Life of Power: Theories in Subjection.* Stanford, CA: Stanford University Press.
Cameron, Deborah. 1985. *Feminism and Linguistic Theory.* New York: Macmillan.
———. 1992. *Researching Language: Issues of Power and Method.* New York: Routledge.
Cheng, Anne Anlin. 2001. *The Melancholy of Race.* New York: Oxford University Press.
Chodorow, Nancy. 1978. *The Reproduction of Mothering: Psychoanalysis and the Sociology of Gender.* Berkeley: University of California Press.
Chow, Rey. 1998. *Ethics after Idealism.* Bloomington: Indiana University Press.
Collins, Patricia Hill. 1990. *Black Feminist Thought: Knowledge, Consciousness, and the Politics of Empowerment.* New York: Routledge.
———. 1998. *Fighting Words: Black Women and the Search for Justice.* Minneapolis: University of Minnesota Press.
Combahee River Collective. 1982. "A Black Feminist Statement." In *All the Women Are White, All the Blacks Are Men, But Some of Us Are Brave: Black Women's Studies*, ed. Gloria T. Hull, Patricia Bell Scott, and Barbara Smith, 13–22. Old Westbury, NY: Feminist.
Corea, Gena. 1985. *The Mother Machine: Reproductive Technologies from Artificial Insemination to Artificial Wombs.* New York: Harper and Row.

Cornell, Drucilla. 1998. *At the Heart of Freedom.* Princeton, NJ: Princeton University Press.

———. 1995. *The Imaginary Domain.* New York: Routledge.

Crenshaw, Kimberle. 1991. "Mapping the Margins: Intersectionality, Identity Politics, and Violence against Women of Color." *Stanford Law Review* 43 (6): 1241–99.

Davis, Angela. 1981. *Women, Race, and Class.* New York: Random House.

de Lauretis, Teresa. 1994. *The Practice of Love.* Bloomington: Indiana University Press.

———. 1998. "The Stubborn Drive." *Critical Inquiry* 24: (4): 851–77.

Derrida, Jacques. 1996. *Archive Fever.* Trans. Eric Prenowitz. Chicago: University of Chicago Press.

———. 1999. "Le siècle et le pardon." In *Le Monde des Débats* (December).

———. 2001a. "On Forgiveness." In *Cosmopolitanism and Forgiveness,* 26–60. Trans. Michael Hughes. London: Routledge.

———. 2001b. "To Forgive: The Unforgivable and the Imprescriptible," and "On Forgiveness: A Round-Table Discussion with Jacques Derrida." In *Questioning God,* ed. John D. Caputo, Mark Dooley, and Michael J. Scanlon, 21–51. Bloomington: Indiana University Press.

Doane, Mary Ann. 1987. *The Desire to Desire: The Woman's Film of the 1940s.* Bloomington: Indiana University Press.

———. 1991. *Femmes Fatales: Feminism, Film Theory, Psychoanalysis.* New York: Routledge.

Douglas, Mary. 1969. *Purity and Danger.* New York: Routledge.

Du Bois, W. E. B. 1969. *The Souls of Black Folk.* New York: New American Library.

Ellison, Ralph. 1947. *Invisible Man.* New York: Vintage.

Eng, David, and Shinhee Han. 2000. "A Dialogue on Racial Melancholia." *Psychoanalytic Dialogues* 10 (4): 667–700.

Fanon, Frantz. 1965. *A Dying Colonialism.* Trans. Haakon Chevalier. New York: Grove.

———. 1967. *Black Skin, White Masks.* Trans. Charles Lam Markmann. New York: Grove.

———. 1968a. *Toward the African Revolution.* Trans. Haakon Chevalier. New York: Grove.

———. 1968b. *The Wretched of the Earth.* Trans. Constance Farrington. New York: Grove.

Faraone, S. V., and J. Beiderman. 1997. "Do Attention Deficit Hyperactivity Disorder and Major Depression Share Familial Risk Factors?" *Journal of Nervous Mental Disorders* 185 (9): 533–41.

Ferrell, Robyn. 2002 "The Pleasures of the Slave." In *Between the Psyche and the Social,* ed. Kelly Oliver and Steve Edwin. New York: Rowman and Littlefield.

Fischer, Lucy. 1996. *Cinematernity: Film, Motherhood, Genre.* Princeton, NJ: Princeton University Press.

Frankenberg, Ruth. 1993. *The Social Construction of Whiteness: White Women, Race Matters.* Minneapolis: University of Minnesota Press.

Freud, Sigmund. 1915a. "Repression." In *The Complete Psychological Works of Sigmund Freud,* ed. James Strachey. Vol. 14, 143. London: Hogarth.

———. 1915b. "The Unconscious." In *The Complete Psychological Works of Sigmund Freud*, ed. James Strachey. Vol. 14, 161–204. London: Hogarth.

———. [1914] 1955. "Remembering, Repeating, and Working-Through." In *The Complete Psychological Works of Sigmund Freud*, ed. James Strachey. Vol. 12, 147. London: Hogarth.

———. [1923] 1955. "The Ego and the Id." In *The Complete Psychological Works of Sigmund Freud*, ed. James Strachey. Vol. 19, 12–66. London: Hogarth.

———. 1961. *Civilization and Its Discontents*. Trans. James Strachey. New York: Norton.

———. [1894] 1962. "The Neuro-Psychoses of Defense." In *The Complete Psychological Works of Sigmund Freud*, ed. James Strachey. Vol. 3, 45–61. London: Hogarth.

———. [1895] 1962. "Obsessions and Phobias, Their Mechanism and Their Aetiology." In *The Complete Psychological Works of Sigmund Freud*, ed. James Strachey. Vol. 3, 74–82. London: Hogarth.

———. [1927] 1972. "Fetishism." In *Sexuality and the Psychology of Love*, ed. Philip Reiff, trans. Joan Riviere, 214–19. New York: Collier.

———. [1913] 1989. *Totem and Taboo*. In *The Freud Reader*, ed. Peter Gay. New York: Norton.

———. [1917] 1989. "Mourning and Melancholia." In *The Freud Reader*, ed. Peter Gay. New York: Norton.

Gaines, Stanley. 1996. "Perspectives of Du Bois and Fanon on the Psychology of Oppression." In *Fanon: A Critical Reader*, ed. Lewis Gordon, T. Denean Sharpley-Whiting, and Reneé T. White, 24–34. Malden, MA: Blackwell.

Gallagher, Shaun, and Jonathan Cole. 1998. "Body Image and Body Schema." In *Body and Flesh*, ed. Donn Welton, 131–48. Malden, MA: Blackwell.

Gallagher, Shaun, and Andrew Meltzoff. 1996. "The Earliest Sense of Self and Others: Merleau-Ponty and Recent Developmental Studies." In *Philosophical Psychology* 9: 211–36.

Gentile, Mary. 1990. "Feminist or Tendentious? Marleen Gorris's *A Question of Silence*." In *Issues in Feminist Film Criticism*, ed. Patricia Erens, 395–404. Bloomington: Indiana University Press.

Gibson, Nigel. 1996. "Jammin' the Airwaves and Tuning into the Revolution: The Dialectics of the Radio in *L'An V de la révolution algérienne*." In *Fanon: A Critical Reader*, ed. Lewis Gordon, T. Denean Sharpley-Whiting, and Reneé T. White, 273–82. Malden, MA: Blackwell.

———. 1999. *Rethinking Fanon*. Amherst, NY: Humanity.

Gilligan, Carol. 1982. *In a Different Voice*. Cambridge, MA: Harvard University Press.

Gilman, Sander. 1985. *Difference and Pathology*. Ithaca, NY: Cornell University Press.

———. 1998. *Disease and Representation: Images of Illness from Madness to AIDS*. Ithaca, NY: Cornell University Press.

Gilman, Sander, et al. 1993. *Hysteria beyond Freud*. Berkeley: University of California Press.

Goldberg, David Theo. 1996. "In/Visibility and Super/Vision: Fanon on Race, Veils, and Discourses of Resistance." In *Fanon: A Critical Reader*, ed. Lewis Gordon, T. Denean Sharpley-Whiting, and Reneé T. White, 179–202. Malden, MA: Blackwell.

Gordon, Lewis. 1995a. *Bad Faith and Antiblack Racism.* New Jersey: Humanities.

———. 1995b. *Her Majesty's Other Children.* New Jersey: Rowman and Littlefield.

———. 1996. "The Black and the Black Body Politic: Fanon's Existential Phenomenological Critique of Psychoanalysis." In *Fanon: A Critical Reader*, ed. Lewis Gordon, T. Denean Sharpley-Whiting, and Reneé T. White. Malden, MA: Blackwell.

———. 1997. *Fanon and the Crisis of European Man.* New York: Routledge.

———. 2000. *Existentia Africana: Understanding Africana Existential Thought.* New York: Routledge.

Grosz, Elizabeth. 1995. *Space, Time, and Perversion.* New York: Routledge.

———. 2001. *Architecture from the Outside.* Cambridge, MA: MIT Press.

Hall, Stuart. 1995. *Frantz Fanon: Black Skin, White Mask*, dir. Isaac Julien. California Newsreel.

Hansberry, Lorraine. 1958. *A Raisin in the Sun.* New York: Vintage.

Hansen, Jennifer. 1999. "Remembering the Self: Gender, Melancholia, and Philosophical Method." Ph.D. diss., State University of New York at Stony Brook.

Head, Henry, and Gordon Holmes. 1911. "Sensory Disturbances from Cerebral Lesions." *Brain* 34:102–254.

———. 1920. *Studies in Neurology*, vol. 2. London: Oxford University Press.

Hegel, G. W. F. 1977. *Phenomenology of Spirit.* Trans. A. V. Miller. Oxford: Oxford University Press.

———. 1948. "The Spirit of Christianity." In *Early Theological Writings*, 182–301. Trans. T. M. Know. Philadelphia: University of Philadelphia Press.

Heidegger, Martin. 1962. *Being and Time.* Trans. John Macquarrie and Edward Robinson. New York: Harper and Row.

Henry, Paget. 2000. *Caliban's Reason.* New York: Routledge.

Hinchman, Lewis P. 1984. *Hegel's Critique of the Enlightenment.* Gainesville: University Presses of Florida.

Holmes, Helen Bequaert, and Laura Purdy, eds. 1992. *Feminist Perspectives in Medical Ethics.* Bloomington: Indiana University Press.

Holzer et al. 1998. "Clinical Depression and African Americans." National Mental-Health Association Web site, DiscoveryHealth.com.

Honneth, Axel. 1991. *The Critique of Power: Reflective Stages in a Critical Social Theory.* Trans. Kenneth Baynes. Cambridge MA: MIT Press.

———. 1996. *The Struggle for Recognition.* Trans. Joel Anderson. Boston: MIT Press.

hooks, bell. 1990. *Yearning: Race, Gender, and Cultural Politics.* Boston: South End.

———. 1994. *Teaching to Transgress: Education as the Practice of Freedom.* New York: Routledge.

Howe, Michael. 1999. *Genius Explained.* Cambridge: Cambridge University Press.

Hubbard, Ruth. 1990. *The Politics of Women's Biology.* New Brunswick, NJ: Rutgers University Press.

Hyppolite, Jean. 1974. *Genesis and Structure of Hegel's Phenomenology of Spirit.* Trans. Samuel Cherniak and John Heckman. Evanston, IL: Northwestern University Press.

Kaplan, E. Ann. 1992. *Motherhood and Representation.* New York: Routledge.

Kardiner, Abram, and Lionel Ovesey. 1951. *The Mark of Oppression: Explorations in the Personality of the American Negro.* New York: Meridian.

Keller, Evelyn Fox. 1985. *Reflections on Gender and Science.* New Haven, CT: Yale University Press.

———. 1992. *Secrets of Life, Secrets of Death.* New York: Routledge.

King, Deborah. 1988. "Multiple Jeopardy, Multiple Consciousness: The Context of Black Feminist Ideology." *Signs* 14 (autumn): 42–72.

Kristeva, Julia. 1982. *Powers of Horror: An Essay on Abjection.* Trans. Leon S. Roudiez. New York: Columbia University Press.

———. 1984. *Revolution in Poetic Language.* Trans. Margaret Waller. New York: Columbia University Press.

———. 1987. *Tales of Love.* Trans. Leon S. Roudiez. New York: Columbia University Press.

———. 1989. *Black Sun: Depression and Melancholy.* Trans. Leon S. Roudiez. New York: Columbia University Press.

———. 1995. *New Maladies of the Soul.* Trans. Ross Guberman. New York: Columbia University Press.

———. 1997. *The Portable Kristeva.* Ed. Kelly Oliver. New York: Columbia University Press.

———. 2000a. *Crisis of the European Subject.* Trans. Susan Fairfield. New York: Other.

———. 2000b. *The Sense and Non-sense of Revolt.* Trans. Jeanine Herman. New York: Columbia University Press.

———. 2001. *Hannah Arendt,* vol. 1 of *Feminine Genius.* Trans. Ross Guberman. New York: Columbia University Press.

———. 2002a. "Forgiveness," interview with Kristeva. *PMLA* 117 (2): 278–323.

———. 2002b. *Intimate Revolt: The Powers and Limits of Psychoanalysis,* vol. 2. Trans. Jeanine Herman. New York: Columbia University Press.

———. 2002c. *The Portable Kristeva.* Ed. Kelly Oliver. 2nd ed. New York: Columbia University Press.

Kruks, Sonia. 1996. "Fanon, Sartre, and Identity Politics." In *Fanon: A Critical Reader,* ed, Lewis Gordon, T. Denean Sharpley-Whiting, and Reneé T. White, 122–33. Malden, MA: Blackwell.

Kuhne, M., et al. 1997. "Impact of Comorbid Oppositional or Conduct Problems on Attention-Deficit Hyperactivity Disorder." *Journal of American Academy of Child Adolescent Psychiatry* 36 (12): 1715–25.

Lacan, Jacques. 1977. *Ecrits.* Trans. Alan Sheridan. New York: Norton.

———. 1981. *The Four Fundamental Concepts of Psycho-Analysis.* Trans. Alan Sheridan. New York: Norton.

Lakoff, Robin. 1975. *Language and Woman's Place.* New York: Harper and Row.

Lane, Christopher. 2000. "The Experience of the Outside: Foucault and Psychoanalysis." *Lacan in America.* New York: Other.

———. 1998. *The Psychoanalysis of Race.* New York: Columbia University Press.

Laplanche, Jean, and J.-B. Pontalis. 1973. *The Language of Psycho-Analysis.* Trans. Donald Nicholson-Smith. New York: Norton.

Larsen, Nella. [1928] 1998. *Quicksand and Passing.* Ed. Deborah McDowell. New Brunswick, NJ: Rutgers University Press.

Lee, C. M., and I. H. Gotlib. 1989. "Clinical Status and Emotional Adjustment of Children of Depressed Mothers." *American Journal of Psychiatry* 146: 478–83.

Lewis, Helen Block. 1976. *Psychic War in Men and Women.* New York: New York University Press.

———. 1981. *Freud and Modern Psychology: The Emotional Basis of Mental Illness.* New York: Plenum.

———. 1985. Depression versus Paranoia: Why Are There Sex Differences in Mental Illness? *Journal of Personality* 53:150–78.

———. 1986. "The Role of Shame in Depression." In *Depression in Young People: Developmental and Clinical Perspectives,* ed. Michael Rutter, Carroll E. Izzard, and Peter B. Read, New York: Guilford.

———. 1987a. "Resistance: A Misnomer for Shame and Guilt." In *Techniques of Working with Resistance,* ed. Donald S. Milman and George D. Goldman. New York: Aronson.

———. 1987b. "Shame and the Narcissistic Personality." In *The Many Faces of Shame,* ed. Donald L. Nathanson, 93–132. New York: Guilford.

Lorde, Audre. 1984. *Sister Outsider.* Trumansburg, NY: Crossing.

MacCannell, Juliet Flower. 2000. *The Hysteric's Guide to the Future Female Subject.* Minneapolis: University of Minnesota Press.

Marcuse. Herbert. 1955. *Eros and Civilization.* Boston: Beacon.

Marx, Karl. 1975. *Marx's Early Writings,* ed. Lucio Colletti, trans. Rodney Livingstone and Gregor Benton. New York: Random House.

———. 1977. *Capital,* vol. 1. Trans. Ben Fowkes. New York: Random House.

Matlock, Jann. 1993. *Scenes of Seduction: Prostitution, Hysteria, and Reading Difference in the Nineteenth-Century France.* New York: Columbia University Press.

McCumber, John. 1993. *In the Company of Words: Hegel, Language, and Systematic Philosophy.* Evanston, IL: Northwestern University Press.

McGary, Howard. 1998. "Alienation and the African-American Experience." In *Theorizing Multiculturalism,* ed. Cynthia Willett. Malden, MA: Blackwell.

Meltzoff, Andrew, and Keith Moore. 1977. "Imitation of Facial and Manual Gestures by Human Neonates." *Science* 198:75–78.

———. 1983. "Newborn Infants Imitate Adult Facial Gestures." *Child Development* 54:702–9.

Merleau-Ponty, Maurice. 1964. "The Child's Relations with Others." In *The Primacy of Perception*, ed. James Edie, trans. William Cobb., 96–155. Evanston, IL: Northwestern University Press.

Miller, Susan. 1985. *The Shame Experience.* Hillsdale, NJ: Analytic.

Mitchell, Juliet. 2001. *Mad Men and Medusas: Reclaiming Hysteria.* New York: Basic.

Morrison, Toni. 1987. *Beloved.* New York: Plume.

Mulvey, Laura. 1975. "Visual Pleasure and Narrative Cinema." *Screen* 16 (3): 6–18.

———. 1996. *Fetishism and Curiosity.* Bloomington: Indiana University Press.

Nathanson, Donald, ed. 1987. *The Many Faces of Shame.* New York: Guilford.

National Mental Health Association. 1998a. "Clinical Depression and African Americans." DiscoveryHealth.com. 21 May.

———. 1998b. Homepage. DiscoveryHealth.com. 20 July.

Nietzsche, Friedrich. 1966. *On the Genealogy of Morals.* Trans. Walter Kaufman. New York: Random House.

Nunez, Sigrid. 1995. *A Feather on the Breath of God.* New York: Harper.

Oliver, Kelly. 1995. *Reading Kristeva: Unraveling the Double-Bind.* Bloomington: Indiana University Press.

———. 1997. *Family Values: Subjects between Nature and Culture.* New York: Routledge.

———. 1997. "Kristeva's Revolutions." In *The Portable Kristeva*, ed. Kelly Oliver, xi–xxix. New York: Columbia University Press.

———. 2001. *Witnessing: Beyond Recognition.* Minneapolis: University of Minnesota Press.

———. 2002. "Psychic Space and Social Melancholy." In *Between the Psyche and the Social: Psychoanalytic Social Theory*, ed. Kelly Oliver and Steve Edwin, 44–66. New York: Rowman and Littlefield.

———. 2003. "Witnessing and Testimony," *At Theory's Limits*, special issue of *parallax* 10 (1): 79–88.

Oliver, Kelly, and Benigno Trigo. 2003. *Noir Anxiety.* Minneapolis: University of Minnesota Press.

Otto, Frei, ed. 1967. *Tensile Structures.* Cambridge, MA: MIT Press.

Pelcovitz, D., et al. 1998. "Post-traumatic Stress Disorder and Family Functioning in Adolescent Cancer." *Journal of Traumatic Stress* 11 (2): 205–21.

Perry, Bruce. 1999. "Post-traumatic Stress Disorders in Children and Adolescents." *Current Opinions in Pediatrics* 11 (4).

Petry, Ann. 1946. *The Street.* New York: Mariner.

———. 1953. *The Narrows.* Boston: Beacon.

Restuccia, Francis. 2000. *Melancholics in Love.* New York: Rowman and Littlefield.

Royce, Josiah. 1919. *Lectures on Modern Idealism.* New Haven, CT: Yale University Press.

Russon, John. 1991. "Selfhood, Conscience, and Dialectic in Hegel's Phenomenology of Spirit." *Southern Journal of Philosophy* 29 (4): 533–50.

Saner, Senem. 2004. "Who Inherits the White West? Intersections of Racial and Cultural Hegemony." *Studies in Practical Philosophy: A Journal of Ethical and Political Thought* 3 (1): 105–17.

Sartre, Jean-Paul. 1956. *Being and Nothingness.* Trans. Hazel Barnes. New York: Washington Square.

———. 1960. *Critique of Dialectical Reason: Theory of Practical Ensemble,* vol. 1. Trans. Alan Sheridan-Smith. London: Verso.

———. 1964. *Colonialism and Neocolonialism.* Trans. A. Haddour et al. London: Routledge.

Sax, Benjamin. 1983. "Active Individuality and the Language of Confession: The Figure of the Beautiful Soul in the *Lehrjahre* and the *Phänomenologie.*" *Journal of the History of Philosophy* 21 (4): 437–66.

Schott, Robin May. 1993. *Cognition and Eros: A Critique of the Kantian Paradigm.* State College: Pennsylvania State University Press.

———, ed. 1997. *Feminist Interpretations of Immanuel Kant.* State College: Pennsylvania State University Press.

Sedgwick, Eve Kosofsky. 2002. "Shame and Performativity: Henry James's New York Edition Prefaces." http://www.duke.edu/~sedgwic/writing/prefaces.htm.

Seshadri-Crooks, Kalpana. 2000. *Desiring Whiteness: A Lacanian Analysis of Race.* New York: Routledge.

———. 2003. "Being Human: Bestiality, Anthropophagy, and the Law." *Umbr(a): A Journal of the Unconscious*: 97–114.

Sharpley-Whiting, T. Denean. 1998. *Frantz Fanon: Conflicts and Feminisms.* New Jersey: Rowman and Littlefield.

———. 1999. *Black Venus: Sexualized Savages, Primal Fears, and Primitive Narratives in French.* Durham, NC: Duke University Press.

Shepherdson, Charles. 1995. "History and the Real: Foucault with Lacan." *Postmodern Culture: An Electronic Journal of Interdisciplinary Criticism* 5 (2): 65.

Showalter, Elaine. 1998. *Hystories.* New York: Columbia University Press.

Skapinakis, Petros, Glyn Lewis, and Howard Meltzer. 2000. "Clarifying the Relationship between Unexplained Chronic Fatigue and Psychiatric Morbidity." *American Journal of Psychiatry* 157: 1492–98.

Sontag, Susan. 1979. *Illness as Metaphor.* New York: Vintage.

Sophocles. 1982. *Antigone.* In *The Three Theban Plays,* trans. Robert Fagles. New York: Penguin.

Souffrant, Eddy. 1996. "To Conquer the Veil: Woman as Critique of Liberalism." In *Fanon: A Critical Reader,* ed. Lewis Gordon, T. Denean Sharpley-Whiting, and Reneé T. White, 170–78. Malden, MA: Blackwell.

Speight, Allen. 2000. "The Beautiful Soul and the Language of Forgiveness." In *Metaphysik der praktischen Welt: Perspektiven im Anschluß an Hegel und Heidegger,* ed. Andreas Großmann and Christoph Jamme, 238–45. Amsterdam: Rodopi.

Spivak, Gayatri Chakravorty. 1999. *A Critique of Postcolonial Reason.* Cambridge, MA: Harvard University Press.

Tapper, Melbourne. 1998. *In the Blood: Sickle Cell Anemia and the Politics of Race.* Philadelphia: University of Pennsylvania Press.

Tate, Claudia, ed. 1983. *Black Women Writers at Work.* New York: Continuum.

Tomkins, Silvan. 1995. *Exploring Affect.* Ed. E. Virginia Demos. Cambridge: Cambridge University Press.

Trigo, Benigno. 2000. *Subjects of Crisis: Race and Gender as Disease in Latin America.* Hanover, CT: Wesleyan University Press.

———. 2002. "Thinking Subjectivity in Latin American Criticism." In *Foucault and Latin America: Appropriations and Deployments of Discoursive Analysis,* ed. Benigno Trigo, 164-84. New York: Routledge.

Tuana, Nancy. 1993. *The Less Noble Sex: Scientific, Religious, and Philosophical Conceptions of Woman's Nature.* Bloomington: Indiana University Press.

Turner, Lou. 1996. "On the Difference between the Hegelian and Fanonian Dialectic of Lordship and Bondage." In *Fanon: A Critical Reader,* ed. Lewis Gordon, T. Denean Sharpley-Whiting, and Reneé T. White, 134–54. Malden, MA: Blackwell.

Vilar, Irene. 1996. *The Ladies' Gallery.* New York: Random House.

Weiss, Gail. 1999. *Body Images: Embodiment as Intercorporeality.* New York: Routledge.

Welton, Donn, ed. 1999. *The Body: Classic and Contemporary Readings.* New York: Blackwell.

West, Cornell. 1994. *Race Matters.* New York: Random House.

Willett, Cynthia. 1995. *Maternal Ethics and Other Slave Moralities.* New York: Routledge.

———. 2001. *The Soul of Justice: Social Bonds and Racial Hubris.* Ithaca, NY: Cornell University Press.

———. 2002. "A Dialectic of Eros and Freedom: Beauvoir and Marcuse." In *Between the Psyche and the Social,* ed. Kelly Oliver and Steve Edwin. New York: Rowman and Littlefield.

Williams, Patricia J. 1991. *The Alchemy of Race and Rights.* Cambridge, MA: Harvard University Press.

———. 1995. The Rooster's Egg: On the Persistence of Prejudice. Cambridge, MA: Harvard University Press.

———. 1998. *Seeing a Color-Blind Future: The Paradox of Race.* New York: Noonday.

Wright, Richard. 1953. *The Outsider.* New York: Harper and Row.

Zahar, Renate. 1974. *Frantz Fanon: Colonialism and Alienation.* Trans. Willfried F. Feuser. New York: Monthly Review.

Ziarek, Ewa Plonowska. 2001. "Rethinking Dispossession: On Being in One's Skin." *parallax* 7 (2): 3–19.

INDEX

Kelly Oliver is W. Alton Jones Professor of Philosophy at Vanderbilt University. She is the author of six books: *Noir Anxiety* (coauthored with Benigno Trigo; Minnesota, 2002); *Witnessing: Beyond Recognition* (Minnesota, 2001); *Subjectivity without Subjects: From Abject Fathers to Desiring Mothers*; *Family Values: Subjects between Nature and Culture*; *Womanizing Nietzsche: Philosophy's Relation to "the Feminine"*; and *Reading Kristeva: Unraveling the Double-Bind*. She has edited *The Portable Kristeva* and *French Feminism Reader*.